DATE DUE			

DS 376.8
.S52
1990

PAKISTAN

Isobel Shaw

Photography by Photobank

PASSPORT BOOKS

Trade Imprint of National Textbook Company
Lincolnwood, Illinois U.S.A.

Dedicated to my husband Bob

Published by Passport Books in conjunction
with The Guidebook Company Ltd.

This edition first published in 1989 by Passport Books,
Trade Imprint of National Textbook Company, 4255 West Touhy
Avenue, Lincolnwood (Chicago), Illinois 60646-1975 U.S.A.

Printed in Hong Kong

ISBN: 0-8442-9918-9

Series Editors: May Holdsworth and Sallie Coolidge
Contributing Editor: Peter Fredenburg
Picture Editor: Carolyn Watts
Text by Isobel Shaw
Additional text contributions by John Elliott, Peter Fredenburg and Kent Obee

Photography by Photobank. Additional photographs by Alain Evrard (7, 24); Peter
Fredenburg (45, 139, 148−149 left, 186, 191, 196); James Montgomery (33 upper right,
167); Isobel Shaw (33 all except upper right, 86, 200).

Design by Rican Design Associates
Mapwork by Bai Yiliang

Contents

Garland vendor in Lahore

Introduction

Pakistan is the land of the Indus River, which flows through the country for 2,500 kilometres (1,600 miles) from the Himalaya and Karakoram mountain ranges to the Arabian Sea. It is a land of snow-covered peaks and burning deserts, of fertile mountain valleys and irrigated plains. Created in 1947 as a homeland for the Muslims of the Indian subcontinent, it is peopled by some 100-million inhabitants representing an array of ethnic groups but united by the Islamic faith.

'The Land of the Pure' (as the Urdu *Pakistan* translates into English) is strategically placed at the crossroads of Asia, where the road from China to the Mediterranean meets the route from India to Central Asia. For thousands of years, this junction has been a melting pot of diverse cultures, attracting traders and adventurers, pilgrims and holy men. Now the old Chinese trade route is reopened; the spectacular Karakoram Highway threads its way through the Himalayas, Karakorams and Pamirs, following the ancient Silk Route and entering China over the 4,733-metre (15,528-foot) Khunjerab Pass, the highest metalled border crossing in the world.

Pakistan's 4,000-year history is richly illustrated by archaeological sites and imposing monuments scattered the length and breadth of the country. Brick cities from the Indus Civilization, which flourished around 2000 BC, stand beside Buddhist ruins contemporaneous with the birth of Christianity. Magnificent Muslim tombs from the 12th century vie with the palaces, mosques and forts of the Moghul emperors of the 16th and 17th centuries.

The country's main cities reflect the many influences, both historical and modern, that have made Pakistan what it is. Lahore, close to the Indian border, is the cultural centre of the country, with an elegant core of Moghul architecture embellished by the flowery exuberance of Victorian Britain. Peshawar, on the North-West Frontier with Afghanistan, is a city straight out of the Arabian Nights, with tribesmen in turbans nonchalantly carrying rifles through the colourful bazaars. Islamabad, the federal capital, is a modern garden city planned by Greek architects. Finally, vivacious Karachi, with its population of eight million, is a huge, bustling port and industrial centre.

Pakistan is striking in the variety of its colours: the fruits and vegetables carefully stacked in the bazaars, the ornately decorated trucks and buses, the bright red and orange turbans and veils, the gold and amber of the autumn leaves against snow-clad mountains.

Various also are the country's attractions, with something for everyone. Pakistan boasts some of the best mountaineering and trekking in the world, exciting archaeological sites, beautiful monuments, lively cities and friendly people. Though tourism is still in its infancy here, the four main cities offer first-class hotels, with simpler but adequate accommodation available elsewhere.

To the spirit hungry for exploration and adventure, Pakistan calls.

General Information for Travellers

Getting There

By Air

Over 20 international airlines fly to Pakistan from more than 40 countries. Most flights arrive at Karachi, but a few go to Islamabad/ Rawalpindi, Lahore and Peshawar. Pakistan International Airlines (PIA) flies to a number of destinations in South Asia and the Gulf (and on to Nairobi) and has direct flights to the main Mediterranean and European destinations, with flights continuing to New York. It also has a limited Far East network.

Pakistan's international airports have banks that change travellers' cheques and foreign currency. There are taxis and public buses from the airports to the city centres, but it is best to bargain with the taxi driver and agree on a fare before setting off. From the airport to the downtown Karachi hotels should cost about Rs90 by taxi, Rs10 by airport coach and Rs2 by bus. From Islamabad airport to the downtown area is about Rs70 by taxi, Rs5 by minibus and Rs3 by bus; to central Rawalpindi, it is Rs50 by taxi and Rs2 by bus.

Overland

From China The Khunjerab Pass is open (weather permitting) from 1 May to 31 October for tours and to 30 November for individual travellers. Customs, immigration and health formalities at Sost, the border post, can be completed daily until 11 am for outgoing travellers and 4 pm for incoming travellers. Travel time from Sost to Tashkurgan, the first Chinese town, is five hours, not counting formalities at the Chinese border post at Pirali.

From India Due to unrest in the Indian Punjab, the border at Wagah, near Lahore, is open only a few days a month and only to organized convoys. Check with other tourists and the authorities for the latest information. India and Pakistan have agreed to open the railway line from Jodhpur in Rajasthan to Hyderabad in Sind, but as we go to press this has not yet happened.

From Iran The border is open only at Taftan, from where it is a 15 to 24-hour bus ride to Quetta in Baluchistan. (Quetta is the only place in Baluchistan open to foreign tourists without a special permit.)

From Afghanistan Afghanistan is closed to foreigners due to the troubles. The two possible entry points from Afghanistan, from Kabul via Torkham and the Khyber Pass, and from Kandahar via Chaman and the Khojak Pass, are both closed except to local traffic.

By Sea

No boats for the general public sail to or from Pakistan. A few pilgrim boats do, however, ply between Karachi and the Gulf states.

When to Go

The climate in Pakistan is so varied that, no matter what time of year you go, the weather will be pleasant somewhere. Winter (November to February) is the best time to visit Sind and the southern Punjab. The rest of the country is at its most colourful in spring (March to May, depending on altitude), when flowers bloom, and autumn (mid-September to mid-November), when the leaves change. For trekking and mountaineering, June to September is the recommended time.

During Ramazan, the month of fasting, the dates of which vary from year to year, no food or drink is sold during the day except in a handful of Chinese restaurants and the dining rooms of large hotels. Poolside service is usually suspended. Tourists visiting at this time should be careful not to eat, drink or smoke in public.

Visas

All visitors must have a valid passport. Nationals of Hong Kong, Ireland, Malaysia, Singapore, Tanzania, Tonga, Trinidad and Tobago, and Uganda can stay as long as they like without a visa. Nationals of the following countries can stay without a visa for one to three months, depending on the country: Fiji, Japan, South Korea, Maldives, Mauritius, Nepal, Philippines, Romania and Western Samoa. (Confirm before departure that the above regulations are current.) All other nationalities need a visa. Israelis and South Africans are not admitted. A maximum of three months' stay is allowed on a tourist visa, but visa extensions can (in theory) be obtained from the Passport Offices in Islamabad, Karachi, Lahore, Peshawar and Quetta (in Quetta, tel 71275; for other offices, see listings). The length of the extension is up to the officer in charge. Contact the Pakistan Embassy or Consulate or Pakistan International Airlines for further information.

Departure

Antiques may not be exported from Pakistan. Only jewellery and precious stones worth less than Rs10,000 and carpets worth less than Rs25,000 are allowed out, and you may be asked to produce foreign exchange certificates sufficient to cover the purchase price. Unaccompanied baggage needs an export permit.

Airport tax is Rs350 on international flights and Rs10 for domestic flights.

Customs

Alcohol is not admitted to Pakistan, and bags are almost always searched and any alcohol found impounded. A non-Muslim can buy liquor if he has a liquor licence, which is obtainable in some large hotels authorized to sell alcohol to hotel guests and from government liquor shops in the main cities, provided that he has a permit from the Excise and Taxation Department of that area.

Official import limits for other items are 200 cigarettes, ½ pint of perfume, and one camera, tape recorder or typewriter. Officials are not strict with most tourists, but visiting Pakistanis and Indians are thoroughly searched.

Health

Visitors need cholera and yellow fever vaccination certificates if coming from an infected area. Malaria exists year round in the whole of Pakistan below 2,000 metres, so malarial prophylactics are essential. Chloroquine-resistant malaria has not yet surfaced in Pakistan, but ask your doctor for the latest information.

Typhoid, tetanus and polio vaccinations should be up to date. Cholera vaccine is only 50 percent effective and may have quite severe side-effects, so it is not universally recommended. Discuss this with your doctor. Some doctors suggest a gamma globulin injection a few days before departure. This gives 80 percent protection for five months against hepatitis, which is prevalent in Pakistan.

The major towns have good doctors, all of whom speak English. Chemists stock a wide range of medicines that are cheap and often obtainable without a prescription. There are hospitals in many towns, the best being the Aga Khan University Hospital in Karachi.

Money

The unit of currency is the rupee, which is divided into 100 paise. Rates are about Rs17.60 to one US dollar, Rs33.30 to one pound sterling, and Rs12.60 to one Deutsche mark.

Any amount of foreign currency or travellers' cheques may be brought into Pakistan, but only Rs100 in Pakistani cash may be taken in or out. Also, you may reconvert only Rs500 into foreign currency. (Save your encashment slips, as you may need to show them.) It is an offence to sell foreign currency except to authorized dealers (foreign banks, the National Bank of Pakistan, the Habib Bank and some big hotels and tourist shops), and the black market rates are not much better anyway.

US currency in cash or travellers' cheques is handiest, but sterling and Deutsche marks are also widely accepted. Travellers' cheques can be changed in the major cities. Rates differ slightly depending on the town and the bank, with unfavourable rates especially in hotels, tourist shops and the Northern Areas. (As we go to press, there are no legal foreign exchange facilities between Gilgit and the Chinese border.) American Express has offices in Karachi, Lahore, Islamabad and Rawalpindi, but the Islamabad and Rawalpindi branches are notorious for their inefficiency and delays. Big hotels accept credit cards.

If you need money sent to you in Pakistan, it is quicker and more reliable to have a bank draft sent by registered mail to an address you can use than to have it transferred bank to bank.

Travelling Within Pakistan

By Air PIA flies to Badin, Bahawalpur, Bannu, Chitral, Dera Ismail Khan, Faisalabad, Gilgit, Gwadar, Hyderabad, Islamabad/Rawalpindi, Jacobabad, Jiwani, Karachi, Khuzdar, Kohat, Lahore, Mianwali, Moenjodaro, Multan, Nawabshah, Panjgur, Pasni, Peshawar, Quetta, Saidu Sharif, Sargodha, Sibi, Sindhri, Skardu, Sui, Sukkur, Turbat and Zhob.

Flights to Gilgit, Skardu and Chitral are extremely good value. These tickets are cheaper if bought in Pakistan, working out at about twice the bus fare. However, these flights operate only when visibility is good and so can be delayed for some days.

Journalists and groups are eligible for discounts. Apply to the public relations officer at the PIA office in Karachi, Lahore, Rawalpindi, Peshawar, Multan or Quetta.

Domestic airport tax is Rs10.

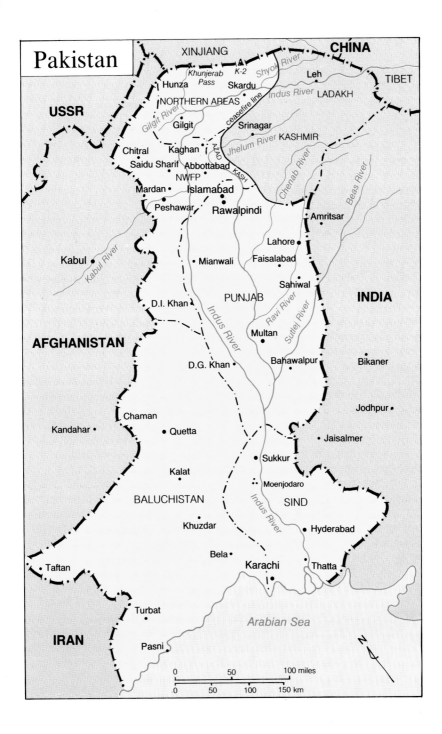

Pakistan

By Train This is the best way to get around if you have enough time. The trunk lines run from Karachi via Multan, Lahore and Rawalpindi to Peshawar, and from Karachi via Sukkar and Quetta to the Iranian border. There is an extensive network of branch lines. Trains run frequently, but they are slow, unpunctual and crowded. Train classes are express and ordinary; compartment classes are air-conditioned, first and second. Air-conditioned and first class have sleeper compartments, and there are special ladies' compartments recommended for women travelling alone. Air-conditioned class is almost as expensive as flying, and you usually need to book several days in advance, especially for sleepers. Most passengers bring their own bedding, but it can sometimes be hired at major stations. Since buying a ticket can be time-consuming and frustrating, ask an agency or hotel employee to handle it for you. If all else fails, you can pay a station porter (recognizable by his red turban and armband) to buy you a ticket and find you a seat.

Parties can hire a luxurious tourist car complete with dining and sitting room, which can be attached to certain trains and detached at any railway station for as many hours as the party wishes. The cost is reasonable if divided among a large party. Contact the Divisional Superintendent's Office, Pakistan Railways, Karachi.

Foreign tourists can get a 25 percent discount (50 percent for students) on most rail fares. Apply to the Divisional Superintendent with your passport and student card at Karachi, Lahore, Rawalpindi, Peshawar, Quetta, Sukkur or Multan railway station for the necessary concession order before you buy your ticket. You may also need a tourist certificate from the local tourist officer to claim your rail discount. Indians and visiting Pakistanis are not eligible.

By Bus Buses are the cheapest but most uncomfortable and dangerous way to travel in Pakistan. They go everywhere. Bus stations are usually near the railway station, if there is one, or near the bazaar in smaller places. On longer journeys, buses make scheduled stops for food, but it is wise to take food (especially fruit) and drink with you. Seats cannot be reserved in advance.

Minibuses are faster, more comfortable and only slightly more expensive than buses. Seats can be booked in advance. Minibuses generally use different stations than the regular buses. Several luxury bus services ply the route between Rawalpindi and Lahore.

By Jeep-taxi Jeep-taxis are the public transport in northern valleys with roads too narrow for buses. The drivers are excellent, but the jeeps themselves are neither cheap nor comfortable, with as many passengers as possible perched on top of the cargo (usually sacks of grain or fertilizer) and crouched on the front and back bumpers. They run to no timetable and, in the remoter valleys, are quite rare.

The Northern Area Transport Company (NATCO) runs buses and jeeps up the Karakoram Highway and into some of the side valleys off the main road. They offer a discount to a limited number of Pakistani and foreign students on each vehicle.

By Car The main roads are surfaced and generally in reasonable condition, but drivers are not conscientious about observing traffic rules, so those unused to driving in Asia — or on the left — may find it harrowing and dangerous. The main Karachi-Lahore-Rawalpindi-Peshawar highway is always very crowded with particularly reckless drivers. The minor roads are often impassable for ordinary cars, so four-wheel-drive vehicles with high clearance are recommended. Stick to small 4WD vehicles in the mountains, as the roads and bridges are very narrow.

Signposts are few and often written only in Urdu, which makes finding your way difficult and frustrating — particularly in big cities. Driving at night is especially hazardous as trucks, bicycles and bullock carts rarely have lights. In parts of Sind, night drivers are prey to bandits.

If you still want to drive, you need only a valid driving licence.

Self-drive **car rentals** are not usually available, but cars with drivers can be hired at the airport and big hotels. Hotel cars are fairly expensive (more so if air-conditioned), but may be worth the extra cost as the drivers speak some English. Make sure with the hotel rental agency that the driver knows where you want to go before you set off. If you wish to visit several places, the best solution is to hire a local taxi (black with a yellow roof) in the street, which costs about Rs300 for the day. Local taxi drivers usually know only the main locations in town and will expect you to direct them to offices or private homes.

Jeeps with drivers are readily available in the mountains. The government-approved rate in the Punjab, on the Karakoram Highway and in Gilgit District is Rs6 per mile and Rs75 overnight charge. In Chitral, the rate is Rs8 per mile and Rs30 overnight charge, and in Skardu it is Rs10 per mile and Rs200 halt charge.

Maps

Good maps are difficult to find in Pakistan. The best overall map is Bartholomew's road map covering the entire subcontinent. The best road map of Pakistan is the 1:2,000,000 map dated 1976, but more generally useful — despite their faults — are the 1:1,000,000 contour maps issued by the Survey of Pakistan. They are reprints of old maps,

so new roads and lakes — and even the present border with India —
are not shown. Road grading is often 50 years out of date, and the
printing is sometimes blurred. Occasionally you can find some of these
in bookshops or hotel lobbies, but your best bet is the Survey of
Pakistan office on Murree Road in Faizabad, between Islamabad and
Rawalpindi. (The office is 200 metres (yards) from the intersection of
Airport and Murree roads, on the right going towards Rawalpindi.)
The Survey of Pakistan office in Karachi near the Metropole Hotel
may also have them.

The Pakistan Tourism Development Corporation publishes
pamphlets with much useful information, including sketch maps.

Accommodation

Karachi, Islamabad, Rawalpindi, Lahore and Peshawar have
international-class hotels, but good accommodation outside these
major cities is in short supply. The situation is improving, however,
with the Serena chain building and taking over hotels at Quetta,
Faisalabad, Swat and Gilgit, and the Shangrila chain building in the
Northern Areas at Chilas, Skardu, Sost and Fairy Meadows. These
hotels are all comfortable but relatively expensive, costing US$30–100
a night. The best hotels are usually heavily booked, especially in
Islamabad and Lahore, so advance reservation is essential.

The **Pakistan Tourism Development Corporation** runs motels and
guest houses at the most popular tourist sites and resorts: at Besham
and Gilgit on the Karakoram Highway, Miandam and Kalam in Swat,
Balakot and Naran in the Kaghan Valley, Chitral town, Skardu,
Taxila, Moenjodaro and Keenjhar Lake. Rooms cost US$20–35 a
night, and the staff is usually very helpful.

Every town has a wide range of **locally run hotels** varying greatly in
price (US$1–40) and standard. Many are cheap by Western standards
and give adequate accommodation. Some are exceptionally good
value, but it is usually prudent to check the room and sanitary facilities
before signing in.

Local hotels usually provide only a bottom sheet and a well-used
blanket, so you may want to carry your own sheet and pillow case (or
sleeping bag liner), and certainly a towel and soap. In winter or in the
mountains, you will need a sleeping bag.

You should order any food you want for the next 24 hours as soon
as you arrive in a local hotel — or, better still, go out and find a food
stall or local restaurant.

At the bottom end are *mussafar khanas*, local inns in which *charpois* (rope beds) are provided without bedding in a communal dormitory or a courtyard. These local inns and the really cheap hotels usually refuse foreigners except in very remote areas, where there is no other accommodation.

There are **youth hostels** at Lahore and Taxila. YMCA hostels are at the major cities of Karachi, Lahore, Peshawar and Abbottabad; Bhurban and Khanpur in the Murree Hills; Balakot, Sharan, Naran and Bat Kundi in the Kaghan Valley; and Ketas in the Salt Range. Karachi and Lahore have YWCA hostels.

Railway retiring rooms, a hold-over from the British Raj, are rooms with beds for passengers holding air-conditioned or first-class tickets. These are good value at Rs20−40 and are available at Karachi City and Cantonment, Lahore City and Cantonment, Multan Cantonment, Rawalpindi Cantonment, Peshawar Cantonment, Sargodha, Taxila, Bahawalpur and Quetta.

Islamabad has the only official campsite in Pakistan, but **camping** is often possible in the gardens of small hotels, rest houses and youth hostels, with access to their facilities. Camping by the roadside, in tribal areas or in some parts of the northern valleys is prohibited. It can also be uncomfortable to camp in the open, as the locals are very curious and in some areas hostile.

Food and Drink

The best Pakistani food is varied and delicious. Chicken, mutton and beef are on the menu in most restaurants, served with *daal* (lentils), *subzi* (vegetables) and *dahi* (yoghurt), and scooped up with *chapatis* or *naan* (two types of unleavened bread, usually made with wheat flour). Lahore is famous for its Moghul cuisine, Karachi for its seafood, and Peshawar for its kebabs, naan and green tea. Pakistani curries are usually not as hot as Indian, and many dishes have no chillies at all, though they are well seasoned with other spices.

Chinese restaurants of varying quality operate in the major cities, and international-class hotels serve European dishes. All restaurant prices are very moderate by international standards.

Visitors should be sensible about what they eat. It is easy to avoid an upset stomach by taking a few simple precautions. Seasoned travellers in Asia will have developed some immunity, but new arrivals should avoid eating anything that has not been freshly cooked, especially salads, sliced tomatoes and even sliced raw onions. Remember: 'Boil it, bake it, peel it or forget it!'

Buffet meals in first-class hotels may also pose risks, as food kept warm for long periods may be contaminated.

Food from roadside stalls is perfectly safe, but make sure it comes from a boiling pot on to a clean, dry plate. Chapatis and daal make a good, cheap, high-protein meal and are available anywhere. Eat where the crowds are, as the most popular stalls have the best — and freshest — food.

To save on meat consumption, Tuesdays and Wednesdays are designated meatless days in most areas. Most restaurants serve only chicken and fish on those days.

Fruit is particularly good in Pakistan, but peel it with a clean knife. (You can buy a good folding knife in the bazaar.) Cut fruit, mixed fruit juices and ice cream sold in the bazaar spell danger to all but the most seasoned of travellers.

Avoid drinking water that has not been boiled or purified. Avoid ice everywhere, even in major hotels, as it is made with unboiled water. Tea is usually safe if it is poured into a clean, uncracked, dry cup. It is a Pakistani custom to boil milk, so that, too, is safe in your tea. International-class hotels claim that their water is safe, but do not risk it unless you know you have built up some immunity. Bottled drinks are safe and are available in all major towns and many smaller ones.

What to Take

Loose cotton clothes are recommended for hot weather. In winter and in the mountains you will need sweaters and something to fend off wind and rain. Pakistanis wear a large cotton or woollen shawl day and night, which is an idea worth copying.

Women should dress modestly in loose trousers and a long, loose shirt. Legs and shoulders should be covered at all times, ruling out dresses. The light-weight scarf or *dupatta* (usually two metres long and half a metre wide) worn by Pakistani women is handy to drape around your shoulders and head in remoter areas and when visiting mosques and shrines. The women's national dress, the *shalwar-kameez*, is very comfortable and can be bought ready made in Karachi, Lahore and Islamabad. Elsewhere, a dressmaker can run one up quickly and inexpensively.

Men should wear shorts only while playing sports and should wear a track suit to and from the sports ground.

A packing checklist includes: sunglasses, some sort of head gear to protect against the sun and dust, lavatory paper, water-purifying

tablets and pills for an upset stomach, insect repellent, sunscreen, a zippered bag for cameras and other possessions to keep out dust, a plastic water bottle and a pocket knife. If you are using cheaper hotels, take a universal plug for washbasins, soap, insect powder and sheets or a sleeping bag. Women should take a complete supply of moisturizing cream and tampons, as these are difficult to find in Pakistan.

Procedure when Visiting Mosques and Shrines

Tourists are welcome in mosques and shrines, provided they remove their shoes, show respect and are suitably dressed. Women should cover their heads and shoulders. A pair of socks (or the little bootees that airlines hand out in business class) will keep your feet off the stones, which can get painfully hot in summer. Women are not allowed into the inner sanctum at some shrines but may look in through a side window. Many mosques close their doors to tourists half an hour before prayers.

Shopping — Best Buys

Pakistan has some beautiful handicrafts. Specialities include rugs and carpets, leather goods, furs, embroidered and appliquéd bedspreads and table linen, pottery, copper and brassware, onyx ornaments, woodwork, and gold and silver jewellery. Prices are controlled in government-sponsored handicraft shops, and you must bargain in the bazaars.

Business Hours

Business hours are 7.30 am−2.30 pm in summer and 9 am−4 pm in winter. Government office hours are 8.30 am−2 pm in summer and 9 am−2.30 pm in winter. Friday is the weekly holiday, when all shops and offices are closed. Most offices remain closed on Saturday.

Time

Pakistan is five hours ahead of GMT. Darkness falls at about 5 pm in winter and 7.30 pm in summer.

Electricity

Electricity is 220−240 volts, with brown-outs down to a few volts. In the north, the electricity supply is very erratic, and paraffin lamps or candles are usually supplied in hotels. Electric hairdryers and razors are usable only in large cities.

National Holidays

23 March — Pakistan Day
1 May — Labour Day
31 July — Bank holiday (banks only)
14 August — Independence Day
6 September — Defence of Pakistan Day
11 September — Anniversary of the death of M.A. Jinnah, the Quaid-e-Azam
9 November — Allama Iqbal Day
25 December — Birthday of the Quaid-e-Azam
31 December — Bank holiday (banks only)

Religious holidays occur on different dates each year, as the Muslim calendar is ten to 12 days shorter than that of the West.

Newspapers and Periodicals

Three English-language daily newspapers — *Dawn, The Pakistan Times* and *The Muslim* — are available in most towns, with others circulated only in Karachi. Foreign newspapers and periodicals are available at large bookstalls and the big hotels, as are English-language books.

Sports and Activities

Fishing There is excellent deep-sea fishing off Karachi and equally good fresh-water fishing in the northern valleys. Fishing permits usually cost Rs10 per day and are available from the local fishing authorities.

Bird- and game-watching Over 740 species of birds have been identified in Pakistan. The Indus is one of the major migration routes of the world, so the lakes and reservoirs of the Punjab and Sind are alive with migrant birds during the winter months. The coastline and deserts are also good places to see unusual birds. Pakistan has seven national parks, 72 wildlife sanctuaries and 76 game reserves.

Sports Pakistanis are sports mad and play all sorts of ball games. They excel at cricket, field hockey, badminton and squash. They are also famous for polo and, in the northern areas, play a local variety of the game that is faster and more exciting than the staider international game. In many areas tourists can hire horses for riding. There are golf courses in Islamabad, Murree, Quetta, Abbottabad and Swat.

Desert safaris Travel agents can arrange camel safaris in the Cholistan Desert.

Trekking The Himalayas, Karakorams and Hindu Kush offer some of the best trekking in the world.

Mountaineering Pakistan has five peaks over 8,000 metres (26,250 feet) and 101 over 7,000 metres (23,000 feet), some of which are still unclimbed. In 1985, some 54 expeditions attempted 62 peaks. Applications for permission to climb K-2 must be made two years in advance, and applications for other peaks one year in advance. For regulations and application forms, write to the Tourism Division, College Road, F-7/2, Islamabad, Pakistan, or to any Pakistani Embassy or Pakistan International Airlines office abroad.

Rafting and Kayaking These sports are permitted on the Indus, Hunza, Gilgit, Swat and Kunhar (Kaghan) rivers, but they are in their infancy in Pakistan, so the rivers have not yet been graded for difficulty. Apply to a good travel agent for details.

Hunting Boar is the only officially sanctioned game animal.

Photography Pakistan and its people are superbly photogenic, but the noon-day sun tends to flatten subjects and rob colours of their brilliance. Though few travellers have time to wait for perfect light, they should remember that the best results are achieved before 10 am and after 3 pm in winter and 4 pm in summer. Underexposing midday shots by half a stop or more can help as will the use of a daylight or haze filter, but the colours in the resulting pictures may still be disappointing.

Colour print film is available in many towns, but it is often old and heat damaged. Film for colour slides and black and white prints is available only in Karachi, Lahore and Islamabad, where it is expensive. Enthusiasts should bring all the film they need and store it in as cool a place as possible.

Photographing military installations, airports and bridges is forbidden. People like to be asked before being photographed, at which point men usually assume manly poses and stare straight into the camera. If you take that shot, you might get your candid a few seconds later. Also, a telephoto lens can be useful for spontaneous shots, but remember that a foreigner in Pakistan does nothing in public completely unobserved. Men should not attempt to photograph women, though female photographers usually have no problem at all, especially if there are no men around to disapprove and if a little time is first spent making friends and asking permission.

One Other Thing

Pakistani women never travel alone. Indeed, many never even leave the house unless accompanied by a family member, friend or servant. Foreign women tourists are therefore advised not to travel alone in Pakistan, not because it is dangerous, but because it offends good Muslim males to see women so immodest as to travel unaccompanied.

Geography

The Indus River forms the axis of Pakistan and, with its tributaries, drains the whole of the country, except for the sparsely populated western province of Baluchistan.

The Indus is also one of the four riverine cradles of early civilization. Like the Nile and the Tigris-Euphrates, it flows across the vast arid zone that spans North Africa and Asia from Morocco to Mongolia. (The Yellow River, in northern China, flows out of this zone to the east.) Almost the entire zone has long since converted to Islam, providing a common culture and identity to the many desert peoples who live here.

Pakistan stretches from the Arabian Sea to the high mountains of Central Asia over a maximum length of 1,800 kilometres (1,120 miles). It covers an area of 803,944 square kilometres (310,322 square miles), making it three times as large as Great Britain or about the size of Texas and Louisiana. The country is bordered on the west by Iran, on the northwest by Afghanistan, on the northeast by China and on the east by India. Its southern coastline is nearly 1,000 kilometres (620 miles) long.

Politically, Pakistan is divided into four provinces: Sind, Baluchistan, Punjab and the North-West Frontier Province (usually abbreviated to NWFP). In addition, there are two other regions, the Northern Areas, which include Gilgit, Hunza, Chilas and Skardu, and Azad (Free) Kashmir and Jammu. These regions are claimed by India on the strength of the maharajah of Kashmir's accession to India at Partition but are on the Pakistani side of the line of control. They are administered directly from Islamabad, with the local inhabitants enjoying only limited voting rights.

Geographically, Pakistan comprises three main regions: the mountainous north, where meet three of the world's great mountain ranges (the Hindu Kush, the Karakorams and the Himalayas); the enormous but sparsely populated plateau of Baluchistan in the southwest, which covers 44 percent of the country's total area; and the Punjab and Sind plains of the Indus River and its five main tributaries. Apart from these irrigated plains, Pakistan is largely barren mountains and arid plateaux.

As vast as Baluchistan is, it is not described in this guide because it is off the normal tourist route. Foreign tourists need permits to travel anywhere in the province except the capital, Quetta.

The Himalayas and Karakorams are the newest mountains in the world. About 55 million years ago, the northward-drifting Indian geological plate collided with the Asian plate, its northern edge nosing

under the Asian plate and pushing up the mountains. The Indian plate is still driving northwards at about five centimetres (two inches) per year, causing the mountains to rise about seven millimetres (¼ inch) in the same period. Pakistan boasts the densest concentration of high mountains in the world, with 82 peaks over 7,000 metres (23,000 feet) within a radius of 180 kilometres (112 miles).

But it is the Indus River that gives Pakistan life; together with its tributaries it provides water for the largest irrigation system in the world. Many of the canals were dug in the last century, but since Independence many new dams and canals have been built, providing water not only for irrigation but also for generating electricity. The dam at Tarbela in northern Punjab, built in the 1970s, is the biggest earth-filled dam in the world, both in terms of the amount of earth used to build it and its electricity-generating potential.

The Indus River is 3,200 kilometres (2,000 miles) long, making it the third-longest in Asia, after the Yangzi and Yellow rivers. It rises at Mount Kailas in Tibet, passes through Ladakh in eastern Kashmir and enters Pakistan, flowing north-westwards between the Himalayas and the Karakorams. It plunges through some of the world's deepest gorges as it twists among the mountains, finally finding an exit south to the plains of the Punjab and Sind. Then the river meanders, becoming as wide as 30 kilometres (20 miles) in places as it flows in numerous channels separated by large islands.

The river floods every summer, when the melting of the mountain snows coincides with the monsoon in the Punjab. In recent years, the flooding has been controlled, but in times past the force of the floodwaters frequently caused the Indus to change course. The many ruined cities in the desert of Sind were all flourishing, riverside commercial centres until the Indus abandoned them.

Finally, the Indus oozes into the Arabian Sea over a giant delta filled by the millions of tons of silt the river deposits annually. This delta measures 150 kilometres (100 miles) in length and 250 kilometres (150 miles) in width, stretching from Karachi to the Indian border.

Climate

Pakistan is dry. A quarter of the country has less than 120 millimetres (4.7 inches) of rain a year, and over three-quarters of Pakistan has less than 250 millimetres (9.8 inches) of rain annually. Rainfall exceeds 500 millimetres (19.5 inches) a year over a mere seven percent of the land, primarily extending from Lahore to the mountain slopes north of

Islamabad. This is the only area reached by the monsoon, which blows across the northern Punjab from India, causing heavy summer storms in this area from July to September. The rains usually reach Islamabad about a week after arriving in Delhi. Occasionally, rain comes to this area from the west in winter. The rest of the country, the north, west and south, are deserts dependent on irrigation for agriculture.

June and July are the hottest months, with midday temperatures in the 40s°C (over 104°F) in most places. In upper Sind and neighbouring Baluchistan, the temperature occasionally goes into the 50s°C (over 122°F). Naturally, it is cooler at higher altitudes, especially in the mountain valleys of Swat and Kaghan and around Murree, where there is rain, but it can get very hot in summer along the dry northern valleys of the Indus and Gilgit rivers, where the heat radiates off the bare mountains. Above 2,500 metres (8,000 feet), temperatures are usually pleasant during the day and cool at night.

December, January and February are the coldest months. At this time, Sind, the southern Punjab and the lower areas of Baluchistan are cool, with daytime temperatures of 10°–25°C (50°–77°F). Islamabad in winter is crisp during the day and cold at night. Above 1,500 metres (5,000 feet), days are cold and nights very cold.

Population

Pakistan's population was estimated at 100 million in 1987. The last census was in 1981, when 83.79 million Pakistanis were counted, not including some three million Afghan refugees and two to three million Pakistanis working abroad. The 1981 figure represents a five-fold increase since the turn of the century.

A quarter of Pakistan's population live in the big cities, the biggest being Karachi (population eight million), Lahore (three million), Faisalabad (1.25 million), Rawalpindi-Islamabad (one million), Hyderabad (one million), Multan, Gujranwala and Peshawar (750,000 each), and Sialkot, Sargodha and Quetta (500,000 each). About three-quarters of all Pakistanis live in the Indus Valley, leaving the desert areas almost empty.

Though united in Islam, the people represent many ethnic groups and speak a variety of languages, the major ones being Punjabi in the Punjab; Sindhi in Sind; Baluchi, Pushtu and Brahui in Baluchistan; Pushtu, Kashmiri, Khowar, Kohistani and Kafiri in the North-West Frontier Province; and Balti, Shina, Burushaski and Wakhi in the Northern Areas. The linguistic picture is further complicated by the

Clockwise from upper left: Afridi chieftain in the Khyber Pass; Kafir Kalash girl; bagpiper of the Khyber Rifles; merchant of Islamkot in the Thar Desert in Sind; two Baluchi girls.

32

multiplicity of dialects that tribal populations have evolved in isolated valleys.

The *lingua franca* of Pakistan is Urdu, which means 'army' or 'camp', reflecting that the language was formed of local languages and the Persian spoken by invaders from the north. Though it is the mother tongue of only a fraction of the population, it is understood by the majority. Many educated Pakistanis speak English as well as Urdu.

Economy

Pakistan's economy is heavily dependent upon agriculture, which accounts for a third of the gross national product and employs nearly three-quarters of the population. Most of the agriculture relies on water supplied through some 64,000 kilometres (40,000 miles) of irrigation canals, almost all of which are on the Indus plain. Rising salinity, caused by poor drainage, is a growing problem, affecting about half of all irrigated fields.

Wheat is the main food crop, followed by rice, millet, maize, barley and pulses. Cotton is by far the most important cash crop and accounts for five percent of world production. High-quality Basmati rice, grown mainly in Lahore Division, is also a major export. Other crops include sugar-cane, oil-seeds (mustard, rape, sesame, linseed and castor), tobacco, fruit, vegetables, chillies and fodder crops.

Textile manufacture is Pakistan's most important industry, followed by light engineering (electrical goods, metal working, precision equipment), food processing (vegetable oils, sugar, drinks), cement, pharmaceuticals, leather and rubber. Pakistan has a substantial fertilizer industry, and Russia has helped to build an iron and steel works near Karachi.

Hydro-electric generation is Pakistan's largest source of energy. Baluchistan has reserves of natural gas, while oil has been found on the Potwar Plateau and, recently, in southern Sind.

Nearly half of Pakistan's foreign exchange earnings come from remittances sent home by the country's two to three million expatriates, most of whom work in the Middle East. This income is important to the many poorer families of Pakistan who have at least one member working in the Gulf, but it is threatened by the economic stagnation that continues to affect the region.

Pakistan's tourism industry remains largely undeveloped, in spite of the great potential it holds.

34

History

The story of Pakistan divides into six distinct periods: prehistory; the ancient empires, from about 3000 BC to the sixth century AD; the coming of Islam, from 711 to the late 14th century; the Moghul period, from 1526 to the 18th century; the British period, from the mid-18th century to 1947; and Pakistan since Partition.

Prehistory

Ten million years ago, the common ancestors of both men and apes roamed the open woodland south of what is now Islamabad. Our own genus, *Homo*, a meat-eater and user of stone tools, evolved here about two million years ago. Modern man, the species *Homo sapiens*, has been living here for at least 50,000 years, according to the carbon dating of fossils liberally scattered along the banks of the Soan River. About 9,000 years ago, man learned to tame animals and to plant crops, and farming villages dating from 6000 BC have been excavated in Baluchistan, the North-West Frontier Province and the Punjab.

The Ancient Empires

These farm communities were the forerunners of the great Indus Valley Civilization, which developed at roughly the same time as the Mesopotamian and Egyptian empires, around 3000 BC. The Indus Valley Civilization was a well-organized urban society able to develop a (still-undeciphered) pictogramic form of writing and to unite the Indus Valley under a strong central government. The sites of the two major excavations of this civilization are at Moenjodaro in Sind and Harappa in the Punjab.

The 18th century BC brought an invasion from Central Asia of Aryans, whose culture was at the time less advanced than the one they replaced, but who were to develop into Hindus. It is through their authorship of the Rigveda, the oldest religious text extant, that we know of their battles against the city dwellers of the Indus.

Buddhism evolved in the sixth century BC, at about the same time that Gandhara, in northern Pakistan, became the easternmost province of the Achaemenid Empire of Persia, then at its height under Darius the Great. Gandhara was a semi-independent kingdom with capitals at Pushkalavati (now called Charsadda) and Taxila, where, from the fourth century BC, there existed one of the greatest universities of the ancient world.

Alexander the Great conquered the region between 327 and 325 BC, taking Gandhara and visiting Taxila before marching across the Salt Range (south of modern Islamabad) to the Beas River. He then sailed down the Beas to the Indus and the sea, finally returning west with a march across the Makran Desert in Baluchistan.

Alexander's empire was short-lived, and in 321 BC, Chandragupta founded the Mauryan Empire, which took in modern Pakistan but had its capital far to the east at Patna, on the Ganges River. His grandson, Ashoka, promoted Buddhism and built Buddhist shrines all over the empire.

History records little of Sind and Baluchistan from the third century BC to the sixth century AD, these provinces being effectively lost at the western edge of Indian influence and the eastern edge of Persian influence. Northern Pakistan, on the other hand, has a fully documented history. Wave after wave of invaders from Persia, Afghanistan and Central Asia entered through the passes of the North-West Frontier and swept across the Punjab towards Delhi.

The Bactrian Greeks, descendants of Alexander the Great's soldiers in Bactria (now Balkh, in north-central Afghanistan), arrived in 185 BC, about 50 years after the death of Ashoka. They built new Greek cities at Taxila and Pushkalavati and were followed in 75 BC by the Scythians (Sakas), Iranian nomads from Central Asia, and in about AD 20 by the powerful Parthians, from east of the Caspian Sea.

The Parthians had already defeated the Romans in 53 BC by waving silken banners, from which the Roman soldiers had fled, thinking such fine, light-weight fabric must be a product of sorcery. The Parthians had then grown rich as middle men in the trade that developed along the Silk Route between China and the Roman Empire.

The Kushans, from Central Asia, overthrew the Parthians and assumed their position at the centre of the lucrative silk trade. By the second centry AD, the Kushans had reached the height of their power, with an empire that extended from eastern Iran to the Chinese frontier and south to the Ganges River. They made their winter capital at Peshawar and their summer capital north of Kabul. Under their most famous king, Kanishka (ruled c 128–151), Buddhism prospered and thousands of monasteries and stupas were built. The Gandharan school of art developed, named after the commercial and spiritual centre of the empire. It combined the artistic traditions of East and West to produce a style so dynamic that it flourished for five centuries.

As the Kushans declined, the northern reaches of their empire were absorbed by the Sassanian Empire of Persia, and the southern

areas by the Gupta Empire. In the fourth century, a new dynasty of
Kidar (Little) Kushans came to power, with their capital at Peshawar.

In about 455, the White Huns (Hephthalites) invaded Gandhara
from the northwest and sacked its cities. The White Huns worshipped
Shiva and the sun god Surya. Buddhism declined, though it continued
in altered form for many centuries and did not finally die out in the
Swat Valley until the 16th century. The White Huns were converted to
Hinduism and may have become the Rajput warrior class.

The Sassanians and Turks overthrew the Huns in 565, but by late in
the sixth century Hindu kings ruled again what is now Pakistan: the
Turki Shahi rulers of Kapisa in Afghanistan controlled the area west of
the Indus, including Gandhara; the rajah of Kashmir ruled east of the
Indus and in northern Punjab; and numerous small Hindu kingdoms
occupied the rest. Brahmanical Hinduism spread at the expense of
Buddhism.

In 870, Hindu Shahis from Central Asia overthrew the Turki Shahis
and established their capital at Hund on the Indus. They ruled an area
from Jalalabad in Afghanistan to Multan, and extending east to include
Kashmir, until 1008.

The Coming of Islam

Islam reached Pakistan from both south and north. In 711, an Arab
naval expedition under Muhammad bin Qasim arrived to suppress
piracy on Arab shipping and ended up establishing control over the
Indus Valley as far north as Multan. Most of the local rulers remained
in power but now paid tribute to the caliph of Baghdad.

In the 11th century, the Turkish rulers of Afghanistan began the
Islamic conquest of India from the northwest. Mahmud of Ghazni
(979–1030) led a series of raids against the Rajput kingdoms and the
wealthy Hindu temples. Gandhara, the Punjab, Sind and Baluchistan
became integral parts of the Ghaznavid Empire, which had its capital
at Ghazni in Afghanistan. The Ghaznavids developed Lahore as their
centre of Islamic culture in the Punjab, and mass conversions to Islam
began at this time.

The Ghaznavid kingdom was destroyed near the end of the next
century by the Ghorids, the Turkish Muslim rulers of Ghor in
Afghanistan. Muhammad of Ghor swept down the Indus into India,
defeated the Rajput confederacy there in 1192 and captured Delhi the
following year. This marked the beginning of the Sultanate Period,
which lasted for over 300 years, with five dynasties of Muslim sultans
succeeding one another in Delhi. The Mongol, Genghiz Khan, harried
the Delhi sultans during the 13th century, never succeeding in
overthrowing them. Tamerlane, the great Turkish conqueror who had

his capital at Samarkand, penetrated India soon after in 1398–9 and sacked Delhi.

The Moghul Period

In the early 16th century, Babur, a descendant of Tamerlane and Genghiz Khan, raided the Punjab from Afghanistan, finally defeating the last of the Delhi sultans, the Lodis, at the battle of Panipat in 1526. Thus began the Moghul Empire.

Four years later, Babur was succeeded by Humayun, who proved to be more of an intellectual than a statesman and was ousted by a Pathan, Sher Shah Suri, who ruled the empire until his death in 1545. Humayun returned from exile in Persia and regained the throne in 1554 but died two years later after falling down his library stairs.

He was succeeded this time by his son, Akbar, the greatest of the Moghul emperors. By the time of his death in 1605, his empire stretched from central India to Kashmir and included Sind and Rajasthan. Akbar improved Sher Shah Suri's centralized administrative system and was a great patron of Moghul art and literature.

Moghul art and architecture reached its height under Akbar's son, Jahangir, and grandson, Shah Jahan, who between them left a legacy of magnificent mosques, palaces, forts and gardens embellished with luxurious and delicate decorations.

Aurangzeb, who ruled from 1658 to 1707, was a pious man and an efficient administrator, but within a few decades of his death the empire disintegrated into several independent states and Muslim power declined.

Then, in 1739, Nadir Shah of Persia invaded the subcontinent and sacked Delhi, but annexed only the territories west of the Indus. After his death, Ahmad Shah Durrani founded the Kingdom of Afghanistan and acquired the Indus territories, the Punjab and Kashmir.

Early in the 19th century, the martial Sikhs, whose religion split from Hinduism in the 16th century, asserted themselves in the Punjab and, by the 1830s, had pushed the Afghans back across the Indus and as far northwest as the Khyber Pass. Ranjit Singh, their greatest leader, consolidated Sikh power in the Punjab and ruled from his capital at Lahore from 1799 to 1839.

The British Period

The British, meanwhile, had arrived in the subcontinent some two centuries earlier, at the beginning of the 17th century. British East

India Company traders started as humble petitioners begging concessions — first from local rulers and later from the Moghul emperors — to trade in cotton, wool, opium, indigo, sugar, jute, diamonds and anything else on which they thought they could turn a profit. Slowly, through force, bribery, usury and intrigue, they consolidated their trade privileges.

By the middle of the 18th century, the British (in the guise of the British East India Company) had become deeply enmeshed in the politics of India and, after the battle of Plassey in 1757, began the systematic conquest of the subcontinent. As Moghul power waned, the Sikhs rose to power in the Punjab and the north, while the British rapidly extended their influence over the rest of the country. By 1843, Sind was in British hands, taken because it was a useful corridor to Afghanistan. British territories met those of the Sikhs at the Sutlej River in the Punjab. In 1845, the British defeated the Sikhs in the First Anglo-Sikh War and set up a British political resident at Lahore. Four years later, the British won the Second Sikh War and annexed the Punjab and the North-West Frontier area.

After the First War of Independence in 1857 (also called the Indian or Sepoy Mutiny), the British government assumed sovereignty over the lands of the British East India Company, bringing half a century of steadily increasing government control to its logical conclusion in the British Raj — *raj* meaning 'rule'. Queen Victoria's Indian realm continued to expand, until Hunza, the remote kingdom bordering China, fell into British hands in 1891, bringing expansion to an end.

The frontier separating British India from Afghanistan was delineated by the British in 1893. The resulting Durand Line cut straight through the tribal area of the Pathans. (There are now about ten million Pathans on the Pakistani side of the border and about half as many in Afghanistan.) The British left the tribal areas to govern themselves under the supervision of British political agents, a system still used by the Pakistani government.

In other ways as well, the influence of the British Raj persists in Pakistan. Elements of the colonial administrative and legal systems, reflecting the traditions of Great Britain, survive to this day. The British mapped the country, demarcated its borders and supplied it with impressive networks of roads, railways and canals. Not only the English language, but also British culture, art and architecture are still in evidence. The architecture is concentrated in the separate cantonments the British built for themselves beside most major towns. These cantonments feature wide, tree-lined avenues and imposing public buildings that are a curious mixture of Victorian gothic and classic Moghul styles.

The Emergence of Pakistan

Following the unsuccessful First War of Independence in 1857, the British resolved to suppress and weaken the Muslims, whom they held mainly responsible for the uprising. Sir Syed Ahmed Khan (1817–98), one of the first to set about restoring Muslim status, founded the Aligarh Movement, later to evolve into the Muslim League. The League was initially part of the Indian National Congress, which had been founded in 1885 to promote political freedom for all communities of the subcontinent. The Muslims broke away, however, because they felt that the Congress neglected their interests.

In 1930, the great Muslim poet and philosopher, Dr Muhammad Iqbal, proposed the creation of a separate Muslim state comprising those areas of the subcontinent with a Muslim majority. His goal was adopted by Muhammad Ali Jinnah, a British-trained lawyer who was to lead the struggle for Pakistan and become its first head of state. When the British realized that they had to relinquish their imperial hold on the subcontinent, they tried to keep the country intact by suggesting that there be autonomous Muslim states under a central government. They failed, however, to devise a plan acceptable to both the Muslim League and the Hindu-dominated Congress. The British finally agreed that the subcontinent should be partitioned into two states upon Independence in 1947.

The division of the subcontinent proved a difficult task. Not only did it coincide with separation from Great Britain, it had to be executed within a limited period of time. Pakistan was to consist of the Muslim-majority areas of the northeast and northwest, while India would retain the predominantly Hindu central region. The most explosive problem area was the fertile Punjab, where Hindu, Muslim and Sikh populations were inextricably mixed. At Independence, an estimated six million Muslim refugees, mainly from the Punjab, streamed across the border into Pakistan, while some four and a half million Sikhs and Hindus went the other way. This migration was accompanied by some of the most grisly communal violence of modern times, resulting in the loss of perhaps half a million lives.

The accession of hundreds of princely states scattered over the subcontinent provided considerable scope for disagreement between India and Pakistan. Though the vast majority were Hindu and readily acceded to India, control of two Hindu-majority states under Muslim rulers was achieved only by sending in the Indian army.

It was in Muslim-majority Kashmir that war broke out. The Hindu maharajah of this beautiful and strategic state had let the Independence Day accession deadline pass without joining either Pakistan or India — an apparent bid for independence or at least a favourable autonomy arrangement. Two months later, the Pakistanis invaded Kashmir, and the maharajah turned to India for help. This led to a military stalemate and the division of Kashmir. Both Pakistan and India still claim the whole of Kashmir, which remains the prime bone of contention between the two countries. The conflict is unlikely to be resolved until India makes good its 30-year-old promise of a plebiscite to determine the wishes of the Kashmiris now living under Indian rule.

The Muslim-majority states that acceded to Pakistan were Khairpur (in Sind), Bahawalpur (in the Punjab), Kalat and Las Bela (in Baluchistan), Dir, Swat and Chitral (in North-West Frontier Province) and Gilgit, Hunza, Punial, Ishkoman, Gupis and Yasin (in the Northern Areas).

Another problem of Partition was that the headwaters of all of Pakistan's main rivers lie in India, requiring a bilateral agreement on water rights for irrigation. A solution was not found until 1959, when the World Bank facilitated the drawing up of a treaty.

Pakistan after Independence

The greatest difficulties facing the new Pakistan were that it consisted of two parts — West and East — separated by nearly 2,000 kilometres (1,250 miles) of hostile Indian territory and that its two divisions were ethnically distinct, with little in common except religion. West Pakistan dominated politically and economically, despite having the smaller population.

The writing of a new constitution took nearly a decade; then, almost immediately in 1958, the constitution was abrogated by the martial-law government of General Ayub Khan, who in 1969 was succeeded by General Yahya Khan. All the while, East Pakistan was becoming increasingly dissatisfied with its position in the power structure. Things came to a head in 1970, when conditions in the East were exacerbated by a disastrous cyclone. In December of that year, elections resulted in wins for the Pakistan People's Party in the West and the Awami League in the East. The dispute over which party would form the government led first to strikes in East Pakistan, then to outright revolt. With a declaration of war on Pakistan, India supported the creation of independent Bangladesh.

Zulfikar Ali Bhutto remained prime minister of Pakistan until 1977, pursuing a policy popular with the urban masses and rural poor, especially in Sind. He nationalized basic industries, banks and insurance, began to democratize the civil service and initiated reform of the health and education systems. When Britain recognized Bangladesh, Bhutto pulled Pakistan out of the British Commonwealth.

He also strengthened ties with China in an attempt to balance the threat from India. Bhutto's downfall came after the general elections in 1977, which opposition parties alleged were rigged in the Punjab.

General Zia-ul-Haq took over the administration of Pakistan, and the state charged Bhutto with the murder of the father of a political opponent. His conviction was followed by a retrial and a second conviction. Bhutto was hanged on 4 April 1979.

Under martial law, Pakistan saw steady economic growth led by the private sector. It also saw efforts towards Islamization of the political, legal and economic structures. 'Non-party' elections were held in 1985, resulting in a civilian government under President Zia and the lifting of martial law the following year.

Afghan Refugees

An estimated three million refugees who fled the Soviet invasion of Afghanistan now live in Pakistan, housed in some 350 refugee camps, mostly in the North-West Frontier Province. With the help of international refugee agencies, Pakistan provides tents, clothing, food, fuel, schooling and medical care. The influx of such a large number of people and livestock into an arid area with a delicately balanced ecology is causing many problems, not the least of which is overgrazing.

Historical Dates

3000−1500 BC	Indus Civilization
1700 BC	Aryans invade from Central Asia
516 BC	Northern Pakistan becomes easternmost province of Achaemenid Empire of Persia. Gandhara is semi-independent kingdom
327−325 BC	Alexander the Great invades Pakistan
272−236 BC	Mauryan Emperor Ashoka promotes Buddhism
185 BC	Bactrian Greeks conquer northwest Pakistan
75 BC	Arrival of Scythians (Sakas) from Central Asia
20 AD	Parthians conquer northern Pakistan
60	Kushans from Central Asia overthrow Parthians
3rd century	Kushans decline and are dominated by Sassanian Empire of Persia
4th century	Kidar (Little) Kushans come to power
455	White Huns invade Gandhara and are converted to Hinduism
565	Sassanians and Turks overthrow Huns

Late 6th–7th century	Turki Shahis control area west of Indus, including Gandhara
711	Muhammad bin Qasim conquers Sind and southern Punjab
870	Hindu Shahis arrive from Central Asia
1001–26	Mahmud of Ghazni invades. Mass conversions to Islam
1034–1337	Sind ruled by Sumrahs, a Sindi tribe
1150	Ghaznavid Kingdom destroyed by Ghorids
13th century	The consolidation of the Muslim sultanate of north India
1221	The Mongol Genghiz Khan invades Punjab
1337	Sammah Rajputs overthrow the Sumrahs in Sind
1398–9	Tamerlane invades from Central Asia
15th century	Decline of Delhi Sultanate. Founding of Sikh religion
Early 16th century	Babur, first Moghul emperor, raids Punjab
1524	Sind conquered by Shah Beg Arghun from Kandahar. Amir Chakar Rind unites Baluchi tribes and defeats Sammahs
1526	Babur defeats Lodis, last of Delhi sultans, and establishes Moghul Empire

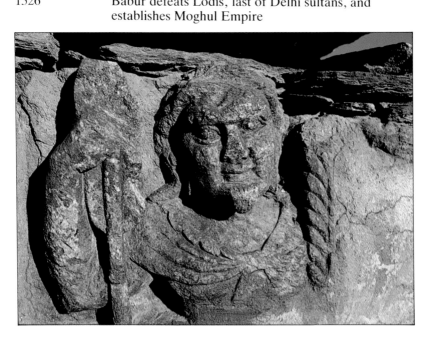

1530–56	Humayun, Babur's son, is emperor, but is forced into exile in Persia by Sher Shah Suri
1545	Death of Sher Shah Suri. Tarkhans take power in Sind
1556–1605	Akbar, son of Humayun, is emperor
1605–27	Jahangir is emperor
1627–58	Shah Jahan is emperor
1658–1707	Aurangzeb is emperor. Sikhs organize as warrior sect
1736	Founding of Kalhora Dynasty in Sind
1739	Nadir Shah of Persia invades subcontinent
1747–73	Ahmad Shah Durrani founds Kingdom of Afghanistan and acquires Indus territories, Punjab and Kashmir
1760s–1830s	Sikhs become dominant force in Punjab
1789	Talpur Baluchis overthrow Kalhora Dynasty in Sind
1799–1839	Ranjit Singh rules Punjab from Lahore
1843	British annex Sind. First British-Afghan War
1845–6	First British-Sikh War
1848–9	British defeat Sikhs in Second Sikh War, annex Punjab and NWFP
1857	First War of Independence (Indian or Sepoy Mutiny)
1858	British government assumes direct rule of British East India Company lands, establishes British Raj
1887	All districts of Baluchistan in British hands
1889	British establish Gilgit Agency
1891	British conquer Hunza and Nagar
1906	All India Muslim League founded
1930	Muhammad Iqbal proposes creation of separate Muslim state
1947	Independence and Partition
1948	Muhammad Ali Jinnah dies. Indo-Pakistani clash over Kashmir
1949	UN sponsors ceasefire in Kashmir
1958	General Ayub Khan sets up military government
1965	17-day Indo-Pakistan War. UN sponsors ceasefire
1969	General Yahya Khan takes over government
1970–7	Pakistan People's Party government under Zulfikar Ali Bhutto
1971	Bloody secession, assisted by India, of East Pakistan, which becomes Bangladesh
1977	General Zia-ul-Haq takes over government
1985	Non-party elections held, returning Zia
1986	Zia ends martial law

Religion

Islam

In few countries does religion play as important a part in the lives of its people as in Pakistan, which was created specifically to provide the Muslims of India with a state of their own. Islam pervades every facet of society. The muezzin's call to prayer from the minarets of the mosques; men bowed in prayer in the fields, shops and airports; *qibbla* (Urdu for 'the direction of Mecca') marked in every hotel bedroom; the veiled women in the streets — all are constant reminders of the devotion and religious fervour of the Pakistanis.

Muslims make up nearly the entire population of Pakistan. Hindus, mostly nomads living in the south, account for only 1.6 percent, and the Christian and Zoroastrian communities are even smaller.

Islam — Arabic for 'submission to God' — was founded by the Prophet Muhammad, who was born in the Arabian city of Mecca in AD 570 and died in Medina in 632. As a prophet, Muhammad was convinced that there was but one God and that there should be one community of believers, while as a statesman he possessed an unparalleled ability to unify the Arab nation. As a prophet and a statesman, he is one of the towering figures of history.

Muhammad saw himself as God's messenger and preached a universal brotherhood in which all men were equal in the sight of God. The masses of the Middle East had exhausted themselves with a long series of wars and were ready to accept Muhammad's new monotheistic religion. The Islamic Empire expanded rapidly and, within a century, stretched from Spain to India.

Islamic dogma holds that the teachings of Islam were first revealed at Creation and that prophets have been sent from time to time to reconvey God's word. These divinely inspired prophets are the Hebrew patriarchs, such as Abraham and Moses. Jesus, too, is revered as a great prophet, though not regarded, as he is by Christians, as divine in himself. Muslims call those who follow the prophets — that is to say, Jews and Christians as well as Muslims — *ahl-e-kitab*, or 'people of revealed books'.

Muslims believe that, despite the teachings of the early prophets, man has continually erred and the prophecy has become obscured and overladen with false interpretations. Muhammad was sent to restore purity and bring to mankind the true word of God. He was the last prophet, to be followed only by the Messiah.

Each Muslim, or adherent of Islam, has five fundamental religious duties, called the Pillars of Islam. He must recite the creed, '*La illaha*

illa 'llah Muhammad Rasulu 'llah' ('There is no God but Allah, and Muhammad is his prophet'). He must also pray five times a day, fast during the month of Ramazan and give alms (*zakat*) for distribution among the poor. Finally, he must save for a pilgrimage to Mecca.

The Koran, the holy book of Islam, is a distillation of the written and oral records compiled during Muhammad's lifetime and in the decades following his death. It lays down the philosophy of Islam and its moral code. As the exact word of God as revealed through Muhammad, the Koran is infallible; it is the supreme authority to which a Muslim looks for guidance.

Islam suffered a major split almost from its beginning. Muhammad died without clearly naming a successor, and there followed a struggle for power, with the result that most of the early leaders of Islam suffered violent deaths. Two main sects of Islam emerged: the larger sect, the Sunnis, followed elected leaders called *caliphs* (*khalifa* is Arabic for 'representative' or 'deputy'); the smaller sect, the Shias (or Shi'ites), followed a line of hereditary leaders called *imams*, who were descended directly from Muhammad through Fatima, his daughter, and Ali, his son-in-law and cousin. The Ismailis, the followers of the Aga Khan, are an offshoot of the Shias and are very active in Pakistan.

Today, most Pakistanis are orthodox Sunnis; most of the rest are Shias, with a smaller number being Ismailis. There are also a few Ahmadis (or Ahmediyas), adherents of Islam's newest sect, which is branded as heretical by other Muslims. The Ahmadis are also called Qadianis, after the Punjabi town of Qadian, where the sect was founded in 1908.

Islam arrived in Pakistan 80 years after the death of Muhammad with the Arab conquest of Sind in AD 711. (The ruins of a mosque dating from 726 have been found at Banbhore, near Karachi.) Holy men subsequently travelling to the subcontinent were able to convert many to Islam, as the new religion offered more hope of salvation than Hinduism, with its fatalistic cycle of reincarnation and its rigid caste structure. In the 11th century, Mahmud of Ghazni brought Islam into the north from Afghanistan, and Islam became the dominant religious force in all the areas of modern Pakistan.

Today, Islamic principles guide the development of Pakistani society, from the government's introduction of interest-free banking and the systematic collection of *zakat* (the welfare tax prescribed by Islam) to the ban against the purchase of alcohol except by permit-holding non-Muslims.

Sufism

Sufism is Islam's mystical tradition, and Sufis are Muslim holy men who develop their spirituality through prayer and meditation. *Sufi* comes from the Arabic *safa*, meaning 'purity', so Sufis are those whose hearts and souls are pure.

The first Sufis were ascetic wanderers in the ninth century who, by fasting, meditation and self-denial, found nearness to God. They wandered around the Islamic world, through Persia and Afghanistan and into the subcontinent, preaching a message of love, peace and brotherhood and teaching by pious example. Many were scholars, poets and musicians able to attract large followings to their gentle form of Islam. Some of Pakistan's finest music and literature were written by Sufi saints: verses set to music that extol the love of God, and morality stories in which virtue receives its reward. The saints portrayed life at its most perfect, embodying the noblest moral teachings of Islam.

The places where Sufi saints settled and died have become important centres of pilgrimage, attracting devoted followers who admire their piety and hope for their intercession to secure God's grant of health, fertility, peace or success. In this way, the saints have given hope to the poor and sick for over a thousand years.

The greatest saints in Pakistan, each with hundreds of thousands of devotees, are Lal Shahbaz Qalandar, whose shrine is in Sehwan Sharif, Data Ganj Baksh of Lahore, Baba Farid Ganj-e-Shakar of Pakpatan, Shah Latif of Bhit Shah near Hala, Pir Baba of Buner, Bari Imam of Nurpur near Islamabad and Shah Shams Tabrez of Multan. All over the country, hundreds of other shrines draw pilgrims who come to pray and make offerings.

Foreign visitors are always welcome at Sufi shrines, provided they remove their shoes, cover their heads and otherwise show respect. The shrines are centres of religious, cultural and social interest. Rich and poor alike come to pray. The best time to go is on Thursday evening, when the shrines are crowded and there is often devotional singing and dancing. Some Sufi followers use music, dancing and incense to reach a trance-like state of communion with God.

Every shrine has a festival (*urs*) each year on the anniversary of its saint's death. The shrine then becomes a fairground, with musicians playing traditional instruments and singers performing mystical folk songs, while dervishes and mendicants dance themselves into a devotional frenzy. Trade fairs also take place, as do sports competitions and, at the larger festivals, exhibition matches of such traditional martial arts as wrestling, swordsmanship, riding, fighting with daggers, and tent-pegging (in which horsemen riding at full gallop pluck pegs from the ground with lances).

Hinduism

Pakistan has played an important role in the historical development of
Buddhism and Hinduism, the latter taking its very name from the
Indus River, along the banks of which it evolved sometime after the
Aryan invasion in 1700 BC. About four million Hindus left Pakistan at
Partition in 1947, and fewer than 1.5 million remain in the country
today.

Buddhism

Buddhism developed in the Ganges Valley and spread to the Indus
Valley in the third century BC, about 230 years after the death of
Buddha. From the second to the fifth century AD, Gandhara, in
northern Pakistan, was Buddhism's most important centre, from where
the religion spread to Tibet and China. Tantric Buddhism evolved in
the Swat Valley in northern Pakistan.

Though no Buddhist community remains in Pakistan today, the
museums are full of Buddhist art dating from the first to the seventh
century. These works, mostly statues of Buddha and scenes from his
life carved in stone or modelled in plaster, were excavated from
archaeological sites all over the country.

Siddhartha Gautama, the Buddha, was born in Nepal in 624 BC.
The son of a wealthy prince, he led a sheltered existence until the age
of 29, when his first sight of human suffering resolved him to renounce
all worldly pleasures. He left his wife and young son and surrendered
himself to the search for peace. He tried fasting and penance without
success, finally receiving enlightenment through meditation. He then
devoted the rest of his life to teaching the way of righteousness and
truth. He died at the age of 80 in 544 BC in Gorakpur, an Indian town
just across the border from his Nepalese birthplace.

Buddhists do not believe in a supreme god, but look instead to the
Buddha, the teacher of truth, to guide them along the Middle Path,
between worldliness and asceticism, to perfection and a higher life.
Buddhists endeavour to avoid suffering by suppressing their sensual
passions, depending on themselves and their own efforts to purify their
lives through charity, compassion, truthfulness, chastity, respect and
self-restraint. The final goal is nirvana, a state of mind beyond human
existence, beyond sin and care.

When Buddha died he was cremated and his ashes divided up and
buried under stupas at various places across northern India. Several of
the stupas in Pakistan are thought to have once contained his ashes.

Though Buddha did not visit Pakistan during his final incarnation,
he is believed to have been there in some of his earlier lives. The

legends of these former lives are told in the Jataka stories, and
Buddhist shrines were built at the places described therein, several of
which are near Peshawar.

Sikhism

The founder of the Sikh religion, Guru Nanak (1469–1538), was born
near Lahore. Taking some elements of Hinduism and combining them
with new ideas, he formed a monotheistic religion with no caste
system. The religion evolved over two centuries and became a strong
military brotherhood. The Sikhs achieved the height of their power
under Ranjit Singh at the beginning of the 19th century, when they
controlled an empire centred on the Punjab, with Lahore as their
temporal capital and nearby Amritsar (in India) as their religious
capital.

   At Partition, the Sikhs migrated *en masse* to India, where they are
now agitating for a separate Sikh state in the Indian part of the Punjab.
Their shrines in Pakistan are maintained by the government and are
visited at festival times by Sikh pilgrims.

Sind

The southern province of Sind takes its name from the Indus River, which flows down its middle, making fertile an otherwise arid, barren land. The province has three distinct landscapes: the lush, irrigated plains along the river, the sparsely populated deserts on either side of the irrigated belt, and the mangrove swamps of the Indus delta. It is flat except at its western edge, where the Kirthar Hills form its border with Baluchistan. The climate is pleasant in winter, with temperatures ranging from 10° to 30°C (50° to 85°F), and hot in summer, when the mercury moves between 25° and 50°C (75° and 120°F).

The irrigated alluvial soil forms some of Pakistan's best farmland. As far as canals can carry water from the Indus, farmers grow wheat, rice, millet, pulses, oil-seeds, cotton, sugar-cane, chillies and such fruits as bananas, mangoes, dates and varieties of citrus. Most of the 70 percent of Sind's rural population that live by agriculture are tenant farmers tilling soil belonging to feudal landlords of Baluch descent. Their way of life has changed little over the centuries, despite some mechanization.

The deserts begin immediately the irrigation ends, the line between green fields and sandy scrubland strikingly abrupt. Desert tribes, some settled around wells, some nomadic, eke out a bare subsistence by breeding camels and goats, growing pulses and millet, and hiring themselves out as migrant labourers.

The Indus delta is a vast marshy tract stretching from Karachi to the Indian border some 250 kilometres (150 miles) away. Through its myriad sluggish channels meandering around thousands of mangrove islands, the Indus empties into the Arabian Sea. Each year, the river deposits millions of tons of silt in the coastal waters, extending the delta and enriching the marine food chain. Fishing is the main occupation on the coast, providing Karachi's restaurants with the seafood for which they are justly famous.

The history of Sind goes back 5,000 years to the Indus Civilization. Moenjodaro was one of the great cities of antiquity, and its ruins, visible on the right bank of the Indus, reveal the remarkably advanced urban organization of a centrally administered empire that sprawled from the Indus as far northwest as Kabul and as far east as Delhi.

Alexander the Great arrived in Sind in 326 BC and captured the main towns along the river. In the third and second centuries BC, Sind was part of the great Mauryan Empire of India. The Buddhism embraced at that time was subsequently supplanted by Hinduism and its caste system.

An Arab expedition under Muhammad bin Qasim conquered Sind in AD 711, which marked the beginning of the Islamic era in the subcontinent, and the province was governed until 874 by the Abbassid Caliphat, the Sunni court at Baghdad described in 'The Thousand and One Nights'.

From the ninth to the 19th centuries, seven different dynasties ruled in Sind. The capital city moved whenever the summer flooding of the Indus carried the river away into a new channel, causing old cities to be abandoned and new ones built. Mansura, Thatta, Alor, Sehwan, Khudabad and Hyderabad were each at one time or another the seat of government — each at one time or another situated on the banks of the river.

The cultural life of Sind revolves around the shrines of the Sufi saints, where religious music and devotional singing constitute a major part of the traditional ceremonies. The Sufi saints are also responsible for the best of Sindhi literature, having written poetry and narratives of great beauty and intensity that are recited and sung all over Pakistan. Sufi shrines are everywhere, and the people who come to them do so in the faith that the saints will intercede with God for the granting of some favour — be it health, fertility or success in some endeavour.

Religion is intensely important to Sindhis, who mark out prayer areas beside their homes and along the roads. These areas are about two metres square and surrounded by stones, with the *mehrab* or prayer niche oriented towards Mecca. Anyone can stop, remove their shoes and pray. (Tourists should take care not to inadvertently step into one of these areas while wearing their shoes.)

Sind is famous for its handicrafts, particularly its textiles, pottery and lacquered woodwork. Patchwork quilts and fabrics with woven stripes or block-printed designs are available in bazaars all over the province. Blue-glazed tiles from Sind decorate most shrines and mosques in Pakistan, and the town of Hala has developed into a centre for the woodworking industry.

The Sindhis are the most colourfully and variously dressed people in Pakistan, with men in the centre of the province favouring turbans in shocking pink. Others wear embroidered caps set aglitter by tiny mirrors, colourful long-tailed shirts worn over *lunghis* (men's sarongs), and traditional embroidered slippers with long, pointed, upturned toes. Women of the desert dress in red skirts cut long and flowing and in bright, tie-dyed shawls. In Sind, the loose-fitting and warm-hued clothes reflect the relaxed and friendly personalities of their wearers.

The Sindhi language, which has its own script, is only one of several spoken in the province, some of the most important being Thari in the Thar Desert, Kutchi in the Rann (Marsh) of Kutch, Lari

in Lower Sind, and Saraiki in Upper Sind. Urdu is the language of
Karachi, a city now populated primarily by Partition-era immigrants,
known as *Mohajirs*, who brought the language with them from India.

Karachi

With a population of eight million, Karachi is the largest city in
Pakistan. A century ago, however, it was a small, isolated collection of
fishermen's huts clustered on the three islands of Manora, Bhit and
Baba in what is now Karachi harbour. The British built Karachi up and
made it the capital of Sind, and, since the creation of Pakistan in 1947,
the city has grown into an international port and the commercial and
industrial hub of the country. It boasts an unusual mixture of modern
skyscrapers and solid, 19th century Victorian Gothic buildings, tree-
lined boulevards and narrow, dusty alleys. Because it is a
comparatively new city, it has no Moghul mosques or tombs. Its main
attractions are, instead, its colourful bazaars, its modern monuments
and the sea.

Getting to Karachi

Karachi has an international airport and a harbour and is connected to
the rest of the country by rail and two major roads, the National
Highway and the newer Super Highway. Most visitors arrive at the
airport, which is ten kilometres from the Saddar Bazaar (the city
centre), a journey costing Rs90 by taxi, Rs10 by airport coach or Rs2
by public bus.

When to Go

Karachi is best during the winter months from mid-November to
mid-February, when the daytime temperature is 15°−20°C (60°−
70°F). In summer the temperature hovers at 35°−45°C (100°−115°F).
During the monsoon season in July and August, the city is very humid,
though little rain falls.

Sights

The Bazaars

The one attraction not to be missed, even by those with only a few
hours in Karachi, is the sprawling bazaar in the **old city** north of M A
Jinnah (Bundar) Road, behind Boulton Market. Hindu women

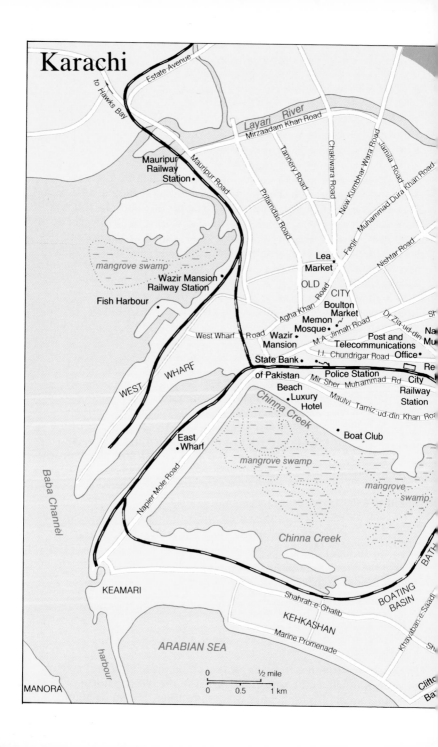

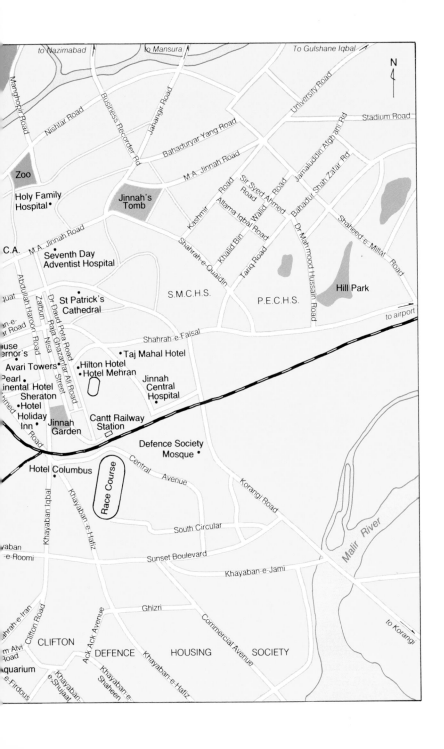

wearing bright, full skirts over baggy trousers, and tribal Baluch men in huge, colourful turbans jostle with camel and donkey carts in the narrow streets. Closer to the market's heart, the alleyways become too narrow for carts and are crammed instead with tiny box-like shops. Each lane specializes in a different commodity.

To get there, ask the driver to drop you in **Sarafa (Silver) Bazaar**, where exquisite old tribal silver jewellery is sold by weight.

Enter a narrow lane opposite a shop called Bombay Jewellery Mart to get to the heart of the bazaar. At the end of Sarafa Bazaar, you come to **Bartan Galli**, where pots and pans of copper, aluminium and steel in all sizes stand stacked against the walls. They, too, are sold by weight. Tinsmiths sit on the ground in front of their stalls coating the copper pots with tin, as the copper is poisonous and must be coated before it can be used for cooking.

Next comes the wholesale cloth bazaar, the most colourful of all. Gold and red, turquoise and blue, the lengths of cloth festoon the alleys. This is the best place to buy traditional Sindhi fabrics: *sussi*, a striped hand-loom; *ajrak*, with block-printed geometric designs; and *bandini*, which is tie-dyed.

There follows a wider area, the **Khajoor (Date) Bazaar**, where tarpaulin awnings flap in the wind over piles of dried fruit. Hawkers wander up and down offering everything from embroidered Sindhi hats and coloured pyjama cords to strips of walnut bark for cleaning the teeth.

Further east, **Saddar Bazaar**, modern Karachi's central shopping area, stretches for about a kilometre (half a mile) from north to south between the two main streets, Abdullah Haroon (Victoria) Road and Zaibun Nisa (Elphinstone) Street.

It is divided into several distinct markets. First on the right as you go north along Abdullah Haroon Road is **Zainab Market**, with dozens of little shops selling new copper and brass, onyx, inlaid wood, lacquer work, hand-printed cloth and appliqué bedspreads or *rillis*. Look for the shops with excellent old embroidered Sindhi cloth, traditional wedding dresses with mirror embroidery work and old tribal silver jewellery. (Marvi Handicrafts and Village Handicrafts are recommended.) Also available at Zainab Market are very good and extremely cheap cotton shirts, ready-made *shalwar kameez* (women's national costumes), export rejects and tee-shirts that proclaim, 'I caught crabs in Karachi.'

A little further up Abdullah Haroon Road are carpet shops selling new Pakistani carpets and old tribal rugs from Baluchistan, Afghanistan and Iran.

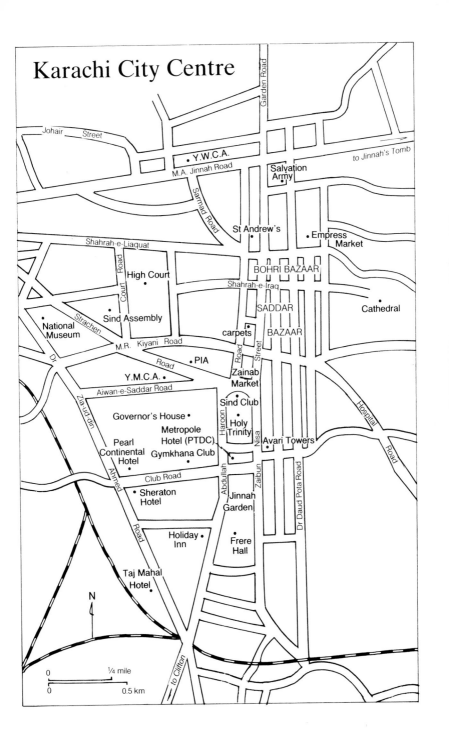

Art on wheels: Trucks and buses serve as canvasses for garish paintings that celebrate all aspects of life, religious and secular.

Oriental Carpets
by Kent Obee

Pakistan is an excellent place to shop for oriental carpets from neighbouring countries or from Pakistan itself, which is now ranked among the top four producers of hand-knotted carpets in the world.

The carpet industry developed in Pakistan only after Partition, so Pakistani carpets are all 'new' and mostly copies of Persian and Turkoman designs. At their best, however, they are as well made as the Iranian or Afghan originals — only less expensive. They are a sensible choice for the buyer wishing to avoid the uncertainties of older rugs or interested in coordinating the carpet with a particular colour scheme.

Pakistan is also an entrepot for carpets from Afghanistan, Iran and Chinese Turkestan (Xinjiang). Afghan carpets are the most readily available, and doubly so in recent years as a result of the upheaval in that country. Most Afghan carpets are 'tribal' pieces made by either Turkoman or Baluch weavers — though many of the newer carpets are actually made in refugee camps in Pakistan. Smuggled Iranian carpets are available in smaller numbers in the major cities at prices as high or higher than the same carpets would fetch in Europe or America. Tribal carpets from Chinese Turkestan have become increasingly available on the market since the opening of the Karakoram Highway.

Any one of Pakistan's major cities — Karachi, Islamabad, Peshawar, Lahore or Quetta — is a good place to shop for carpets. Lahore is the manufacturing and wholesaling centre of the indigenous carpet industry. Peshawar and Quetta are entry points for goods coming from Afghanistan and Iran, but the better pieces soon make their way to the markets of Islamabad and Karachi, drawn by the more numerous foreign buyers and the resulting higher prices.

Caveat emptor is the golden rule of carpet buying in Pakistan. Although many dealers are well informed and genuinely interested in sharing their enthusiasm for their wares, others are neither particularly knowledgeable nor above duping a gullible tourist with a story that a chemically washed product from a refugee camp is a hundred-year-old Bokhara. Shops in the major tourist hotels can be especially bad in this respect. The collector's knowledge (or that of a friend) of carpets and the current market is the best guarantee of making a worthwhile purchase.

The prospective buyer should be prepared to bargain — and bargain hard. The amount dealers come down varies greatly from shop to shop; it can be as little as five or ten percent, or it might be 50 percent. Many residents of Islamabad, when shopping at the popular Juma (Friday) Market, use as a rule of thumb a reduction of a third.

While there are inherent risks, there are also genuine carpet bargains to be had in Pakistan. Few antiques or museum pieces appear on the market, but the discerning shopper can find carpets of true quality and artistic merit. The pursuit of these can be enjoyable and educational — even addictive.

Bohri Bazaar, down the side lanes north of the carpet shops, is another cloth bazaar offering a wide selection of fabrics. It is usually full of women dressed in traditional *purdah* shopping elbow to elbow with thoroughly modern Karachi ladies.

Empress Market, further north and dating from 1889, is a huge Victorian Gothic structure crowned by a clock tower 50 metres (165 feet) high. Inside are hundreds of stalls selling fruit, vegetables, meat, fish and other groceries. Housewives hire assistants to haggle for the best produce (for a small commission) and carry their shopping bags. A stall behind the market sells hookahs of every conceivable shape and size.

The Sea

The most romantic way to spend an evening in Karachi is to go crabbing in Karachi's harbour in a traditional lateen-sailed craft, an activity that begins at sunset and ends with a crab feast under the stars.

Keamari Harbour, as it is called, is a 15-minute ride by minibus or taxi from central Karachi. (If you take your own car, it is safe parked in the guarded lot.) At the end of the wharf, dozens of boatmen clamour for your attention. Bargain hard for a rate of Rs50–100 per hour for a private boat seating ten. Aim to set sail about an hour before sunset and plan to stay out for three or four hours. Before you leave, check that your boatman has on board potatoes, onions, seasonings and — well — crabs, in case your luck is bad. Bring your own drinks.

The wharf business settled, a boy shins up the mast to unfurl the sail and the boat slides out into the harbour. The captain finds a spot to drop anchor, and passengers receive handlines and bits of fish to use as bait. Meanwhile, the crew fry up the potatoes and onions and heat a pot of water. The crabs can then be either boiled or fried with spices.

As the sun sets, dangling V-formations of cormorants wing westward to their roosts and flamingos fly close to the shoreline.

If there is a moon to light your way, a romantic sail further up the harbour takes you to **Sandspit**, the nine-kilometre-long (six-mile) sandbank that divides the sheltered harbour from the open sea. Wade ashore and walk 100 metres (yards) over the spit to the seaward side, where from July to November giant sea turtles lumber ashore to lay their eggs in the sand. To find them, look along the shoreline for their tracks, which look like tractor tracks about a metre and a half (five feet) wide. Follow these up the beach. The turtle is skittish while she is digging her nest, but once she starts laying her eggs, talking and even a weak light will not disturb her.

In season, turtles lay on all the sandy beaches from the mouth of the harbour west to Cape Monze. The Sind Wildlife Management Board arranges guided tours of the turtle projects at Sandspit and Hawkes Bay (see Karachi listing on page 206).

Daytime visitors to Keamari harbour can chug around in public launches that cast off when they are full. The crossing to Manora Point or to the islands of Bhit or Baba costs only Rs1 and takes about ten minutes from Keamari. Photography is forbidden in the harbour area.

Sandspit now runs to **Manora Point**, once an island and the site of the original fishing village of Karachi. Manora is less than an hour by car from central Karachi, but going by boat is easier and more fun. Once there, travel is by public Suzuki or on foot. The beach is clean enough for swimming. Kilometres of sand beg to be walked across, and there are even camel rides. Manora also has a large naval base, a lighthouse, two British Raj-era churches and a ruined Hindu temple.

The harbour islands of **Bhit** and **Baba** are still inhabited by descendants of Karachi's original fishing population. They are members of the dark-skinned Mohana tribe (thus related to the fishermen on Manchar Lake) and are very friendly.

Other daytime options at Keamari include bird-watching in the swampy creeks between Karachi and the mouths of the Indus and deep-sea fishing.

The **fish harbour** is at the end of West Wharf Road, where hundreds of fishing boats with coloured sails or outboard motors bring their daily catch. The wharf is always bustling with men unloading fish or loading ice and with children sluicing down boats and sitting in circles peeling shrimps. Further upstream, boat builders work shisham wood with bow drills and hand adzes and saws. No metal is used in the boats; hull planks are pegged to the ribs with wooden dowels.

The Beaches

The most popular outing for tourists with children is **Clifton Beach**, about five kilometres (three miles) south of central Karachi along Abdullah Haroon (Victoria) Road, only ten minutes by taxi or bus number 20 from Shahrah-e-Iraq Road. The beach has a well-stocked aquarium and an amusement park with a roller-coaster, ferris wheel, merry-go-round and bumper cars. Visitors can also ride camels and horses along the beach or sample the fare at the many food stalls. The water, however, is too polluted for swimming.

Clifton was once a tiny coastal village. Attracted by the cool sea breeze, the British developed it in the 19th century into a health resort for the military. Along its tree-lined streets survive many graceful old colonial houses set in spacious, shaded gardens.

Clifton Viewpoint, atop the hill beside the amusement park, overlooks the whole of Karachi. In the foreground stands **Mohatta Palace**, a turn-of-the-century Moghul Gothic pile of red sandstone complete with domes and cupolas. Jinnah's sister, Fatima, lived here until she died in 1978, but it is now empty. The seaward view has Oyster Rocks protruding from the water halfway to Manora Lighthouse, and to the right (west) you can see the tops of the loading cranes at Keamari Harbour.

At the top of the hill near Clifton Viewpoint is the **Shrine of Abdullah Shah Ghazi**. Its tall, square chamber and green dome are typical of Sufi shrines everywhere in Pakistan. Abdullah Shah Ghazi was a ninth-century saint descended directly from the Prophet Muhammad. He is revered as the patron saint of Karachi and has one of the largest followings in Pakistan, with devotees flocking to his shrine at a rate of 1,000 per day or as many as 10,000 at weekends. His intercession with God is considered particularly beneficial to women with marital problems such as an inability to conceive.

Foreigners are welcome in the shrine if they are suitably dressed (heads, legs and arms covered) and remove their shoes at the entrance. The best time to visit is Thursday evening, when Sind's most famous devotional singers gather for the *qawwali* ceremony, the singing of mystical songs. Many devotees spend the night in the shrine wrapped in their shawls.

This shrine, like others, is well supplied with beggers, who are attracted by the distribution of free food and provide the faithful with the opportunity of gaining a blessing through the giving of alms.

Beaches clean enough for swimming stretch west for hundreds of kilometres along the coast of Sind and Baluchistan to the Iranian border, but only those near Karachi are open to foreigners.

Hawkes Bay, 25 kilometres (16 miles) from central Karachi, offers beach huts with cooking facilities, bathrooms and changing space. The swimming is particularly good in March and April, and in winter the sea is cold but still pleasant. However, from May through October the sea is dangerously rough, making swimming inadvisable. Camel rides and other seaside amusements are available.

Baleji Beach, about 45 minutes west of Karachi, is a succession of secluded bays divided by rocky outcrops. There is no greenery or, apart from that provided by a few private huts, shade of any kind. The rock pools are interesting, and body surfing is good, though swimmers should beware of the undertow.

Beyond Baleji Beach is Karachi Nuclear Power Plant (KANUPP), around which the road detours for about three kilometres (two miles), returning to the coast at **Paradise Point**. Here the waves crash through a rock with a hole in it. From here on, the road follows the top of a low cliff with quiet little coves along its base. From December through March, the snorkelling here is very good. **Cape Monze**, about 25 kilometres (15 miles) beyond the nuclear power plant, has a lighthouse and some more isolated coves.

Gaddani Beach, about 50 kilometres (30 miles) from Karachi across the Hub River in Baluchistan, is famous as the world's biggest ship-breaking yard. Ships displacing up to 20,000 tons are beached by running them full speed on to the sand at high tide. They are then taken apart with a minimum of mechanization. Foreign visitors in private cars may be turned back at the check-point at the bridge over the Hub River unless they have a permit obtainable (not very conveniently) from the provincial government of Baluchistan in Quetta. However, those taking the public bus that leaves from Lee Market in Karachi in the morning and afternoon are likely to get through unchallenged.

National Museum

One of the best museums in Pakistan, the National Museum, located off Dr Zia-ud-din Ahmed Road, houses a well-displayed collection of 4,500-year-old Indus Civilization artefacts, impressive 1,500-year-old Gandharan Buddhist stone sculpture, tenth-century Hindu sculpture from Bangladesh and Muslim art objects. There is also an interesting ethnological gallery, a room of coins and illustrated manuscripts, and a special exhibition hall.

Architecture

The Tomb of Muhammad Ali Jinnah is Karachi's most impressive monument. Jinnah, called the *Quaid-e-Azam* or Father of the Nation, led the movement for a separate Muslim state, which started in the 1930s. At Partition in 1947, he became the governor-general of Pakistan, an office he held for little more than a year before dying of tuberculosis. The square tomb stands on a hill at the east end of M A Jinnah Road, from where there is a good view over the city. The crystal chandelier inside is a gift from the People's Republic of China, the blue-tiled ceiling comes from Japan, and the silver railing was given by Iran. The colourful ceremony of the changing of the guard takes place every two hours: at 10 am, noon, 2 pm, and so on.

Defence Society Mosque, Karachi's largest and best-known modern mosque, supports a huge, flattened dome on a low red brick wall. It has excellent acoustics, enabling the unamplified voice of the *maulana* to be heard clearly by 20,000 worshippers.

Holy Trinity Cathedral, on Abdullah Haroon Road north of the Metropole Hotel, was built as the garrison church in the mid-19th century and survives as an example of colonial church architecture. Its many brass and marble memorials set round the inside wall recall the history of British life in Sind.

Several other 19th-century churches survive in Karachi, including **St Andrew's Church** and **St Patrick's Cathedral**. There are no graveyards near the churches; all Christians are buried in the Christian cemetery near the airport.

The **Sind Club**, on Abdullah Haroon Road, is of interest to enthusiasts of British social history. Founded in the mid-19th century exclusively for the enjoyment of British civil servants, the club did not accept Indian or Pakistani members until the early 1950s, some years after Independence. Though only members and their guests may eat at the club (and, in the evening, only if attired in dark suit and tie), casual visitors may wander in to gawk at the spacious halls and wide verandahs overlooking beautifully tended gardens. Particularly evocative are the billiards and reading rooms.

Frere Hall, set in the spacious Jinnah Gardens opposite the Holiday Inn, is a singularly charming Victorian Gothic hotchpotch. Built as a social and cultural centre in 1865, it is now a public library. The ceiling was recently painted by Sadequain, an eminent Pakistani artist.

The **Sind High Court**, on Court Road, is a 19th-century red sandstone assemblage of cupolas, balconies and pillars. Opposite is the **Sind Assembly Building**, which was built late in the 19th century in typical British colonial style with wide verandahs and high ceilings.

A drive west on I I Chundrigar Road takes one past the vast **Cotton Exchange Building** and the new **Habib Bank Plaza**, an elegant round tower. Further along on the left is the 19th-century, Greek-porticoed **State Bank of Pakistan**, beside which stands the new **State Bank Building**.

Trips from Karachi

National Highway to Thatta

A day trip along the National Highway to Thatta takes one past Chaukundi, Banbhore and Makli Hill on a tour of scenic and historical interest.

The **Chaukundi Tombs** are the first stop, 27 kilometres (17 miles) east of Karachi, where acres of stone tombs stretch along the crest of a low ridge. Built between the 15th and 19th centuries by Baluchis (a tribe originating in Syria) and Burpats (who arose from a cross of

Baluchis and Rajputs), the tombs are of various sizes and designs but fall into two basic types: some support roofs on pillars, but most consist of solid, oblong pyramids standing two to four metres (seven to 14 feet) high and completely covered with finely carved geometric designs. The small rosette is a frequent motif that may have some forgotten connection with pre-Islamic sun-worship, as may the sunflowers, wheels and chrysanthemums, which also suggest the sun. Squares, diamonds, triangles, swastikas, herringbones, zig-zags and crosses are also used in every possible combination. The same patterns also appear on local wood carvings and textiles.

Men's graves are those surmounted by a stylized turban atop a pillar carved with weapons and sometimes horses and riders, a design that may have originated in the Rajput custom of temporarily burying a fallen soldier at the battlefield and marking his grave with his upright sword capped by his turban. At any rate, such representation of animals and people is extremely rare in Muslim culture and bespeaks pre-Muslim influence.

Women's graves are often decorated with stylized jewellery, the earrings, bangles and necklaces resembling those still worn today. Similar groups of tombs exist at over 100 sites along the coast of Pakistan and as far inland as Sukkur.

Banbhore, an archaeological excavation with a museum, lies 62 kilometres (39 miles) from Karachi on the north bank of Gharo Creek and a few kilometres south of the highway. The foundations of a mosque and the city wall both date from the eighth century, making the mosque the earliest yet found in the subcontinent. It was about 40 metres (130 feet) square and consisted of an open courtyard surrounded by covered cloisters on three sides and the prayer chamber on the fourth. The roof of the prayer chamber was supported by 33 pillars arranged in three rows. The city wall was built of limestone blocks and had semi-circular bastions at regular intervals and three gates, the main gate opening south to the creek. The other gates, on the north and east sides, led to a lake that served as the city's main water supply.

Once a port near the mouth of the Indus, Banbhore may have been founded by Alexander the Great in 325 BC; certainly, Greek-style pottery dating from the first century BC has been found here. For the next 700 years, Buddhists and Hindus ruled the town as it grew in size and importance.

Banbhore has been identified with Debal, the port taken in AD 711 by the first Arab invader of the subcontinent, Muhammad bin Qasim. Sent by the caliph of Baghdad, the 17-year-old conqueror arrived by sea with a force of 15,000 infantry augmented by cavalry mounted on

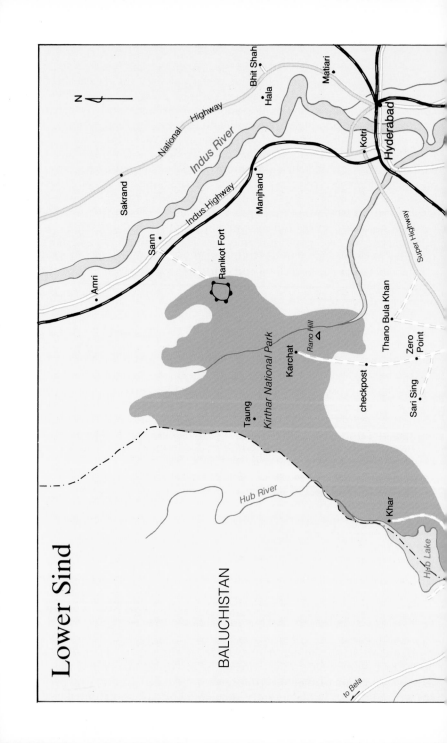

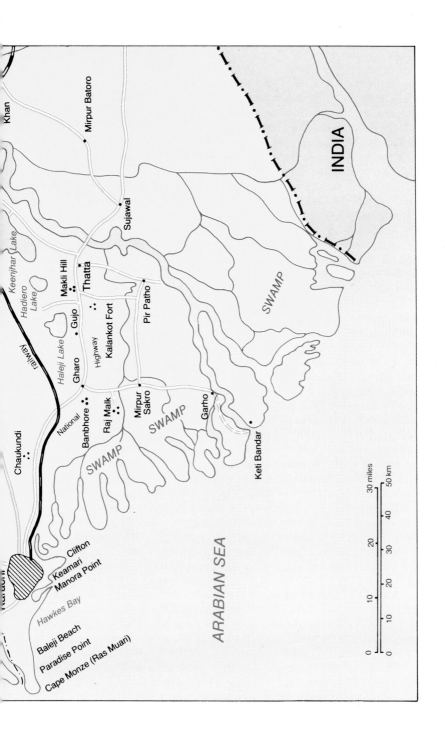

horses and camels. Weapons included rockets, firearms and five catapults, the biggest of which, called 'Wee Bride', took 500 men to operate and had been used by the Prophet Muhammad himself. The catapult destroyed the Hindu temple at Debal, and when the garrison surrendered, Muhammad ordered beheaded every man over 18 — an age he, himself, would never reach.

The precocious conqueror then went on to take Neroon (now Hyderabad), before marching up the Indus, killing King Dahir, packing off the king's two daughters to the caliph of Baghdad, taking Brahmanabad-Mansura, fighting a fierce battle at Alor and proceeding on to Multan.

King Dahir's two spirited daughters, meanwhile, conspired to avenge their father's death by telling the caliph that Muhammad had defiled them before fobbing them off on him. The caliph was furious and sent an order to Muhammad to have himself sewn up in the skin of a freshly killed cow and returned to Baghdad. Ever obedient, Muhammad did as he was ordered and died within three days. The girls subsequently confessed their lie and suffered an even nastier death.

Banbhore was destroyed in the 13th century, when it was sacked and burnt by the Afghan invader, Jalall-ud-din. The coastline has since inched forward in a march that is estimated to have pushed back the sea by at least 80 kilometres (50 miles) since Alexander's time. Also, silting and earthquakes have directed the Indus into different channels, leaving the ruins high and dry.

The coin and pottery displays in the little museum at the site give an idea of what the port was like in its heyday, indicating that Banbhore had trading links with the Muslim countries to the west and with lands as far east as China.

Haleji Lake, 87 kilometres (54 miles) from Karachi, is a nature reserve. In the winter months, birds migrate from the north and settle here in their thousands. On a good day between October and February, bird-watchers can expect to see 100 species here, including flamingos, pelicans, kingfishers and up to 20 different species of birds of prey.

Makli Hill (*Makli* means 'Little Mecca') is reputedly the largest necropolis in the world. With a million graves, tombs and mausoleums, it is an impressive and eerie place. For over ten centuries, the Sindhi people have held Makli sacred, and a spiritual atmosphere persists to this day.

Makli was the graveyard for the nearby town of Thatta, which was the capital of Lower Sind from the 14th century to the 17th, a prosperous port and a great centre of Islamic learning. Here lie the remains of Thatta's elite: kings, queens, generals, saints, scholars, philosophers and poets. The hill is long and low, stretching for about eight kilometres (five miles) north to south and bisected by the National Highway. Some of the tombs, which vary in size and grandeur, are of stone decorated with delicate carving, while others are of brick covered with beautiful tiles glazed blue and white. The most interesting mausoleums are in two groups: the relatively recent tombs of the Tarkhan kings, the rulers of Sind from 1545 to 1614, lie near the highway, and the older tombs of the Sammah kings are clustered three kilometres (two miles) away along the ridge to the north. Permission to take a car to the Sammah tombs can be obtained from the Archaeological Office to the left of the main gate. Accommodation is available at the Archaeological Department Rest House and should be booked through the Archaeological Office in Karachi (see Karachi listing on page 207).

Starting at the gate on the National Highway and working north along the ridge, first visit the unusual well surrounded by a white wall on the left. Half-way down the well is a pillared gallery where soldiers stood guarding the water.

The first tomb on the right is that of Jani Beg Tarkhan, the last independent Tarkhan ruler of Sind, who died in 1601. His octagonal brick tomb stands on a terraced platform in the centre of a courtyard surrounded by a brick wall. Alternate layers of dark blue and turquoise glazed tiles and red unglazed bricks decorate the walls. Inside, the cenotaph (empty tomb) of Jani Beg is inscribed with verses from the Koran. The mosque set in the western wall of the enclosure has an exquisitely decorated *mehrab*, the prayer niche facing Mecca.

The Tomb of Tughril Beg Tarkhan, a general who served the Moghul Emperor Aurangzeb and died in 1679, has a small square pavilion with a conical dome supported by 12 delicately carved stone pillars with honeycombed capitals. Lotus blossoms and sunflowers decorate the niches. The wall mosque to the west has three elegant *mehrabs* in the centre and solid raised minarets at each end.

The Tomb of Baqi Beg Uzbek, who died in 1640, is an open brick court with a raised central platform supporting three graves. The mosque in the west wall has a domed chamber with a brick ceiling patterned in zig-zags.

The finest tomb on Makli Hill, that of Isa Khan Tarkhan II, is a magnificent two-storey stone building in the centre of a square courtyard surrounded by a high stone wall. Isa Khan II died at the age of 90 in 1644, having served as governor of Gujerat (in India) under the Moghul emperor Shah Jahan, then as governor of Thatta for a year. The tomb has a high dome surrounded by a two-tiered verandah,

the upper tier being roofed with small domes and reached by stairs going up the east side. The tomb is decorated inside and out with delicate tracery like that at Akbar's palace at Fatipur-Sikri, near Agra in India. Floral and geometric designs surrounding a lattice window decorate the *mehrab* of the wall mosque in the west wall of the enclosure.

The Tomb of Jan Baba, son of Isa Khan I and father of Isa Khan II, was built in 1608 and stands in a stone enclosure entered through an elegant portico built later. Under a pillared pavilion lie seven graves in a row. The walls are covered in carved tracery that looks like fine brown lace; one wall hides the two ladies' tombs in the northeast corner. The east door offers an excellent view of Thatta.

The best-preserved tomb is that of Dewan Shurfa Khan, a revenue collector who died in 1638. (The richness of the tomb indicates where much of the revenue went.) The square brick building, with heavy round towers at its corners, is placed in the centre of a walled court. When Sir Richard Burton (later to become famous for his discovery of the source of the Nile River) saw it in 1876, he found the tiled dome 'gaudy, with more the appearance of a pleasure house than a mansion of the dead'. In the richly decorated interior (Burton continues) 'your eye rejects the profuseness of square and circle, spiral and curve, diamond and scroll work, flowers, border pattern and quotation from the Koran'. Perhaps time has softened the effect, for a century later the blue, red and white zig-zags of the ceiling and the ornate decoration on the cenotaph delight the eye.

The paved road then twists and turns for a kilometre (half a mile) among thousands of graves of every description before reaching the **Shrine of Abdullah Shah Ashabi**, which is surrounded by the usual food and souvenir stalls catering for pilgrims. The colourful clothes and lively bustle of the saint's devotees make a welcome change after all the empty tombs.

A dirt road leads from the shrine north along the ridge for another 2.3 kilometres (1.5 miles) to the Sammah tombs. The Sammahs ruled Sind from 1337 to 1524 and reached the peak of their power under Sultan Jam Nizam-ud-din (1461–1509), whose square stone mausoleum is the most impressive of the group. The walls are decorated inside and out with bands of medallions, diamonds, sunflowers, calligraphy and, on the north side, even a row of ducks. The loveliest part of the tomb is the richly carved projection of the *mehrab* on the outside of the west wall, with its arched balcony above showing Gujerati Hindu influence. (Possibly the Muslim architects employed Hindu stonesmiths who carried over habits acquired when building Hindu temples.) The tomb remains open to the sky because the architects were unable to build a big enough dome. Stairs lead to the top of the walls, which offer a commanding view of the surrounding countryside.

Next to the tomb are the ruins of a mosque with a view north across the ravine to the next section of Makli Hill. The white shrine in the distance is that of Ali Shah Shirazi, a popular saint who died in 1572.

Thatta, about 100 kilometres (62 miles) east of Karachi, was once called Pattala, and it was here that Alexander the Great rested his troops in 325 BC before marching across the Makran Desert in Baluchistan. Thatta, the capital of lower Sind from the 14th century through the 16th, became part of the Moghul Empire in 1592 and prospered for another 150 years as a port famous for its cotton weaving and wood carving. The city finally fell into decline in the 18th century, not only because the Indus shifted its course away from the town, but also because Britain's newly developed textile industry began to export cotton *lungis* to India that were better and cheaper than the once-famous Thatta product. By 1851, the population had fallen from a high of 300,000 to 7,000. The beautiful wooden houses have rotted away, leaving now only about a dozen near the bazaar.

Thatta's **Jami Mosque** (sometimes called, after its imperial Moghul builder, **Shah Jahan Mosque**) dates from 1647 and is built of red brick tempered with the cool blues and greens of glazed tiles. The mosque consists of a central court surrounded by brick arcades covered with 93 domes. These domes have the accoustical effect of enabling prayers said in front of the *mehrab* to be heard in any part of the building. The domes over the entrance and the *mehrab* are completely lined with glazed tiles of blue, turquoise and white arranged to represent the sun surrounded by stars.

The story of the origin of the mosque is that Shah Jahan, as a young man, took refuge in Thatta when his father, Jahangir, was displeased with him for some reason lost to history. Later, when he became emperor, he built the mosque in gratitude to the people of Thatta for harbouring him.

Thatta Bazaar, behind the mosque, is a good place to buy *sussi* (striped hand-loom) and *ajrak* (hand-block-printed cloth) and to see some old houses with wind-catchers on their roofs and balconies of carved wood hanging over the street. **Khizri Mosque**, a small brick structure dating from 1613 in a tiny courtyard behind a high wall just before the bazaar on the right, also has wind-catchers on the roof to funnel cool air to the faithful below.

Dabgir Mosque is one kilometre (half a mile) south of Shah Jahan's Mosque on the road to Sujawal. Now well out of town, this mosque once stood in the heart of the much bigger Thatta of old. It was built in 1588 by Khusro Khan Charkas, a finance officer who escaped punishment for embezzlement when the governor suddenly died. He atoned for his crime (and disposed of its proceeds, perhaps) by building the mosque.

The **Yahya Khan Bridge**, the last to span the Indus before it reaches the sea, is eight kilometres (five miles) beyond Dabgir Mosque toward Sujawal. The bridge is about one kilometre (half a mile) long. For two or three kilometres on either side, the road runs along a high embankment laid across the flood plain and overlooking surprisingly dense riverine forest.

Keenjhar Lake, lying 22 kilometres (14 miles) from Thatta on the road to Hyderabad, has developed into a resort offering sailboats for hire, fishing facilities and excellent bird watching. It is crowded on Fridays but quiet during the rest of the week. The new Pakistan Tourism Development Corporation motel is bookable through the PTDC office in Karachi (see Karachi listing on page 206).

Beside the lake is the **Tomb of Noori**, a fisher girl of the Mohana tribe who married King Jam Tamachi of the Sammah Dynasty and thus became the subject of a romantic rags-to-riches story very popular in Sind. Jam Tamachi is buried on Makli Hill.

Sonda Graveyard, on the east side of the National Highway 14 kilometres (nine miles) beyond the entrance to Keenjhar Lake, has some excellent Chaukundi-style tombs, almost all of which are decorated with a carving of a horse and rider or of jewellery. The Engineering Department bungalow on the embankment behind the graveyard overlooks, on the one side, the white sands of the Indus flood plain and, far in the distance on the other, Keenjhar Lake.

North of Karachi

Another day trip from Karachi, this time to the north, takes in Mangho Pir, Hub Dam and Khar Wildlife Preserve.

Mangho Pir, 18 kilometres (11 miles) north of Karachi, is the Shrine of Pir Mangho, a 13th-century Sufi saint. It stands on a low hill beside two sulphurous hot springs guarded by crocodiles. These crocodiles are the snub-nosed variety, as distinct from the long-snouted gavial of the Indus, and are considered particularly dangerous.

An amusing legend is attached to their origin. When Pir Mangho first came from Arabia, he inadvertently brought the crocodiles in his hair, where they travelled in the form of lice. Soon after his arrival, there sprang from the desert two oases around hot springs gushing from a clump of date palms. The 'crocodiles' jumped into the springs and have lived there ever since. (Zoologists, for their part, suggest that the crocodiles became stranded in the springs when the Hub River changed course.)

On Fridays the shrine is thronged with pilgrims seeking blessings and cures, particularly for rheumatism, skin diseases and leprosy. They used to enter the pool containing the crocodiles, but now use a separate bathing place built nearby. Supplicants offer goats to the crocodiles and believe that, if the meat is eaten, their prayers will be answered. The five crocodiles currently in residence consequently spend most of their time stuffed to bursting and immobile, with shreds of meat dangling from their jaws. A connection begs to be made between this gorging of crocodiles and the worship of the crocodiles in ancient Egypt, a land with which the people of the Indus conducted trade as long as 5,000 years ago.

From Mangho Pir, a paved road runs northwest for 33 kilometres (20 miles) to the **Hub Dam**. The escarpment overlooking the Hub Valley from the west is the home of several groups of Baluch tribespeople, and small, temporary settlements of wattle houses surrounded by thorn hedges cluster along the top of the ridge. Men may not approach these settlements, but foreign women are welcome to enter and meet the Baluchi women within.

The Hub Dam is almost five kilometres (three miles) long and holds back a shallow lake trapped between low, barren hills. A sandy track passable only by 4WD vehicles continues past the dam for about 20 kilometres (12 miles) along the edge of Kirthar National Park to **Khar Wildlife Preserve**, where there is a guesthouse bookable through the Sind Wildlife Management Board (see Karachi listing on page 206).

In winter, Hub Lake is alive with birds. Swimming is inadvisable, as the lake is also alive with crocodiles. Monitor lizards inhabit the rocks around Khar, and the wildlife complex is a breeding centre for blackbuck, peacocks and urial sheep.

Kirthar National Park

A four-hour drive from Karachi (for 4WD vehicles only) takes the visitor deep into the heart of Kirthar National Park, a game preserve measuring over 3,000 square kilometres in the Kirthar Hills and a good destination for a three-day trip. October to February is the most comfortable — that is, coolest — time to go, but the flowers bloom during the (relatively) wet monsoon in August.

Five furnished rest houses with cooking facilities and running water are situated on the edge of a wide valley in the centre of the park at **Karchat**. They are bookable through the Sind Wildlife Management Board, which also hires out tents to those who wish to camp, which is safe and enjoyable. Some food is available if ordered well in advance, but it is better to take your own food, drink and bedding.

The rolling valleys and contorted, rugged lines of the Kirthar Hills form a natural haven for urial sheep, ibex and chinkara gazelle. Jungle cats, desert cats and even the occasional leopard or desert wolf also prowl the park. Pangolins (scaly anteaters), porcupines and monitor lizards are much in evidence.

Other attractions in the park are the 18th-century Chaukundi-style tombs at **Taung** and the prehistoric archaeological remains at **Koh-Tarash**. The enormous **Ranikot Fort** is also within the park, two hours by jeep from Karchat. Ranikot is about four hours from Karachi via the Indus and Super highways.

Moenjodaro

The 4,000-year-old brick ruins of the Indus Civilization city of Moenjodaro, which means 'Mound of the Dead', stand on the west bank of the Indus in upper Sind, one hour and 20 minutes from Karachi by air.

The Indus Civilization flourished from 3000 to 1500 BC, making it contemporary with the ancient civilizations of Egypt and Mesopotamia. At its height, it comprised at least 400 cities and towns along the Indus and its tributaries, covering most of present-day Pakistan and stretching northwest as far as modern Kabul and east as far as modern Delhi. The waterways were the main highways connecting the empire, and flat-bottomed barges almost identical to those still used today plied the rivers from city to city. Few of the cities have been excavated; what little we know of the civilization comes mostly from Moenjodaro and Harappa, the latter being 550 kilometres (342 miles) to the north, near Lahore.

The Indus people had a strong central administrative system. The cities appear to have been built according to a single, highly organized plan, with a raised citadel in the west and streets laid out in neat blocks defined by wide avenues intersecting at right angles. Much like modern Islamabad, different sectors were reserved for different functions, so that there was an administrative sector, a residential sector for the wealthy, another for the working class, and separate sectors for various kinds of artisans and tradesmen.

A priestly class probably governed the people, collecting taxes in the form of grain, which was stored in state granaries, the period equivalent of modern banks. Weights and measures were standardized throughout the empire. Indeed, regulation was so pervasive that even the dimensions of building bricks were universally prescribed.

The first prerequisite of an urban civilization is a well-organized agricultural system able to produce the surpluses necessary to feed its cities, and the Indus Civilization developed from an aggregate of settled farming communities using relatively advanced farming techniques. Irrigation was probably practised even though the climate at the time was slightly wetter than now, resulting in forested, highly fertile land along the Indus. Crops included wheat, barley, sesame and vegetables. By 2000 BC, cotton had become a major trade commodity — a status it retains today — and all the draught animals and livestock now seen in the subcontinent had been domesticated. That cats and dogs were also tamed is evidenced evocatively by a certain brick on display in the museum at the site. Before baking, the brick was imprinted with the footprints of both animals, thus becoming posterity's record of a dog chasing a cat.

The elaborate and efficient system of waste drainage used in the Indus cities has excited considerable interest. Drains from each house flowed first into cesspits, in which solid matter settled, then liquid waste flowed on through the carefully graded, brick-lined drains that ran down the centre of each street under a cover pierced at intervals with inspection holes. The sewers eventually emptied into the river.

Bathrooms in the homes of the wealthy had floors of snuggly fitting bricks. Some houses had separate lavatories, and most had their own brick-lined wells. Many even had rubbish chutes running through the wall to rectangular brick rubbish bins outside.

Sentry boxes stood at intervals in the streets to shelter the city police from the sun and rain.

An hour at **Moenjodaro Museum** provides some idea of what the ancient city probably looked like and of the cultural and economic basis of the larger civilization.

Two large murals show a reconstruction of the city, with its high outer walls narrowing at the top, along which soldiers patrol from one square watch-tower to the next. Down by the river, cargoes of cotton and grain are unloaded from boats into two-wheeled ox carts like those still used today. In the carts, the grain is transferred to the state granaries, as priests mill around the palace and its great bath nearby. Two-storey, flat-roofed houses stretch into the distance across the prosperous city.

One of the more interesting exhibits shows the traders' seals, which demonstrate the great artistic talent of the Indus people. These seals are exquisitely tiny, generally two to four centimetres (0.8–1.6 inches) square, and fashioned from steatite, a soft, easily carved stone. Each is delicately and realistically engraved with such animals as roaring tigers and rough-skinned rhinoceros or renderings of deities and fighting demons. Across the tops of most seals are inscriptions in Indus Civilization script, presumably naming the merchants who owned them. As no extensive writings have survived and these proper names are complemented by only a few short inscriptions found on bits of pottery, philologists hoping to decipher the script appear to face a hopeless task.

Though the evidence in hand suggests that the Indus Civilization was both larger and better organized than either its Egyptian or Mesopotamian counterpart, we know less about it. (In the case of Egypt, the ancient way of life is known from artefacts preserved in the dry atmosphere sealed within the pyramids and royal tombs.) We do know, however, that trade among the three civilizations and the surrounding tribes was extensive. Merchants from the Indus carried cotton by camel and horse caravan across the hills to Mesopotamia (where cotton came to be called *sindu*, just as in Greece, cloth was called *sindonian*). What they received in return must have been perishable, for no trace remains, but on the way back through Baluchistan, merchants picked up steatite for their seals, bitumen and alabaster.

Silver, lead, tin, turquoise and lapis came from Persia and Afghanistan, red iron oxide pigment from the islands of the Persian Gulf, and copper and various semi-precious stones from India.

Mother goddesses moulded of clay were common throughout the ancient world, and those found in Moenjodaro show that the people here were as devoted to these fertility deities as anyone else. There are, however, no solid clues to the nature of the state religion, though the famous little statue of a haughty priest king (the original is on display in the National Museum in Karachi) indicates the existence of a ruling class of clergy, and the many elaborate baths suggest ritual bathing similar to that practised today by both Hindus and Muslims.

The bronze dancing girl, pert and provocative (and a copy of the original kept but not displayed in Delhi), indicates either a tradition of temple girls or a familiar and lively sense of fun. Some of the numerous terracotta figurines are undeniably phallic, suggesting a crude sense of humour.

The figurines and jewellery displayed show that the women of the Indus Civilization wore short skirts and dressed their hair in high, complicated coiffures. They loved jewellery and wore hair pins, earrings and multiple strings of beads made of carnelian, agate, faience, ivory, cowrie shells and gold. Priests' robes were worn over one shoulder, like those worn by Buddhist monks today, and priests either wore their hair short or gathered it in a bun held at the back of the head by a headband.

The pottery in the museum is not of great beauty, reflecting efficient mass production rather than a striving for elegance. Potters in the village nearby are still churning out the same designs.

Geometric patterns at the Jami Mosque in Thatta (left) contrast with the floral design of a mosque in Lahore.

Moenjodaro was abandoned around 1500 BC, although the civilization lingered on in places for another five centuries. The decline probably resulted from a combination of factors. Climatic change (perhaps a slight easterly shift in the monsoon) compounded the effects of overgrazing and the felling of trees for fuel, causing impoverishment of the soil, which was also becoming saline. A parallel problem on a different plane was general political deterioration. Towards the end, the building of fortifications became fast and furious, presumably to defend the city from the waves of warlike Aryan nomads who started invading the subcontinent from Central Asia about 1700 BC. We know from the Rigveda, the religious hymns of the Aryans, that they overthrew a people with flat noses and a strange language, a people who lived in walled cities. The Rigveda also describes breaking a dam and flooding a city. Some of the more striking finds at Moenjodaro are skeletons lying in contorted positions, as though they lay precisely where they had been slain. However, the picture of the city dying overnight as the result of the slaughter of its inhabitants is probably more dramatic than accurate.

Excavations have uncovered only parts of the city, which was about five kilometres (three miles) in circumference. An embankment for flood control ran 1,500 metres (5,000 feet) along the river bank, but today the river is five kilometres to the east and controlled by a modern embankment.

From in front of the museum and looking south, the visitor first notices the remains of a Buddhist stupa built at the highest point and dominating the other ruins. Built 2,000 years later than the Indus Civilization city, it sits atop the ruins of the ancient acropolis, or fortified citadel, that once crowned the 15-metre (50-foot) high artificial hill. Moenjodaro's administrative and religious buildings — the public bath, state granary, palace and assembly hall — are just to the west of the stupa.

The great bath, more than two metres (seven feet) deep and sealed with a bitumen lining, was probably used for ritual bathing. It has been restored with new brick, so it appears rather as it did to those who used it. Broad steps lead down into the water at either end, and a neatly arched and brick-lined drain accommodates the overflow. A cloister surrounds the bath, and on three sides are a series of small rooms, possibly private baths for the priests. In one of these is a well.

Beside the bath is the state granary, the 'treasury' where taxes in the form of wheat, barley and sesame were stored. Twenty-seven high brick platforms in three rows of nine are separated by ventilation channels. Wooden storage bins were built on these foundations. On the north side, but crumbled so that it is hard to make out, is the loading bay, where the ox-drawn carts pulled up to load and unload.

The palace, or priests' college, is north of the bath and consists of a cloistered court surrounded by rooms. The assembly hall is about 100 metres (yards) to the south and survives as the foundations of a large, square, pillared room adjacent to a portion of the city fortifications. No temple building has turned up, but if there is a great temple it is probably buried under the Buddhist stupa.

The secular and unofficial part of the city lies east of the citadel area and is laid out in a neat, chessboard pattern. Wide thoroughfares divide the city into 12 regular blocks, with narrower side streets leading off to give access to the individual houses.

Only a fraction of the square kilometre (four-tenths of a square mile) that this area covered has been excavated, but the residential district for the wealthy, which has been unearthed, is the most exciting part of Moenjodaro. Here you stroll down narrow side streets between high, forbiddingly blank walls, the shadows of which are cool — but eerie. Even when the city was alive, these alleyways must have been dark and claustrophobic. Periodically, a set of steps leads to a door, but the front of the house is windowless. Inside are the remains of about ten rooms of different sizes opening on to a central courtyard. Most of the houses had two storeys, and a staircase led up to a (probably) wooden balcony that encircled the courtyard and provided access to the upper rooms. Still-visible holes in the walls presumably held the wooden beams that supported the second floor. The only windows were small and high up and, though looking on to the courtyard, were protected by wooden or stone grills.

Odd as it seems, the brick linings of wells tower into the air like factory chimneys, but the explanation is quite simple. As the centuries passed and old houses fell down, new ones were built on top of them, thus raising the general level of the ground. As excavators have worked their way down through the levels and further into the past, they have spared the well linings thus exposed. The workmanship near the top of the wells, which was added as the ground level rose, is coarser than the older work showing lower down, illustrating the decline of the civilization.

On the east side of the wealthy residential area is a wide avenue leading south, and this is where the shops were. Each commodity was sold in its own specific street: jewellers congregated in one street, fabric merchants in the next, coppersmiths occupied a third street and potters still another.

The smaller houses of the working class are about 300 metres (yards) south along the main street. In the northwest corner of this area is a block of 16 single-storey cottages in two rows of eight, one row facing a street, the other a narrow lane. All are identical, comprising two small rooms, and share a nearby well.

Moenjodaro and the knowledge of the civilization that built it lay
undisturbed for thousands of years until it was rediscovered in 1922 by
Sir John Marshall, a British archaeologist. Now the ruins are in
danger. Years of irrigation in an area with inadequate drainage have
raised the water-table and made the water salty. Moisture is creeping
up the brick walls of Moenjodaro, softening them so that they crumble
to the touch. With the water-table now only a few metres from the
surface, the remains of the earliest years of the city's existence are
already many metres below it. UNESCO has provided money to pay
for pumping water out in an attempt to lower the water-table, but
irreparable damage has already occurred, and the earliest remains are
probably lost forever.

Punjab

The Punjab, its name meaning 'Land of Five Rivers' (referring to the rivers Indus, Jhelum, Chenab, Ravi and Sutlej), is the richest, most fertile and most heavily populated province of Pakistan. Here live over 50 million people — slightly more than half the population of the whole country. Geographically, it is a land of contrasts, from the alluvial plain of the Indus River and its tributaries to the sand-dunes of the Cholistan Desert, from the fairy-tale beauty of the pine-covered foothills of the Himalayas to the strangely convoluted lunar landscape of the Potwar Plateau and the Salt Range.

Monsoon rains fall on northern Punjab, making the belt from Lahore to Rawalpindi-Islamabad and continuing north into the foothills the only part of Pakistan to get more than 500 millimetres of rain a year. Further south, the five rivers provide adequate water for irrigating most of the land on the alluvial plains that separate and surround them.

The Punjab grows most of Pakistan's wheat, rice, barley, maize, pulses, oil-seeds and sugar-cane. The area around Multan is the cotton-growing centre of the country. Cotton is Pakistan's most important cash crop, exported both in raw form and in fabrics and clothing. The Punjab is also the home of much of Pakistan's industry. Textiles, steel, sporting goods, electrical appliances, surgical instruments and fertilizers are all made here, mainly around the large cities of Faisalabad, Multan, Sialkot, Gujranwala and the provincial capital, Lahore. The Punjab is also rich in mineral resources, including salt, gypsum, coal and oil.

Geographical position and the fertility of its soil have made the Punjab an important centre of human endeavour from prehistoric times. Man lived on the banks of the Soan River 50,000 years ago, and the Indus Civilization flourished at Harappa and other sites as early as 2500 BC. Taxila, near modern Islamabad, was a centre of culture and learning for a thousand years from 500 BC to AD 500. When Alexander the Great visited Taxila in 326 BC, it was known throughout the ancient world for its university. Islamic learning and architecture developed at Uch and Multan during the 13th and 14th centuries.

In the 17th century, Lahore became one of the greatest Moghul cities in the subcontinent. A town near Lahore had been the birthplace of Guru Nanak, the 15th-century founder of the Sikh religion, and Lahore was the capital from which Maharajah Ranjit Singh ruled his 19th-century Sikh Empire. The British coveted this fertile region, and overthrew the Sikhs in 1849, annexing the Punjab to their Indian dominions, with Lahore as its provincial capital. Finally, it was in

Lahore that the All India Muslim League passed on 23 March 1940 its Resolution for the Creation of Pakistan.

At Partition, which came about seven years later, the wealthy Punjab, like Bengal in the east, was itself partitioned, its multi-communal population of Muslims, Hindus and Sikhs precluding its total inclusion in either India or Pakistan. At the same time, no line drawn through the province could fail to place many millions of people on the wrong side of the border. The result was a nightmare of massacres and mass migrations.

When the Pakistanis decided to build a new capital from scratch, it was in the Punjab, the fertile heart of the country, that a site was chosen. The construction of Islamabad began in 1962 near the most beautiful part of the Punjab, the Murree Hills, adjacent to Rawalpindi and the Grand Trunk Road, Pakistan's east-west axis.

The best time to visit northern Punjab is in the spring, from February to April, and in the autumn, from September to November. Southern Punjab is extremely hot in summer, so Multan is at its best in winter, from November to February.

Lahore

Lahore is Pakistan's most interesting city, the cultural and intellectual centre of the nation. Its faded elegance, busy streets and bazaars, and wide variety of Islamic and British architecture make it a city full of atmosphere, contrast and surprise. Lahore looks south to the great civilization of the Moghul emperors; Peshawar looks north to Central Asia. Those who visit both cities gain some understanding of the cultural influences that have shaped Pakistan.

Getting to Lahore

Air, rail and road links tie Lahore to the other cities of Pakistan — and to India and the Gulf. International flights from Delhi, Jeddah, Riyadh, Dubai and Dhahran and domestic flights from 14 cities (flights from Karachi costing Rs700) land at Lahore's airport, which is some five kilometres (three miles) from the city centre. Buses cover the 280 kilometres (174 miles) from Islamabad-Rawalpindi along the Grand Trunk Road in four to six hours. The same journey takes five or six hours on the safer and more comfortable train. From Karachi to Lahore takes two to three days by road or 16−21 hours by train. Second class on an ordinary train costs about Rs80, a first-class sleeper costs Rs250, and an air-conditioned sleeper on the express, Rs610. The Grand Trunk Road crosses the Indian border 29 kilometres (18 miles) from Lahore at Wagah, but passage is restricted (see General Information for Travellers on page 9).

When to Go

October to March is the best time to visit Lahore. Because it is only 213 metres (700 feet) above sea level, it is hotter than Islamabad and can get very hot in the summer.

History

Lahore has been the capital of the Punjab for nearly a thousand years, first from 1021 to 1186 under the Ghaznavid Dynasty, founded by Mahmud of Ghazni, then under Muhammad of Ghor, and then under the various sultans of Delhi. It reached its full glory under Moghul rule from 1524 to 1752. The third Moghul emperor, Akbar, held his court in Lahore for the 14 years from 1584 to 1598. He built the marvellous Lahore Fort on the foundations of a previous fort and enclosed the city within a red brick wall boasting 12 gates. Jahangir and Shah Jahan extended the fort, built palaces and tombs, and laid out gardens. The last of the great Moghuls, Aurangzeb (1658−1707), gave Lahore its most famous monument, the great Badshahi Mosque.

During their rule centred here in the 18th and 19th centuries, the Sikhs took little interest in the gardens and actually dismantled many of Lahore's Moghul monuments, from which it is said they took enough marble to build the Golden Temple at Amritsar twice over.

When the British took over in 1849, they erected splendidly pompous Victorian public buildings in the style that has come to be called Moghul Gothic. The Lahore Cantonment, the British residential district of wide, tree-lined streets and white bungalows set in large, shaded gardens, is the prettiest cantonment in Pakistan.

Since Independence in 1947, Lahore has expanded rapidly as the capital of Pakistani Punjab. It is the second-largest city in the country and an important industrial centre.

Sights

Except for the old town and the British-built Lahore Central Museum, all of the most impressive sights in Lahore date from the Moghul period. These include Badshahi Mosque, Lahore Fort, Wazir Khan's Mosque, Shalimar Garden and Jahangir's Tomb.

Lahore Central Museum

Housed in a Moghul Gothic structure opened in 1894, this museum is

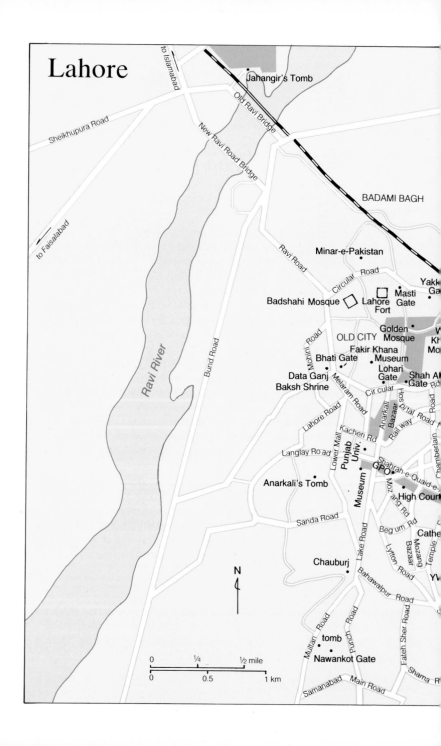

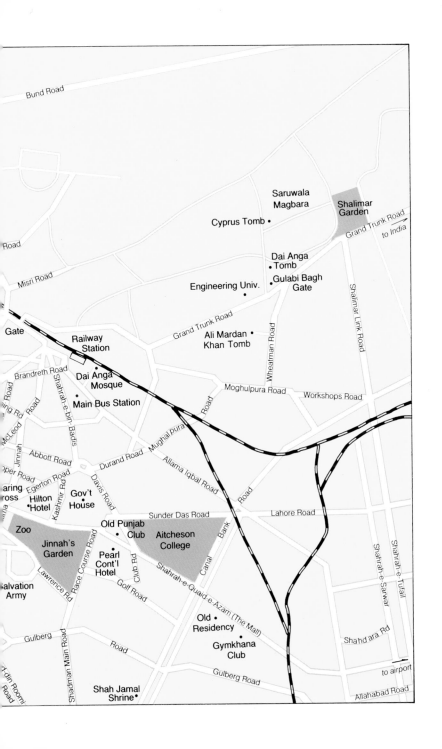

the best in Pakistan, with superb collections of Buddhist stone sculpture from the Gandharan period and Islamic works such as illustrated manuscripts, miniatures, rugs and carvings. The prehistory gallery is excellent, as is the ethnographic display. The museum's first curator was John Lockwood Kipling, Rudyard's father and no doubt the writer's model for the kindly 'white-bearded Englishman' who was curator of the Lahore Museum in *Kim*.

Badshahi Mosque

(Open 5 am–9 pm) With the simple grace of its lines, its pleasing proportions and its airy spaciousness, this mosque, built by Emperor Aurangzeb in 1674, represents the very best of Moghul architecture. It is a huge, walled square with minarets at each corner and a monumental gate at the top of a broad flight of steps. The courtyard is paved with red sandstone — which gets very hot under bare feet in the summer. A square marble fountain stands in the centre of the courtyard, while an arcade of white arches lines its perimeter on three sides. The fourth side, opposite the gate, is the prayer chamber, which is topped by three elegant marble domes. The ceilings inside the prayer chamber are decorated with carved plaster work and floral frescos in subdued colours.

You can climb to the top of one of the minarets for an excellent bird's-eye view of the mosque, the fort opposite and the old city of Lahore. The minarets have 204 steps and are exactly one-third as tall as the courtyard is wide.

Hazuri Bagh

This garden (*bagh*) lies in the square area between Badshahi Mosque and Lahore Fort. Aurangzeb built it as a *serai* (a kind of hotel) and used it for reviewing his troops. The two-storey building by the south gate was a boarding house for scholars studying at the mosque. The north gate, through which nobles passed when visiting the palaces inside the fort, is called Roshnai Darwaza ('Gate of Light') because it was brightly lit at night. Ranjit Singh's grandson was killed by falling masonry — probably murdered — while passing here *en route* from his father's cremation to his own coronation.

Hazuri Bagh Baradari, the marble pavilion in the centre of the garden and one of the few surviving Sikh monuments in Lahore, was built by Ranjit Singh in 1818 using marble taken from various Moghul tombs and the floor of the fort's royal bath house. Its elegant pillars of carved marble support delicately cusped arches. Ranjit Singh held court under the mirrored ceiling of the central area. The pavilion had a second storey until it was damaged by lightning in 1932.

The **Tomb of Allama Muhammad Iqbal**, the great poet-philosopher who lived from 1873 to 1938 and conceived the idea of Pakistan as a separate Muslim state, is on the left as you face the gate of Badshahi Mosque. Built in 1951, this small tomb is constructed of red sandstone. The window grills, door frames and entire interior are of carved white marble. The translucent marble headstone, a gift from Afghanistan, is inscribed with two of the poet's couplets condemning racial discrimination.

Lahore Fort

The massive walls of Lahore Fort, built by Akbar in the 1560s, tower over the old city of Lahore, and the huge rectangle they define, 380 by 330 metres (1,250 by 1,080 feet), is filled with buildings from a variety of periods. A complete tour of the fort takes about two hours.

The entrance is through **Alamgiri Gate** (1), built by Aurangzeb at the same time as Badshahi Mosque in 1674. A ramp leads from Alamgiri Gate to the old Musamman Burj Gate (2) on the left and, on the right, to the royal kitchens (3), which are now occupied by the police and closed to the public. (Note that ground level within the walls is much higher than that outside. The intervening space is filled with many levels of dungeons, all windowless except the rooms against the walls.)

The **Maktab Khana** (Clerks' House) (4) is a small cloistered court surrounded by arcades in which clerks sat recording the names of visitors. The inscription outside tells that it was built by Jahangir in 1618.

The **Moti Masjid** (Pearl Mosque) (5) is entered via steps rising from the corner of the large courtyard north of the Maktab Khana. This little gem was built by Shah Jahan in 1644, ten years before he built a similar mosque in the Red Fort at Agra and 18 years before he built the most exquisite pearl mosque of all in the Red Fort at Delhi. All three are faced in white marble and are charmingly intimate, making their impact through their delicate proportions and purity of line.

The **Diwan-e-Am** (Hall of Public Audience) (6) is an open pavilion with 40 pillars built by Shah Jahan in 1631 to shelter his subjects when they appeared before him. The original building collapsed in 1841 when it was shelled by Sikhs from atop one of the minarets of Badshahi Mosque. Credit for this poor reconstruction goes to the British, who used it as a hospital and covered the spacious lawn in front with barracks and offices.

The marble pavilion and red sandstone balcony at the back of the Diwan-e-Am are originals built by Akbar. Here the emperor appeared daily before the public — who, in his day, crowded under a canvas awning. The serpentine sandstone brackets are typical of Akbar's commissions, with the depiction of animals showing Hindu influence and reflecting Akbar's policy of religious tolerance. His two-storey **Diwan-e-Khas** (Hall of Private Audience) (7), built in 1566, is behind the balcony and is reached by stairs on the right. Visible inside are traces of the original painted and gilded stucco work, and the marble work here is the oldest in Lahore.

Masti (or **Masjidi**) **Gate** (8) is east of the Diwan-e-Am. It was the original main gate to the fort built by Akbar in 1566 and receives its name from the Masjid (Mosque) of Maryam Zamani just outside. The gate is defended by heavy octagonal bastions equipped with battlements, loopholes and machicolations from which attackers were targetted with missiles and boiling oil.

Jahangir's Quadrangle (9), north of the Diwan-e-Am and one of the fort's most attractive areas, was started by Akbar in 1566 and finished by Jahangir in 1617. The buildings on the east, west and south sides of the court reflect typical Akbari style, with richly carved red sandstone columns and elaborate animal-shaped brackets. Behind the buildings to the east is **Akbar's Court** (10), now housing the fort administrative offices and, in the underground rooms, conservation laboratories.

The **Khwabgah-e-Jahangir** (Jahangir's Room of Dreams — or, more prosaically, his sleeping quarters) (11) is the main building running the length of the north side of Jahangir's Quadrangle and is typical of Jahangir's period in its austerity. It is now a museum, containing a huge ivory model of the Taj Mahal (returned from England in 1950), some excellent illustrated manuscripts (including the *Akbar Nama*, the daily chronicle of Akbar's reign), some good Moghul miniatures and a collection of Moghul coins.

The **Hammam** (12), Jahangir's bath house, is in the southwest corner of the quadrangle. It was once quite luxuriously paved with marble and had delicate floral frescos covering the walls. A cascade of water flowed over the carved sandstone of the niche in the south wall. The bath was remodelled (and its floor stripped of marble) in Sikh times. The British used it as a kitchen.

The new **museum** (13), west of the bath, contains a fine collection of Moghul and Sikh arms and paintings dating from the Sikh period. Stairs outside the building run to the second floor, where more Sikh paintings are hung.

From the museum you again enter the quadrangle of the Moti Masjid. **Shah Jahan's Quadrangle** (14) is to the north, entered through the window into Shah Jahan's sleeping quarters, which consist of five connecting rooms built in 1633. The middle room features lattice

Lahore Fort

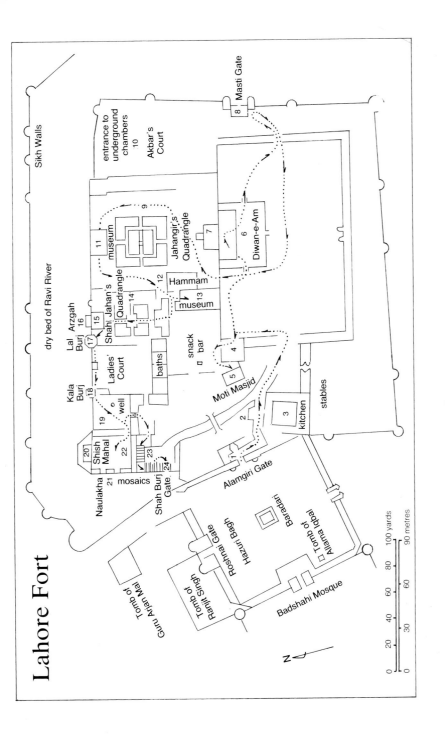

screens, door frames and a central fountain, all of marble. The fresco
of Radha and Krishna dates from the Sikh period.

Shah Jahan's Diwan-e-Khas (Hall of Private Audience) (15) is the
graceful arcaded pavilion of marble on the north side of the
quadrangle, which the emperor built about 1645. Delicately carved
marble lattice screens overlook the now-dry bed of the Ravi River, and
the floor is paved with coloured marble in geometric patterns. The
central fountain was once decorated with *pietra dura* inlay. The British
converted the pavilion into a church.

Below the pavilion at the foot of the fort wall is the ruined **Arzgah**
(16), where nobles assembled every morning to pay their respects to
the emperor. Here, on the outer wall, are some particularly fine tile
mosaics of blue dragons, the emblem carried before the emperor.

The **Lal Burj** (Red Tower) (17) is the octagonal summer pavilion in
the northwest corner of Shah Jahan's Quadrangle. Built between 1617
and 1631 by Jahangir and Shah Jahan, it forms part of the north wall of
the fort. The tower is decorated with beautiful tile mosaics and filigree
work. The paintings inside date mostly from the Sikh period, as does
the third storey of the structure. The floor was originally of marble,
and the water channels, fountains and central pool must have made it
delightfully cool in summer. On the staircase in the northeast corner
survive remains of a gilded and painted honeycomb cornice, indicating
how lavishly decorated the whole pavilion once was.

Adjacent is the **Ghusl Khana** (Ladies' Courtyard), built by Shah
Jahan in 1633. All that remains is a small marble pavilion overlooking
the river in the middle of the north side of the courtyard. This pavilion
was reserved for the emperor when he came to visit the ladies of his
harem. Only the foundations of the ladies' apartments and their
private mosque survive. The almost completely ruined *hammam* (bath
house) on the south side of the courtyard was built in the Turkish style,
with a dressing room, warm bath and hot bath. The marble floor is still
intact in the southwestern room. Note here the terracotta water pipes
built into the wall. The water heater was at the western end beside the
original *baitul khana* (lavatory).

The **Kala Burj** (Black Tower) (18), a twin summer pavilion to the
Lal Burj, is in the northwest corner of the ladies' court. The building's
decoration is completely gone, and its central portion is closed, but it
still serves as passage to the **Garden Court** (19), the ladies' private
garden.

The **Court of the Shish Mahal** (Palace of Mirrors) (20) is the best
preserved and most interesting place in the fort. The Shish Mahal was
built by Shah Jahan in 1631 as private apartments for his empress, and
it was here that the British chose to assume sovereignty over the
Punjab in 1849. The whole of the interior is covered with mirror

mosaics, carved and gilded plaster work and *pietra dura* inlay. The ceiling is original Moghul work; the walls, with frescos and sherds of blue and white china, date from Sikh times. The main hall of the palace is open at the front, with five beautiful cusped arches supported on delicate fluted double pillars. *Pietra dura* inlay decorates the base of each pillar and the tops of the arches. The graceful vine pattern over the two outer arches is particularly fine. The floor is a geometric mosaic of marble.

Surrounding the main hall is a string of nine connecting rooms with views through exquisite marble screens to the dry riverbed. Here, the ladies could look out without being seen and enjoy the cool breezes off the then-flowing river. The easternmost room is covered in frescos and offers excellent views along the outer walls of the fort, showing the windows of the underground rooms and the remains of the brilliantly coloured tile mosaics of animals, people and geometric designs that once decorated the arched niches on the outer face of the wall.

The **Naulakha** (21), named for the nine *lakhs* (hundred-thousands) of rupees it cost to build in 1631, is the small marble pavilion on the west side of the court styled after a Bengali bamboo hut with a curved roof. This dainty pavilion is decorated with the finest *pietra dura* inlay in Lahore; the carefully selected bits of jade, carnelian, lapis, agate, jet and other semi-precious stones are set into the marble in delicate floral and geometric designs. At the top of the double pillars supporting the archway, in one tiny niche, 102 minute pieces of stone are inlaid to make one floral pattern. The view through a lovely marble screen takes in the Badshahi Mosque, Ranjit Singh's Tomb, the gold dome of Guru Arjan's Memorial and the Minar-e-Pakistan.

On the south side of the court is a row of rooms (22), on the back wall of the central one of which is a water cascade. The water once rippled down this wall and filled the water channels and fountains in the courtyard.

The exit is around to the left (east) behind this wall and down the broad, shallow steps of the **Hathi Paer** (Elephant Path) (23). This was the private entrance of the royal family and leads straight to the **Shah Burj Gate** (24). In the western wall above the path are niches from which eunuchs observed and a crier announced the comings and goings of royalty. Servants stood in attendance in the upper gallery above. The door on the right leads to the underground rooms, which are closed to the public.

As you leave through the Shah Burg Gate, look to your right along the wall at the 350-year-old mosaics set into the outer face of the fort wall. This use of glazed ceramic tile is of Persian origin and became popular in the reign of Shah Jahan as a practical means of decorating brick monuments in the Punjab, where stone is scarce. The mosaics decorating the west and north walls of Lahore Fort are unique in style and variety of design, for here the geometric patterns are liberally interspersed with animal and human figures, which, like Moghul miniature paintings, illustrate the ways and amusements of the Moghul court, a curious blend of barbarism and refinement. Vigorous scenes in which elephants, camels and bulls are pitted against each other jostle with depictions of a polo game and of *paris*, Persian winged fairies wearing robes inflated by flight. Around on the north wall are blue dragons and numerous scenes peopled by courtiers.

Other Sights near the Fort

The **Minar-e-Pakistan** (Tower of Pakistan), which looms in the park near Badshahi Mosque, marks the spot at which the Muslim League on 23 March 1940 passed the resolution calling for the creation of the independent Muslim state of Pakistan. Visitors can climb to the top for an excellent view of Lahore Fort, Badshahi Mosque and, outside the walls, the tombs of Guru Arjan Mal and Ranjit Singh.

The **Tomb of Guru Arjan** has elegant fluted domes covered in gold leaf. Guru Arjan was the fifth Sikh guru and is remembered for compiling the *Adi Granth*, the original Sikh holy book, which is now across the Indian border in Amritsar.

The **Samadhi** or **Tomb of Ranjit Singh** is a splendidly ornate example of Sikh architecture, with gilded, fluted domes and cupolas and an elaborate balustrade round the top. It is lined with marble taken from various Moghul monuments in Lahore. The ashes of this greatest Sikh ruler, who controlled the Punjab and Kashmir from 1799 to 1839, are in the lotus-shaped urn sheltered in the centre of the tomb under a marble pavilion inlaid with *pietra dura*. Known as 'the one-eyed lion of the Punjab', the illiterate maharajah ruled his empire with a firm hand and was fond of horses and beautiful women. Other tiny urns in the tomb contain the scanty remains of his four wives and seven concubines, who threw themselves on his funeral pyre.

Old City and Wazir Khan's Mosque

At the same time that Akbar built the fort at the northwest corner of Lahore, he enclosed the city within a high brick wall with 12 gates, six of which still stand. A circular road allows motor traffic to bypass the old city.

Wazir Khan's Mosque is in the old city, 300 metres (yards) from Delhi Gate. It is on the left in a narrow lane lined with tiny shops selling everything from paper money garlands to rat traps.

This unique mosque is one of the most beautiful in Pakistan. It was built in 1634 by Hakim Ali-ud-din, popularly known as Wazir Khan,

Wrestlers show their stuff in Peshawar.

who was governor of the Punjab under Shah Jahan. Craftsmen from the Punjabi city of Chiniot, from where Wazir Khan hailed and which is still famous for its wood-carvers, were brought in to do the work. The mosque is built of brick and faced with mosaics of brightly coloured glazed tiles in Moghul floral motifs on a background of clear yellow. Its frescos and enamel mosaics have been carefully restored by Pakistan's few remaining craftsmen able to do so. The effect is very fine, particularly the mosaic calligraphy, including a Persian inscription over the entrance which translates as: 'Remove thy heart from the gardens of the world, And know that this building is the true abode of man.'

The prayer hall has five chambers, each surmounted by a dome. Octagonal minarets stand at each corner of the courtyard. The custodian will unlock one so that visitors can climb up the 69 steps to the muezzin's gallery for an excellent panorama of the old city. Entombed in the courtyard is the Syed Muhammad Ishaq, a saint otherwise called Miran Shah, who died in the 14th century. To the left of his grave is a well.

The **Sonehri Masjid** (Golden Mosque), named for its three gilt domes, dominates a square some 500 metres (about a quarter of a mile) west of Wazir Khan's Mosque. The way through the bazaar is along a narrow lane overhung by precarious wooden balconies. The mosque was built in 1753 by Bokhari Khan, a favourite of the powerful widow of Mir Mannu until (it is said) he displeased the lady and was beaten to death by her female attendants, who used their shoes to do the job.

In the courtyard behind the mosque is a large well with steps leading down to the water. This is credited to Guru Arjan, the fifth Sikh guru.

Take the alley that runs beside the left (south) wall of the mosque, and continue along a very narrow lane in which are sold pots and pans in all sizes and shapes. This is the **brass bazaar**. The pots and pans are sold by weight, but some fine antique brassware still rewards a search. After 200 metres (650 feet), you come out at a *tonga* (horse cart) and motor rickshaw stand in a wide street. Either vehicle will take you cheaply from the old city via Shah Almi Gate. Where the gate used to be is now an abandoned Hindu temple.

The next gate to the west is Lohari Gate, about 500 metres (a quarter of a mile) into the old city from which, on the right, is **Fakir Khana Museum**. This modest house has a charming collection of family relics, including Moghul miniatures, carpets, Gandhara statues and Chinese silks and jade.

Outside the old city's Bhati Gate is the **Data Ganj Baksh Shrine**, using the popular name (meaning 'one who gives generously') of Syed Ali Abdul Hasan bin Usman. This Sufi saint came from the Afghan city of Ghazni to Lahore in 1039 and died here in 1072. He was a great scholar — the author of the *Kashful Mahjub*, a basic text in Persian on the fundamentals of Sufism — and is one of the most popular saints in Pakistan. Hundreds of pilgrims flock to his shrine every day. Foreign visitors are welcome, with Thursday being the best day to go (see pages 50 and 111). Data Ganj Baksh's *urs* (death festival) — almost a national event — spans the 18th and 19th days of the month of Saffar.

Jahangir's Tomb

This second cluster of Moghul monuments is on the Grand Trunk Road about five kilometres (three miles) toward Rawalpindi from the centre of Lahore. Buses number 6 and 23 take about 20 minutes from Lahore Railway Station. After you have crossed the toll bridge over the Ravi River, a dome and minarets become visible over the palms. Turn right about 700 metres (almost half a mile) beyond the toll booth. If on foot, follow the path across the railway line. If driving, follow the road for 600 metres before turning left to cross the railway level crossing. About 700 metres further on is the massive Moghul gateway leading into the tombs. The entrance fee for the three tombs together is Rs2.

The fresco-covered gateway of plastered red brick leads into **Akbari Serai**, built by Shah Jahan in about 1637 as a travellers' hotel. It is a spacious garden quartered by footpaths and planted with huge chinar, plane, shisham (rosewood), peepul and banyan trees. Around the four sides are 180 small rooms with verandahs.

On the east side, a handsome red sandstone gateway inlaid with marble leads into the **Tomb of Jahangir**, who died in 1627. The tomb was built by his son, Shah Jahan of Taj Mahal fame. It stands in the centre of a large garden divided by paths and water channels into 16 square sections and filled with beautifully spreading mature trees. The flat-roofed mausoleum is low and square, with each corner featuring a tall, octagonal minaret decorated with a zig-zag design and crowned with a marble cupola.

The red sandstone walls are inlaid with marble in intricate geometric patterns. Inside, the floors are of highly polished variegated marble, and the walls and ceilings of the surrounding arcade and its 30 rooms are covered in geometric and floral frescos. Four passages lead into the centre, where the white marble cenotaph (empty tomb) stands on a plinth decorated with *pietra dura* inlay in delicate floral designs.

The Ninety-Nine Attributes of God are inlaid in black marble. The south side of the cenotaph is inscribed: 'The Glorious Tomb of His High Majesty, Asylum of Pardon, Nur-ud-din Muhammad, the Emperor Jahangir', followed by the year of his death. Marble lattice screens fill the arches on all four sides of the cenotaph.

A staircase in each of the five-storey minarets leads up to the roof, which is surrounded by a balustrade and paved with white marble inlaid with geometric patterns in yellow and black. (Ask for the key at the ticket office.) The marble cenotaph surrounded by a marble railing that once occupied the centre of the roof was removed by the Sikhs to Amritsar.

A certain General Amise, a French officer in Ranjit Singh's army, actually converted Jahangir's tomb into a residence. After his death, the tomb was lived in by Sultan Muhammad, the brother of the Afghan ruler Amir Dost Muhammad.

The passage leading through to the **Tomb of Asaf Khan** is left of the handsome red sandstone mosque that stands on the west side of the Akbari Serai, opposite the gate of Jahangir's Tomb. Its bulbous dome is visible from the serai as it looms over the mosque.

Asaf Khan enjoyed close marriage ties with the ruling family. He was brother-in-law to Jahangir through Nur Jahan and father-in-law to their son, Shah Jahan, through Mumtaz Mahal, the lady of the Taj Mahal. Shah Jahan built this huge mausoleum for his father-in-law upon his death in 1641, nearly a decade and a half after Asaf Khan had provided crucial support in his struggle for the succession.

The tomb, which reflects classic Moghul design, is set in the centre of a large walled garden. A particularly graceful, high-pointed dome crowns an arched octagonal base. The whole must have been a glorious sight when the arches were fully faced with glazed-tile mosaics of blue, green, yellow and orange and when its dome was sheathed in shining white marble. The marble cenotaph within, once inlaid with *pietra dura*, still lists the Ninety-Nine Attributes of God in black inlay, but the fountains on the plinth marking the four cardinal points are gone. The northernmost of the two massive gates leading to the garden still retains some of its glazed tiles.

The **Tomb of Nur Jahan**, west of the railway, is reached via the road outside the south wall of Asaf Khan's Tomb. Follow it west, then turn left to cross the railway line, at which point the tomb is immediately on your left.

Nur Jahan lived until 1645, surviving by 18 years her husband, Jahangir, through whom she wielded considerable power. She filled her years of forced retirement by building herself a magnificent square tomb similar in design to that of her husband. Unfortunately, the monument was stripped to its brick core by the Sikhs, but it has been restored recently with new sandstone facing inlaid with marble. The four minarets and the garden wall have collapsed, and the frescos inside survive only in traces. The marble cenotaphs of Nur Jahan and her daughter, Lakli Begum, and the marble platform supporting them are 20th-century replacements, the originals having disappeared.

To return to the Grand Trunk Road, drive on past Nur Jahan's Tomb and turn right.

Shalimar Garden

This impressive Moghul monument is on the Grand Trunk Road, five kilometres (three miles) towards the Indian border from the centre of Lahore. Bus number 20 takes 20 minutes from the railway station. If going by car from Jahangir's Tomb, bypass the city by taking Bund Road after crossing the toll bridge over the Ravi River. Make an effort to be at Shalimar Garden when the fountains are playing, which is daily 10−11 am and 4−5 pm in summer and 11 am−12 noon and 3−4 pm in winter. The flowers are at their best in February and March.

Shah Jahan built the Shalimar Garden in 1642 for the pleasure of the royal household, which often stayed here for days or weeks at a time. In design, it conforms to the classic Moghul conception of the perfect garden and consists of three terraces of straight, shaded walks set around a perfectly symmetrical arrangement of ponds, fountains and marble pavilions, all surrounded by flower beds and fruit trees and enclosed within a wall. (In its rigid symmetry, it is similar to gardens laid out in 17th-century Europe.) Incredibly, the whole garden took less than 18 months to build. The problem of creating sufficient water pressure to feed the hundreds of fountains was solved by carrying water from the Royal Canal into raised tanks outside the garden.

The garden was designed to be entered at the lower terrace, which was open to distinguished members of the public. Honoured guests then moved against the flow of the cool waters to discover new and greater delights at the middle terrace, which was used for entertaining. Only intimates of the royal family were permitted to experience the supreme serenity of the upper terrace, the royal inner sanctum.

These days, visitors troop straight on to the upper terrace from the Grand Trunk Road. The terrace is divided into quarters by ponds splashed with fountains and has nine buildings, including the octagonal towers at each corner. The emperor's sleeping quarters were in the building in the middle of the south wall, just to your left as you enter. The building's three rooms, the walls and ceilings of which were once covered with frescos, open on to a wide verandah overlooking the garden through five gracefully cusped arches.

The empress's sleeping quarters are in the centre of the west wall, across from the Hall of Public Audience, which juts through the wall and out of the garden. The emperor walked through this hall daily to show himself to the public gathered in a separate walled garden outside. The arcaded pavilion on the north side of the terrace is the Grand Hall, which was once covered with frescos and used for ceremonial functions. The little house in the northeast quarter, built by the Sikhs early in the 19th century, was used as a guest house. William Moorcroft, the prodigious English explorer, stayed here in 1820.

The middle terrace is four metres (13 feet) down and reached by two flights of steps on either side of the Grand Hall. Between them, a cascade carries water down from the upper ponds to the great central pond, a broad square of water upon which play 150 fountains. Between the cascade and the pond, and surrounded by a marble railing, is the emperor's marble throne, where he sat in the moonlight listening to his musicians play and watching his *nautch* girls dance.

The Turkish bath house is set in the wall in the southeast corner of the terrace. Its changing room and cold and hot baths were once decorated with *pietra dura* inlay.

Two pavilions on either side of a waterfall guard the steps between the middle and lower terraces. In rows along the marble wall behind the waterfall are hundreds of little cusped niches. Flowers in golden vases occupied them by day, and lamps by night, so that, when viewed from the lower terrace through a double row of five cusped arches, the waterfall was a shimmering sheet of light.

The lower terrace, the least exciting, has two gates decorated with glazed-tile mosaics, two corner towers and a Hall of Private Audience once decorated with white marble and frescos.

Trips from Lahore

Hiran Minar

Emperor Jahangir enjoyed hunting in the area around Sheikhupura, about 30 kilometres (19 miles) from Lahore. There, in 1616, he built a hunting pavilion in the centre of an artificial lake and the Hiran Minar, a tower in memory of his pet deer. Three years later he built the massive brick fort still standing at **Sheikhupura**.

Buses run frequently between Lahore and Sheikhupura. If driving yourself, turn left 700 metres (almost half a mile) past the toll gate on the bridge over the Ravi River and go west along Sheikhupura Road. After two kilometres (one and a quarter miles), take the right fork on to the dual carriageway, an excellent road that goes straight across flat farmland for 30 kilometres (19 miles), to Sheikhupura.

The Hiran Minar and an artificial lake are in a deer park four kilometres (2.5 miles) beyond Sheikhupura toward Sargodha. Turn right where the dual carriageway ends, just past the railway level crossing.

The waters of the large, square lake are held within a brick wall and well stocked with fish. A little arched pavilion stands at each corner of the lake, and steps lead down to the water. An arched causeway leads out to the three-storey octagonal pavilion in the centre, where Jahangir sat in the shelter of the graceful arcade and watched the wild animals drawn to the water. Near the end of the causeway stands the Hiran Minar, dedicated to the memory of the deer Jahangir called Mansaraj. Visitors can climb the 99 steps to the top. An old well is concealed in the bushes near the tower, and boats are for hire on the lake.

Chhanga Manga Wildlife Reserve

This park in a huge forest 70 kilometres (43 miles) southwest of Lahore and half-way to Sahiwal features five small steam trains that pull deer-watchers along narrow-gauge tracks through the woods to large fenced pens stocked with several species of deer. There is a lake with boating, a restaurant and accommodation that is good value.

Harappa

An important excavation of the Indus Civilization, Harappa is just west of Sahiwal toward Multan. The Archaeology Department Rest House is comfortable, with rooms bookable through the Director of Archaeology at Lahore Fort (see Lahore listing on page 211).

Islamabad

Islamabad, Pakistan's new capital, nestles against the Margalla Hills, the foothills of the Himalayas in northern Punjab. Modern, spacious and carefully planned, Islamabad is a city of wide, tree-lined streets, large houses, elegant public buildings and well-organized bazaars. Traffic jams and crowds almost never occur, and narrow lanes and slums are few and far between. Sidewalks are shaded and safe behind rows of flame trees, jacaranda and hibiscus. Roses, jasmine and bougainvillaea fill the many parks, and scenic viewpoints show the city to its best advantage.

The decision to replace Karachi with a new capital in the centre of the country near the hills was made in 1958. Doxiadis Associates, a Greek firm, drew up plans for a huge triangle with its apex towards the Margalla Hills. Within the triangle is a grid divided into eight zones designated governmental, diplomatic, residential, commercial, educational, industrial and so on. The city has no real centre and is very widely spread out, each sector having its own shopping area and its own open space. Construction began in 1961, with the first residents moving in two years later.

Getting to Islamabad

Islamabad shares an airport and railway station with Rawalpindi, its twin city on the Grand Trunk Road. The main bus station is also in Rawalpindi, from where buses leave continuously for Islamabad. A taxi from the airport to Islamabad costs about Rs70, a wagon costs Rs5 and a bus Rs3.

When to Go

At 518 metres (1,700 feet) above sea level, Islamabad is at its best from October to March, when days are crisp and nights are cold. Spring is short but intense, with flowers producing a riot of colour in March. The hottest months are May and June, before the monsoon, but even they are not oppressive. Abnormally hot weather can be escaped by taking a trip to Murree, a hill resort 2,240 metres (7,400 feet) above sea level, less than an hour's drive away.

Getting Around

This can be a problem. Islamabad is too spread out for walking, and public transport runs frequently on only three or four of the main streets. However, good street maps are available in most bookshops, and Morris 1,000 taxis can be hired for about Rs30 per hour. In Islamabad addresses, 'E' is also known as 'Mehran', 'F' as 'Shalimar' and 'G' as 'Ramna'.

Sights

Daman-e-Koh Viewpoint is half-way up the Margalla Hills and gives the best bird's-eye view south over Islamabad, with the President's Palace, the Legislative Assembly and the Secretariat offices dominating the east end of the city (to your left) and the huge Shah Faisal Mosque

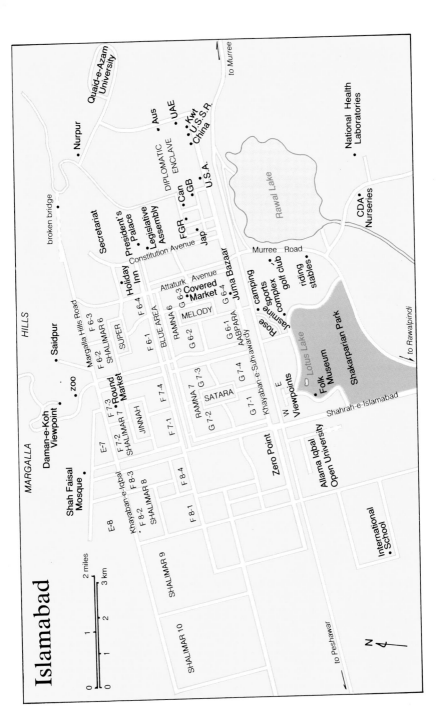

Islamabad

pressed against the hills to the west. In the distance are Rawal Lake and Rawalpindi. On a clear day after rain, you can see far out over the Potwar Plateau beyond Rawalpindi to a horizon serrated by the Salt Range.

The **zoo** and **children's adventure playground** are at the bottom of the hill below Daman-e-Koh Viewpoint. The road rising behind the viewpoint leads to the top of the ridge and then east towards Murree.

Shah Faisal Mosque, superbly sited at the foot of the Margalla Hills, resembles an eight-sided bedouin tent surrounded by four 90-metre-high (300-foot) concrete minarets. The walls hang from four giant concrete girders and are faced with white marble. The interior is decorated with mosaics and a spectacular chandelier. Designed by Vedat Dalokay, a Turkish architect, and financed largely by donations from Saudi Arabia, it is the world's biggest mosque, with room for 15,000 worshippers inside and another 85,000 in its raised courtyard. Below are two storeys housing an Islamic research centre, library, museum, press centre, lecture hall, cafeteria and the offices of the Shariat faculty of the Islamic University.

Shakarparian Park, centred on two low hills between Islamabad and Rawalpindi, has paved paths winding through gardens and past fountains and young trees planted by visiting dignitaries. The hills are crowned by **East and West Viewpoints**, which offer photogenic views of Islamabad against the backdrop of the Margalla Hills. A plan of the city has been laid out in a sunken garden at East Viewpoint, with hedges cleverly trimmed to resemble the hills.

Lok Virsa (the Institute of Folk and Traditional Heritage), also in Shakarparian Park, displays a large collection of art, handicrafts and musical instruments from around the country and has an open-air exhibition of wood carvings. Closed Mondays.

Rawal Lake is the large reservoir surrounded by forest, northeast of Shakarparian Park. It is a protected reserve offering excellent bird watching, with many migrating birds resting here en route between the USSR and India. About 300 species have been spotted in the Islamabad area.

Nurpur village and the Shrine of Syed Abdul Latif Shah, a 17th-century saint, are against the Margalla Hills and near Quaid-e-Azam University at the northeastern edge of town. The saint has an enormous following throughout the country, and a visit to his shrine speaks volumes about the intensity of religious devotion in Pakistan. Invalids who have come to pray for recovery pull threads from their clothing and cut off locks of their hair to hang from the banyan tree in the courtyard, while others anoint their foreheads or wounds with ashes from the sacred fire. The best time to go is on Thursday evening,

Sufism — Muslim Mystics and Saints

The atmosphere in the shrine is hushed, tense and emotional. The crowd shuffles slowly forward to caress the silver railing round the saint's tomb. Reverently, the pilgrims touch the doorpost, the pillars, the stone that once hung around the saint's neck. They slip their offering into one of the locked collection boxes and anoint themselves with holy oil from one of the many lamps.

A man helps his wife, barely able to walk, to the railing, and as she clutches it she cries, her lips moving in prayer. The procession swirls past her. Young women pray for a child, men for success, the poor for strength, the troubled for peace. In the further recesses of the dim tomb sit men and women with Korans open on their crossed knees, fingers tracing the lines of Arabic as they recite from memory, the intensity of their devotion lifting them from the world, blotting out the profane.

Sufi shrines, the tombs of Sufi saints, are scattered in their hundreds all over Pakistan. Thousands of devotees flock to each shrine to beg their favourite saint to intercede with God and secure the granting of some favour.

The mystic side of Islam emerged in the ninth century, when wandering holy men from Arabia, Iraq, Persia and Afghanistan set out from their native lands, carrying messages of love — love for God, love for the Prophet Muhammad and love for one's neighbour. For the next 700 years, wandering ascetics filtered into the subcontinent, spreading their brand of Islam. Each chose an area in which to settle and preach, and many opened kitchens to feed the hungry. (Most shrines still offer free food and shelter.)

The Sufis preached a love for God that went beyond simple obedience. Their teaching was geared to the common man who did not understand Arabic or complicated theological concepts. The Sufis used the local vernacular — be it Punjabi, Sindhi, Baluchi or Pushtu — and composed haunting music, lyrical poems and popular romantic stories to carry their message to the masses. Tales of love and longing and songs of solace and hope could be easily understood by all. Many used dance, moving feverishly to the driving beat of drums, to reach a trance-like state of union with God. These mystics were known in the West as Whirling Dervishes.

The spiritual strength and traditions of the Sufis have survived through the centuries, and the shrines are as active now as in the days of their founders. Each shrine has an annual festival to commemorate the death of its saint with three days of music, devotional singing and prayer. Outside the shrine, the amiable chaos of a fairground prevails, complete with performing animals, street theatre, transvestite dancing, acrobatics and wrestling among the food and souvenir stalls. Wildly dressed fakirs mingle with the crowds, receiving food and coins in return for blessings.

Nothing better reveals the spiritual life of Pakistan than a visit to a shrine during its festival (*urs*), or on a Thursday evening, when the singing and praying continues all night.

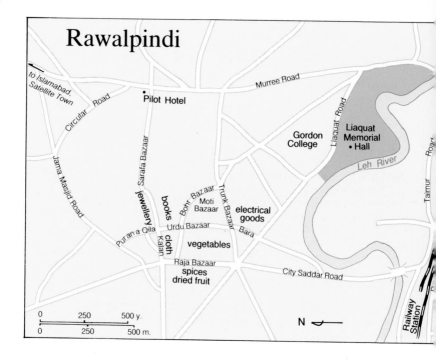

when the shrine is alive with pilgrims and there is usually *qawwali* devotional singing. Take the minibus from Aabpara Market.

The **Holy Man's Cave**, where the saint lived and meditated for 12 years, is a 45-minute climb up the hillside just behind Nurpur.

Rawalpindi

Though Rawalpindi lacks the historical monuments found in other Pakistani cities of its size, it is a lively, bustling place with a lot of local colour in its crowded streets and exciting bazaars. The city developed under the British Raj as a regional military headquarters and is now the supreme headquarters of the Pakistani army, with a large garrison stationed here. The cantonment is typical of residential areas built by the British all over the subcontinent.

Getting to Rawalpindi

Rawalpindi is on the Grand Trunk Road 280 kilometres (174 miles) from Lahore and 173 kilometres (108 miles) from Peshawar. It shares

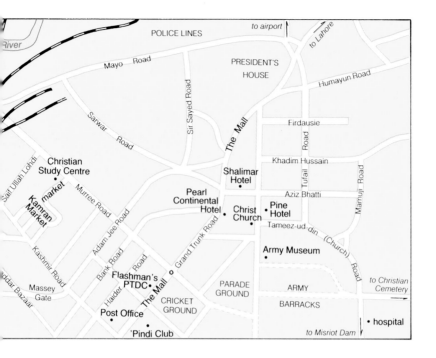

an international airport, a railway station and two bus stations with Islamabad. Murree Road, Airport Road and Peshawar Road connect Rawalpindi and Islamabad.

Good public transport and a broader range of hotels and restaurants (especially in the middle and lower range) make Rawalpindi a better place to stay than Islamabad. A steady stream of buses and minibuses cover the 20 kilometres between the two cities in about as many minutes — or take a taxi from Rawalpindi for a half-day tour of Islamabad.

Sights

The best way to see Rawalpindi is by wending through its bazaars, but you should orient yourself before setting out. The city has two main roads: the Grand Trunk Road runs roughly from east to west and is known as the Mall as it passes through the cantonment; Murree Road breaks north from the Mall, crosses the river and brushes the east end of the old city on its way to Islamabad. The two main bazaar areas are Raja Bazaar in the old city and Saddar Bazaar, which developed as the cantonment bazaar between the old city and the Mall.

Raja Bazaar comprises many smaller bazaars, each a labyrinth of small alleys. As is typical in Asia, shops selling the same items are grouped together. (This was true also in 14th-century European cities, in which trade guilds each had their own area.) In order to get to Raja Bazaar from Murree Road, turn west into Liaquat Road. On your left you will see **Liaquat Park**, where Liaquat Ali Khan, Pakistan's first prime minister, was shot while speaking at a rally of the Muslim League in October 1951. The park's **Liaquat Memorial Hall** is Rawalpindi's main concert hall. Music shops dominate further along on the right under a row of old carved-wood balconies. (The manufacture of musical instruments has become a Pakistani speciality, with more bagpipes made here than in Scotland.)

Raja Bazaar Road, the dual carriageway at the end of Liaquat Road, is the second-hand clothing market. The wholesale vegetable market is half-way down on the right, with the alleys off to the left specializing in spices, nuts and dried fruit. Conical towers of red chillies, orange tumeric, orange and yellow lentils, and green dried peas conspire to evoke bazaar scenes from the Arabian Nights.

Kalan Bazaar is the narrow street on the right at the end of Raja Bazaar in which are sold, on the left, shoes and stockings and, on the right, bales of cloth, chiffon scarves, hats, block-printed bedspreads and oils for the hair and skin. This runs into **Sarafa Bazaar**, the jewellery market. Note on your left a red 19th-century British post-box, Rawalpindi's first. The jewellery bazaar sells gold and silver, and some of the antique tribal silver is particularly lovely. Most of these jewellers maintain separate — and much smarter — shops on Murree Road. Beyond the jewellery shops are those selling household utensils in copper, brass, tin, aluminium and stainless steel. Finally, Sarafa Bazaar Road brings you back to Murree Road.

The **cantonment** evokes the British Raj, with its Christian churches and cemetery, spacious bungalows, club, cricket ground, mall and the colonial-style Flashman's Hotel. Behind Flashman's is **Saddar Bazaar**, the centre not only for shopping but also for hotels, banks, airlines and travel agents. The heart of the bazaar is along Kashmir Road and Massey Gate.

The **Army Museum**, near the Pearl Continental Hotel, houses a fine collection of weapons, uniforms and paintings depicting Pakistan's military history. Hours are 9 am−3 pm in winter, 8 am−noon and 5.30−7 pm in summer.

The **President's House** is behind high walls at the east end of the Mall. Beyond it along the Grand Trunk Road towards Lahore are the jail, Murree Brewery (a Parsee-owned firm that makes whisky and excellent beer for sale to non-Muslims) and **Ayub National Park**. The park has a lake with boats, children's amusement park and playground, mini-golf course, zoo and restaurants, in addition to walkways and bridle paths through the trees.

Trips from Islamabad-Rawalpindi

Murree and the Galis

The Galis are a string of hill resorts along the ridge between Murree, an hour's drive northeast of Islamabad, and Abbottabad, on the Karakoram Highway. Murree, at 2,240 metres (7,400 feet), combines convenience with a cool pine forest, amidst magnificent mountain scenery, to become the first choice for a day's outing from Islamabad.

Founded as a hill station by the British in 1851, Murree was the summer headquarters of the government of the Punjab until 1876, when the honour was transferred to Simla. Murree remained, however, a little bit of England, complete with a mall for promenading, parks, churches, schools, clubs and cafes. Since Independence, Murree has once again become the summer headquarters of the governor of the Punjab and, since Islamabad became the capital of Pakistan in 1962, has expanded rapidly.

Murree is lovely all year round. In summer it is cool — even chilly in the evening — and rain is common. In winter, the snow is piled high along the sides of the streets.

Getting to Murree

Bus and minibus service is frequent between Islamabad-Rawalpindi and Murree. Visitors going by car can return to the capital on the back road via Karor, which like the main road climbs steeply through mature pine forest but takes about 45 minutes longer. Another option is to make a loop from Islamabad to Murree, through the Galis to Abbottabad and back to Islamabad via the Karakoram Highway, Taxila and the Grand Trunk Road. This loop takes five or six hours, driving time.

Sights

Murree spreads along the top of a ridge for about five kilometres (three miles). At the northeast end is **Kashmir Point**, with views across the valley of the Jhelum River into Azad Kashmir. At the southwest end is **Pindi Point**, looking back towards Rawalpindi and Islamabad. Between the two runs **the Mall**, at the centre of which is the main shopping area, where most people congregate. Numerous roads leave the Mall and either follow the contours of the ridge or descend to the

main road. Promenading and shopping are Murree's main amusements. Good buys are cashmere shawls, furs, walking sticks, fruits and nuts. Murree's pistachio nuts are reputed to be the best in Pakistan.

Bhurban is a minor resort eight kilometres (five miles) from Murree on the road leading northeast to Kohala and the Jhelum Valley. The **golf course** here is open to non-members except in the high season.

The Galis

The **Galis** (*gali* meaning 'lane' in the local dialect) are along the road that runs north from Murree to Abbottabad. The hill stations are Barian, Sawar Gali, Khaira Gali, Changla Gali, Dunga Gali and Nathia Gali, this last being the most popular. The road follows the ridge through forests of giant pines and offers on clear days superb views of the snow-covered Pir Panjal Range, in Indian-held Kashmir, and the 8,125-metre (26,660-foot) Nanga Parbat, 170 kilometres (100 miles) away to the northeast.

Regular bus and minibus services connect Murree with Abbottabad, with stops at the various Galis along the way. The road is surfaced but narrow, with steep drops into the valley below. Running mostly at altitudes of 2,000–2,500 metres (7,000–8,000 feet), the road is blocked by snow from December until the beginning of May.

Numerous footpaths cut through the forest, and horses are for hire in every village. At **Ayubia National Park**, between Changla Gali and Dunga Gali, is a chair-lift to the top of the ridge.

Nathia Gali, the most popular of the Galis, is like Murree, with a small timbered church, bungalows, park and governor's house. This is the best place to stay for those who like walking. Walks include following the water pipe from Pines Hotel eight kilometres (five miles) through Dunga Gali to Ayubia or climbing the highest peak along the ridge, the 2,981-metre (9,780-foot) Miranjani.

Taxila and the Road to Peshawar

Along the Grand Trunk Road from Islamabad-Rawalpindi west to Peshawar are some of Pakistan's most important historic sites. Trade routes from the east, west, north and south come together in this area, and all the great invaders of the subcontinent passed this way. Every major epoch of Pakistani history has left its mark here: the ruins of the great civilizations of the three cities of Taxila; the Moghul caravanserai at Attock; Hasan Abdal, one of the spiritual centres of the Sikhs; and the modern Tarbela Dam.

Getting Around

Buses ply continuously between Rawalpindi and Peshawar, with passengers free to alight anywhere along the way. The railway runs parallel to the road.

Taxila

Taxila, about 35 kilometres (22 miles) from Islamabad, is one of the subcontinent's most important archaeological treasures, with the remains of three great cities and dozens of Buddhist monasteries dating from 600 BC to 600 AD. Situated at the meeting place of trade routes linking China, India, Central Asia and the West, Taxila was incorporated in many empires and became the cultural crossroads of the ancient world.

It was the main university town of Gandhara, a kingdom of northern Pakistan from the sixth century BC to the 11th century AD. Students at Taxila studied mathematics, law, history, medicine, social sciences, the arts, astronomy and military science. The level of knowledge was remarkably high for the period, especially in the fields of mathematics, medicine and astronomy. The Greek Alexander the Great arrived in 326 BC and held philosophical discussions with the resident intellectuals. He left a garrison at Taxila, but his empire quickly disintegrated following his death in Babylon at the age of 33.

Ashoka, before he inherited the whole of the Ganges-centred Mauryan Empire in about 275 BC, was viceroy at Taxila. He introduced Buddhism to Gandhara, from where the religion spread to Central Asia, Tibet and China. Ashoka died in 232 BC, and soon afterwards his empire declined.

Gandhara was then ruled by Bactrian Greeks from northern Afghanistan, who built a new city at Taxila. Now called Sirkap, the city was laid out in a regular grid, with streets crossing at right angles. The Sakas and Parthians followed the Greeks. Gondophares, one of the greatest of the Parthian kings, played host at Taxila to St Thomas the Apostle, the first Christian missionary to India.

In about AD 60, the Kushans arrived from Afghanistan and ousted the Parthians. They brought the Gandharan Empire to its greatest height in the second century AD, when it extended from eastern Iran to the valley of the Ganges. The Kushans built a new city at Taxila, which was a regional capital.

The Kushans were also great patrons of Buddhism, which from the first to the fifth centuries AD was the majority religion. Thousands of stupas were built all over the kingdom, with more than 50 in Taxila, one atop every hill. This was the great period of Gandharan Buddhist

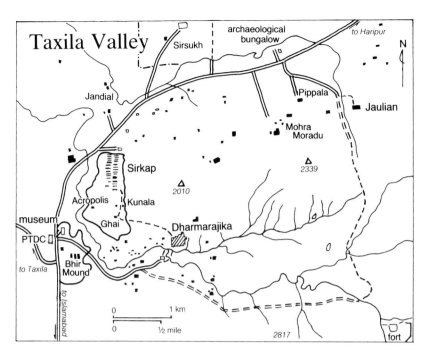

Taxila Valley

art; images of Buddha and scenes from his life worked in stone and plaster decorated every stupa and monastery. Most of the Buddhist sculpture in Taxila Museum is Kushan.

About AD 455, disaster struck Taxila in the form of the White Huns, hordes from Central Asia related to Attila, who was ravaging Europe at about the same time. Taxila never really recovered.

Taxila may at first disappoint those unused to older archaeological sites, appearing as nothing more than heaps of stones and the odd wall dotted about the valley. Stopping first at the museum helps enliven the ruins.

Taxila Museum is open daily 9 am−4 pm in winter and 8.30 am−12.30 pm and 2.30−5 pm in summer. It houses one of the best collections of Gandharan Buddhist art in Pakistan, an interesting coin collection and a display of artefacts — utensils, weights, jewellery and coins — illustrating the daily life of the inhabitants of ancient Taxila. A contour map of Taxila Valley shows the layout of the cities and all the other archaeological sites.

Those with time for only one site should see Jaulian, even though it involves a short walk up a steep hill. Those with three hours should see, in order, Dharmarajika, Sirkap and Jaulian. (Only those who are

quite fit should attempt to explore Taxila in the heat of summer, as
there is little shade.)

Dharmarajika is the site of a Buddhist stupa and monastery. The
stupa was probably the first built in Pakistan and is certainly one of the
largest and most impressive. It was built by Emperor Ashoka in the
third century BC to enclose a small relic chamber containing ashes of
the Buddha. It was subsequently enlarged and restored over the
centuries, and votive stupas and a monastery were added.

The **main stupa** is 15 metres (50 feet) high and 50 metres (165 feet)
in diameter. The great slice cut into its west side is the work of treasure
hunters searching for the golden casket containing the Buddha relics.

Originally, the whole dome of the stupa was plastered and gilded,
with a tall mast rising from its top and supporting seven or more stone
discs (like those on the stone umbrella in the museum). The dome was
surrounded by painted and gilded carvings of Buddha and scenes
depicting his life. All the other buildings in the complex were plastered
and painted in many colours. The forest of smaller stupas surrounding
the main stupa were all topped by spires like those on modern
Burmese or Thai pagodas.

Two processional paths lead round the stupa, with a flight of steps
at each of the four cardinal points. To the left of the eastern flight of
steps is the best-preserved section of the base of the stupa. This broad
band of ornamental stonework dates from the fourth or fifth century
AD. Little niches that once contained Buddhas are framed with trefoil
arches alternating with portals.

Around the main stupa is a galaxy of smaller **votive stupas** built by
wealthy pilgrims hoping to gain a blessing or merit. These monuments
date from the first century BC to the fourth century AD. Beyond the
ring of votive stupas on the south is a larger stupa dating from the
second century AD. It is one of the best-preserved in the complex and
is adorned with rows of Buddhas, atlantes (human figures supporting
the structure) and elephants.

To the north is a **row of chapels** containing four huge lime plaster
feet, the remains of two enormous Buddhas, the larger of which must
have been 11 metres (36 feet) high. On either side of the feet are the
lower parts of other figures, some of which still show traces of red
paint. All were once painted and gilded.

A large **monastery** lies on the northern edge of the complex, its five
courtyards dating from the first century BC to the sixth century AD. In
the centre of each courtyard is a stupa, and round the edges are the
monks' cells. The largest (northernmost) court, with 104 cells on two
storeys and a bath in the northwest corner, dates from the second or
third century AD. In the centre of the monastery was the hall of
assembly, and beyond the north wall was a sturdy watch-tower.

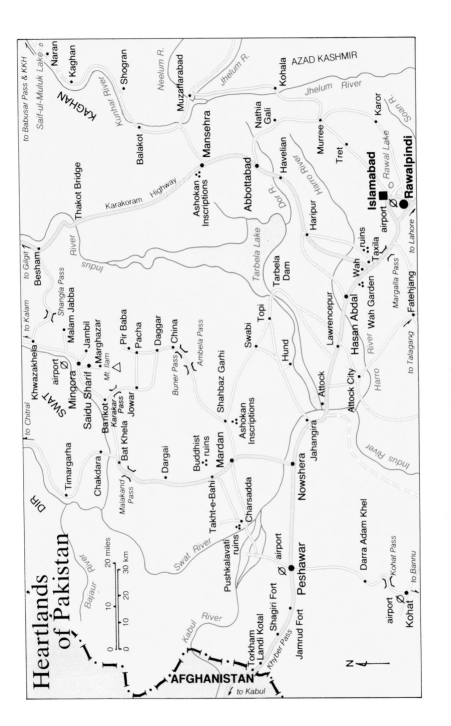

Other ruins in the complex include a building that once housed a reclining Buddha, a water tank for bathing and an apsidal (round-ended) temple built in the first century AD.

From Dharmarajika, a footpath leads over the hill to Ghai Monastery, Kunala Stupa and Sirkap, the second city of Taxila. The city is 30 minutes away by foot, or 15 minutes if you go round by car to the main gate. A walk around the site takes at least 15 minutes, but even this can be uncomfortable in summer except in the very early morning.

Sirkap was built by the Bactrian Greeks in 185 BC and used by the Sakas and Parthians until AD 80. The **city wall** ran five kilometres (three miles) round the roughly rectangular city, enclosing some rugged hills in the southeast, the isolated hill of the acropolis in the southwest and the large, flat area of the city proper. The wall was about six metres (20 feet) thick, six to nine metres (20−30 feet) high and interspaced with tall, square bastions. A large hole excavated beside the wall about 50 metres (165 feet) to the right (west) of the north gate (by which visitors enter the city) bares construction from different eras. The neatly fitted Greek wall, dating from the second century BC, is at the bottom; the Saka wall, from the first century BC, is above it and surmounted in turn by the Parthian wall, which dates from the first century AD. At the bottom of the hole is the original Greek drain.

The north gate leads into the wide **main street**, which is 700 metres (almost half a mile) long. The low walls that line the street are actually the foundations of the Parthian city; the upper parts of the buildings were made of mud and have long since disappeared. Down either side of the street was a row of small shops consisting of wooden platforms under colourful awnings. Behind the shops were two-storey private houses, the windowless walls of which were plastered and painted various colours. The houses were entered through doors opening on to side streets. Each house had up to 20 small rooms on each storey arranged around a small courtyard, with a wooden balcony giving access to the upper rooms. Inside, the rooms were generally plastered and painted, but some had wooden panelling. The flat, mud-covered roof was supported by wooden beams.

In almost every block was a Jain or Buddhist stupa, with its gilded dome and crowning spire of umbrellas rising above the surrounding walls. (Mahavira, the founder of the Jain religion, was a contemporary of Buddha.) The city had no wells, water being carried from the river outside the west wall. Sewage ran down the streets in open drains.

As one walks south from the north gate, the first block on the left contains a **stupa** set in a large court and overlooked by rooms on all sides. The relic chamber of this stupa once contained a Mauryan-period (third-century BC) crystal reliquary.

A large Buddhist **apsidal temple** occupies the whole of the fourth block left (east) of the main street. It was built on the ruins of an earlier temple following an earthquake in about AD 30. Two flights of steps lead up from the main street into the spacious courtyard around the temple. Immediately on either side of the steps are the small cells of the attendant monks. East of these are the bases of two small stupas, around which were found numerous stucco plaster heads and other decorative objects. These are now on view in the museum.

The temple has a round-ended nave with a stupa at its eastern end, around which ran a processional passage entered from the porch. The roof probably consisted of interlocking timbers covered with thatch and mud. The line of plain blocks of stone around the inside wall of the apse marks the level of the original timbered floor.

The **small stupa** in the next block dates from the first century BC, making it the oldest stupa at Sirkap. It has no base, but when unearthed its circular dome was decorated with acanthus flowers boldly modelled in lime stucco and painted. The stupa directly across the street has a double flight of seven steps leading up to it. Its plinth (square base) has thick stone walls radiating from the centre, suggesting to some a sundial. In fact, the walls were buttresses.

In the next block is the Buddhist **Shrine of the Double-Headed Eagle**, a first-century AD stupa mixing classical Greek and Indian styles. The façade boasts a row of Corinthian pilasters alternating with decorated niches in three distinct styles. The pair of niches nearest the steps resemble the pedimental fronts of Greek buildings; the next pair feature ogee arches like Bengal roofs; the outer pair are shaped like early Indian *toranas*, like those at Mathura, south of Delhi.

The double-headed eagle is perched atop the central niche. This motif, common to early Babylon and Sparta, was later adopted by the Scythians; later still, it was used in the imperial arms of Russia, Germany and Ceylon. This stupa originally had a drum and dome topped by a tiered stone umbrella, the whole decorated with finely moulded stucco plaster, gilded and painted.

The small **Jain stupa** in the next block has a rectangular base with five decorative pilasters on each side. The drum, dome and umbrella have all disappeared, but the remains of two Persepolitan columns crowned with lions were unearthed in the courtyard, and parts of these now stand at the four corners of the plinth.

The **Royal Palace** and the houses of wealthy citizens and officials are further south along the main street on the left. The palace differs from private houses only in size. A Greek visitor in AD 44 described it

as 'chaste in style', with wood-panelled rooms set around small courtyards.

Kunala Stupa is a ten-minute walk from the palace, atop a hill in the southeastern part of the city beyond the end of the main street. The site offers an excellent bird's-eye view of the entire city.

Kunala was the faithful son of the third-century BC Mauryan emperor Ashoka. It was his ironic misfortune to have eyes possessing such beauty that they captured the heart of his stepmother. Spurned by her stepson, the spiteful woman first tricked Ashoka into making him viceroy of Taxila, thus removing him far from the capital at Patna. She then sent a dispatch under Ashoka's seal, bringing accusations against him and ordering that his eyes be gouged out. The ministers at Taxila were loath to carry out the command, but the prince, believing it to have come from his father, insisted on its speedy execution.

The stupa was built at the very spot were the prince was blinded. Not surprisingly, it became a place of pilgrimage for the blind. (Taxila is still a haven for those suffering from eye trouble, as it has the best eye hospital in Pakistan.)

A curious feature of the stupa is that it was built over a smaller votive stupa (now exposed by excavators) because a stupa, once built, may not be moved or destroyed. When this little stupa was found in the way, it was simply incorporated into the structure. The smaller stupa dates from the first century BC, the surrounding one from the third or fourth century AD.

Kunala Monastery, also dating back to the third or fourth century, has an open courtyard surrounded by monks' cells. In each cell is a little arched niche in which the monk kept his lamp and books. The assembly hall is south of the courtyard.

Ghai Monastery crowns the next hill, which is still within the city walls. It is unusual in that the monks' cells surround, instead of an open court, a square hall with sloping windows.

Jaulian, with its monastery and stupa, is the best-preserved site at Taxila. It was built in the second century AD and burned by the White Huns in about AD 455.

The entrance leads into the **lower stupa court**, which is surrounded by alcoves or chapels that once contained statues of Buddha. The south side of the court is wired off and roofed to protect the bases of five votive stupas built as offerings by pilgrims early in the fifth century AD. They are decorated with rows of plaster carvings of Buddha with attendants, elephants, lions and contorted nudes. The inscription on the fifth stupa, titling the statues and naming the donors, is carved in Kharoshthi script, the national language of Gandhara.

The **main stupa court** is to the south, approached up five steps. The plaster Buddhas, bodhisattvas, attendants, animals and atlantes crowding around the bases of the central stupa and its 21 votive stupas are now protected by a flat roof. Once, though, the golden dome and umbrellas of the main stupa rose about 20 metres (65 feet) into the open sky, dominating the surrounding forest of gilded spires. The steps up the main stupa, which once led to the processional path round the dome, now give tourists access on to the modern roof.

Of particular interest is the Healing Buddha, the stone figure with the hole at its navel set in the north wall of the main stupa to the left of the steps. The faithful used to put a finger into the hole and pray for a cure. The Kharoshthi inscription below the Buddha records that it was the gift of a certain Budhamitra, who 'delighted in the law'.

Jaulian Monastery is west of the main stupa. The monastery courtyard, once decorated with statues of Buddha and scenes from his life, is surrounded by 28 monks' cells. Access to each cell was through a low wooden door, and the lintels and doorjambs were also of wood. The walls above the doors were constructed of mud and small stones, but these have fallen down. In each cell is a small sloping window and a niche for the monk's lamp. In the fifth century AD, all the walls were plastered and painted. Another 28 cells once occupied the second storey, which was reached by a stone staircase in one of the cells. The upper cells all opened on to a carved wooden balcony that ran, supported by wooden pillars, around the court.

The shallow water tank in the centre of the court collected rainwater off the wooden roof during the monsoon; at other times, the monks carried water up from wells at the bottom of the hill. They bathed in the enclosure in the corner of the tank. The hall of assembly, kitchen, store-room, refectory, stewards' room and latrine are west of the monastery court.

West of Taxila

Hasan Abdal, 13 kilometres (eight miles) west of Taxila along the Grand Trunk Road, is the site of one of Pakistan's few active Sikh temples, some ruined Hindu temples and a Muslim shrine.

Tarbela Dam is on the Indus River 45 kilometres (28 miles) north of the Grand Trunk Road. (The turn-off is about midway between Hasan Abdal and Attock.) You can drive across the dam and continue to Peshawar, making this a worthwhile, two-hour detour. Tarbela is the world's largest earth-filled dam in terms of the volume of earth used to build it and its electricity-generating capacity, and it boasts the two biggest spillways in the world. It is an impressive sight, particularly between July and September, when the lake is full from the melting snows and the monsoon rains and the main spillway is in use to carry the overflow. The dam is 2,743 metres (1.7 miles) long, 600 metres (2,000 feet) wide at its base and 143 metres (470 feet) high.

   Attock is about half-way between Islamabad and Peshawar, where
the Grand Trunk Road crosses the Indus River. It was a small place of
no importance until the 1540s, when Sher Shah Suri chose it as the
crossing place for his new Shahi Road from Delhi to Kabul. Until then,
everyone who crossed the Indus, from Alexander the Great to the
Moghul emperor Babur, did so 20 kilometres (12 miles) further upriver
at Hund.
   The **Caravanserai of Sher Shah Suri** is the most impressive sight at
Attock. It is just east of the new bridge and perched immediately
above the south side of the road, from which it is accessible via a short,
steep flight of steps. It was a 16th-century hotel consisting of four rows
of small rooms set around a huge courtyard. Its walls afford an
excellent view of the river, the new bridge and **Attock Fort**, which was
built in the years 1581–6 by the Moghul emperor Akbar. (The fort is
closed to the public.)
   Readily visible just north of the bridge is the confluence of the
Kabul and Indus rivers. The waters of the Kabul are a muddy brown,
but those of the Indus are a clear blue, the silt having settled behind
Tarbela Dam. The Indus here is a provincial boundary, and by the
time you reach the western shore you have crossed from the Punjab
into the North-West Frontier Province.

North-West Frontier Province

The North-West Frontier Province, or NWFP, runs for over 1,100 kilometres (680 miles) along the border with Afghanistan. Peshawar is its capital, and the Vale of Peshawar, fertile and well watered by the Kabul and Swat rivers, is its heart. This was also the heart of the ancient kingdom of Gandhara and is rich in archaeological remains. The northern half of the province consists of five river valleys running roughly parallel north to south: the Chitral, Dir, Swat, Indus and Kaghan. These valleys are on the northern edge of the monsoon belt, so are fairly green and partly wooded in their southern sections. Northern Chitral and the upper regions of the Indus Valley are mountainous deserts, where cultivation depends entirely on irrigation. The NWFP south of Peshawar is below the monsoon belt and consists of low, rocky mountains and wide, gravelly plains.

The **Tribal Areas**, which cover nearly half of the province along its border with Afghanistan, are autonomous regions governed by tribal law under the supervision of the Pakistani government. Because the government cannot, however, guarantee the safety of people who enter these areas, they are closed to foreigners. Even Pakistanis need permission to enter. The increased cultivation of opium in the Tribal Areas in recent years has intensified the risks faced by outsiders who attempt to slip in for whatever reason.

The **Khyber Pass**, the route from Peshawar to Kabul in Afghanistan, is the feature of the province most widely known (and infused with romance) in the world beyond. It is presently closed to foreigners, however, because of the dangers and official sensitivity arising from its traffic in drugs one way and guns the other.

The warlike **Pathans** (or Pushtuns or Puktuns), who live in the NWFP and the adjoining areas of Afghanistan, number about 15 million, making them one of the world's largest tribal societies. They have always considered themselves a race apart, a chosen people, and no one has ever managed to subdue them. The Moghuls, Afghans, Sikhs, British and Russians have suffered defeat at their hands. The Pathans are divided into numerous sub-tribes and clans, each defending its territory and honour. In addition, the Pathans serve as Pakistan's first line of defence along the Durand Line, the border drawn in 1893 by Sir Mortimer Durand, then foreign secretary of British India.

About three million **Afghan refugees** flooded into Pakistan after the Russian invasion of Afghanistan in December 1979. Most of them live in 350 enormous refugee camps, mostly in the NWFP.

Peshawar

Peshawar, the capital of the NWFP, is a frontier town, the meeting
place of the subcontinent and Central Asia. It is also a place where
ancient traditions rub against those of today, where the bazaar in the
old city has changed little in the past hundred years except to become
the neighbour of a modern university, some first-class hotels, several
international banks and one of the best museums in Pakistan.

No other city is quite like old Peshawar. The bazaar within the
walls is like an American Wild West movie costumed as a Bible epic.
Pathan tribesmen stroll down the street with their hands hidden within
their shawls, their faces half obscured by the loose ends of their
turbans. (With his piercing eyes and finely chiselled nose, the Pathan
must be the handsomest man on earth.) Afghan traders, many of them
in Peshawar to sell drugs and buy arms, stride proudly past in their
huge black and white turbans. Smuggling, drug-trading and arms-
dealing are all in a day's work — as they have been in these narrow
and crowded streets for centuries. Overlooking all are the massive Bala
Hizar Fort — still a military installation — and the elegant Mahabat
Khan Mosque — still a place of prayer.

On the other side of the railway line is the cantonment, its tree-
lined streets wide and straight as they pass gracious administrative
buildings and spacious bungalows commanding equally spacious
gardens. Clubs, churches, schools, the Mall, Saddar Bazaar and the
airport round out the British contribution to the modernization of
Peshawar. Further west is University Town, Peshawar's newest section
and the site of Peshawar University.

A local book, *Peshawar, Historic City of the Frontier*, by A H Dani
and published by Khyber Mail Press in 1969, makes a good first
purchase. It gives a detailed account of Peshawar's history and a tour
of its city walls and ancient monuments.

Getting to Peshawar

Peshawar is linked by air to a dozen Pakistani towns and cities
(including Karachi, Lahore and Islamabad-Rawalpindi) and even to
Europe via Dubai. It is the last stop for tourists on the national rail
system. Bus and minibus services run between Peshawar and
Islamabad (three or four hours), the valleys of Swat, Dir and Chitral to
the north and, for the adventurous, the desert towns to the south
beyond Kohat.

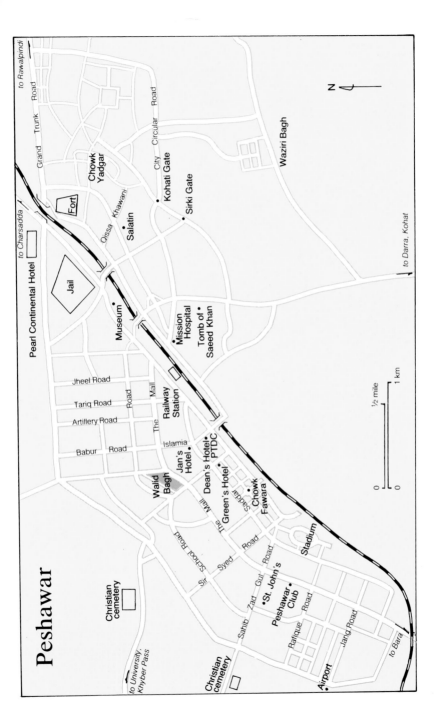

History

The fortunes of Peshawar are inextricably linked to the Khyber Pass, the eastern end of which it guards. The pass seems to have been little used in prehistoric times, and even in early historic times it was generally shunned as too narrow and thus too prone to ambush. Not until the powerful Kushans invaded Gandhara and pacified the area in the first century AD did the Khyber become a popular trade route.

Peshawar owes its founding 2,000 years ago to these same Kushans. In the second century AD, Kanishka, the greatest of the Kushan kings, moved his winter capital here from Pushkalavati, 30 kilometres (20 miles) to the north. His summer capital was north of Kabul at Kapisa, and the Kushans moved freely back and forth through the Khyber Pass between the two cities, from which they ruled their enormous and prosperous empire for the next 400 years.

After the Kushan era, Peshawar declined into an obscurity not broken until the 16th century, following the Moghul emperor Babur's decision to rebuild the fort here in 1530. Sher Shah Suri, his successor (or, rather, the usurper of his son's throne), turned Peshawar's renaissance into a boom when he ran his Delhi-to-Kabul Shahi Road through the Khyber Pass. The Moghuls turned Peshawar into a 'city of flowers' (one of the meanings of its name) by planting trees and laying out gardens.

In 1818, Ranjit Singh captured Peshawar for his Sikh Empire. He burned a large part of the city and felled the trees shading its many gardens for firewood. The following 30 years of Sikh rule saw the destruction of Peshawar's own Shalimar Gardens and of Babur's magnificent fort, not to mention the dwindling of the city's population by almost half.

The British crushed the Sikhs and occupied Peshawar in 1849, but, as much as Sikh rule had been hated, its British replacement roused little enthusiasm. More or less continuous warfare between the British and the Pathans necessitated a huge British garrison. When the British built a paved road through the Khyber Pass, they needed to build numerous forts and pickets to guard it.

Sights

Bazaar Tour

The most exciting part of Peshawar is its old city, elements of which date from Sikh, Moghul and even Buddhist times. It is a labyrinth of narrow lanes and colourful bazaars, a mosaic of traders, travellers, Pathan tribesmen and Afghanis. In typical Asiatic style, shops selling

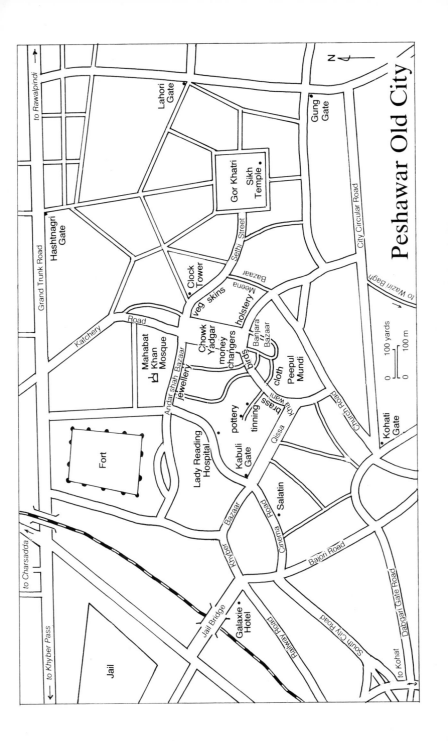

Peshawar Old City

similar wares are found together. They are generally open all day, every day, except during *juma* prayers on Fridays between noon and 2 pm. A tour taking in all the most interesting and picturesque bazaars and some of the specialist shops and workshops can be accomplished in two or three hours.

Khyber Bazaar, full of doctors, lawyers and dentists, features billboards depicting sets of false teeth of nightmarish proportions. This is also the bus terminal for the Khyber Pass and for Kohat. **Kabuli Gate**, one of the walled city's 16 gates, is at the end of Khyber Bazaar. (The wall survived until the mid-1950s, and though the names remain, the gates and the wall have, for the most part, disappeared.)

Qissa Khawani (Story-tellers') Bazaar was described in the mid-19th century by British Commissioner in Peshawar Sir Herbert Edwardes as 'the Piccadilly of Central Asia'. Towering over the street are tall, narrow buildings with intricately carved balconies and window frames enclosing wooden shutters. Here you find many of Peshawar's cheaper hotels and, in the evening, food stalls selling excellent kebabs and fry-ups. Meat is sold by weight and then cooked while you watch.

Brass and copper shops are in the street to the left (northwest) at the end of Qissa Khawani. These sell a range of new and old wares. Ali Brothers on the left is the best known and where all VIP visitors are taken. 'Poor Honest Ali', as he disarmingly calls himself, has Gardner Russian china as well as a selection of high-quality brass and copper. When Ali shows his testimonials from ambassadors and the photo of himself with Jackie Onassis, remember, bargain hard.

The Peshawar Pottery is down a side street on the left, immediately after the brass shops. Here you can watch the potters at work 10 am−4 pm except Fridays. The wide range of ornamental and utilitarian pottery is glazed in strong earth colours.

Tinsmiths work in the street leading to the pottery, using traditional methods to coat brass pots with tin to prevent the brass from poisoning food.

Back on the main street and beyond the copper market are shops selling **blankets and shawls** from the valleys of Swat and Kaghan. Made of hand-spun wool, they are predominantly red and black, with brightly patterned borders. The lane to the right (southeast), opposite the street to the pottery, leads to the **cloth bazaar**. Beyond that is the **basket bazaar**, which is full of baskets from Dera Ismail Khan, at the southern tip of the province. Here, also, is the **Banjara Bazaar**, which specializes in unusual decorative items such as bells, wooden beads and hair braids. Ask here for the way to **Peepul Mundi**, the main grain wholesale market, where there is a peepul tree believed to be descended from the tree under which Buddha preached.

If you choose instead to continue on the main street towards Chowk Yadgar, you pass the **bird market**, where song birds are sold as pets in small cages, as in China. To the left are more cloth shops selling all types of *charders* (multi-purpose sheets) and block prints.

Chowk Yadgar is old Peshawar's central square and the best place to leave your motor rickshaw or car. The monument in the centre commemorates the heroes of the 1965 Indo-Pakistani War and is the traditional place for assembling political rallies and demonstrations.

On the left (west) side of the square, money changers squat on hand-knotted carpets with their safes behind them and their pocket calculators at the ready. They will change any currency (illegally), but will accept only large notes.

From Chowk Yadgar are two interesting walks, one to the west and the other to the east. Running off the square to the west is **Andarshah Bazaar**, a narrow street of gold- and silversmiths selling jewellery (both tribal and modern), antique silver, old coins and military buttons and buckles. While you rummage through the boxes of treasures, trying on nomads' earrings, the shopkeeper plies you with cups of sweet green tea brewed in huge copper samovars.

Mahabat Khan Mosque is at the top of the hill to the right (north), its entrance a narrow gateway between jewellery shops. Built in the 1670s, this beautifully proportioned Moghul structure, named for a regional governor who served under both Shah Jahan and Aurangzeb, is orthodox in design. Its open courtyard has an ablution pond in the middle and a single row of rooms around the sides. The prayer hall occupies the west side flanked by two tall minarets. According to the turn-of-the-century Gazetteer for the NWFP, the minarets were frequently used in Sikh times 'as a substitute for the gallows'. A fire that raged through the Andarshah Bazaar in 1895 (the Gazetteer continues) failed to destoy the mosque thanks only to the 'unremitting efforts of the faithful'. The interior of the prayer hall is sheltered beneath three low fluted domes and is lavishly and colourfully painted with floral and geometric designs.

If you start again at Chowk Yadgar but go east this time, you pass fruit and vegetable stalls on the right and an alley full of hardware shops on the left before coming to **Cunningham Clock Tower**. It was built in 1900 'in commemoration of the Diamond Jubilee of Her Majesty the Queen Empress' but is named after Sir George Cunningham, who came along somewhat later. Cunningham started his Asian career as the political agent assigned to North Waziristan (in the Tribal Areas) and advanced to become governor of the NWFP in 1937−46 and again after Independence in 1947−8. The **leather and skins market** around the clock tower features the skins of very young

Karakul lambs, and many of the shops have tailors on hand to make Astrakhan hats.

The **Meena Bazaar**, for women, is down the alley to the right (south) of the clock tower. Groups of *burqa*-clad (veiled) women shop for beads, trimmings, machine-embroidery and trinkets. Visitors considering adopting *purdah* can buy their *burqa* here in a choice of colours.

Further up the hill from the clock tower is the shoe bazaar, which is down an alley on the right. Next is the block-printing shop, where cloth is hand printed using a variety of carved wooden blocks dipped in an array of dyes.

The way up the hill to the Moghul caravanserai is called **Sethi Street** because most of the old houses here belong to the Sethi family, one of the oldest merchant families in town. The Sethis once had offices in Czarist Russia and Shanghai; they imported silks and china and exported cloth, indigo and tea. The houses are tall and supplied with balconies. Beautifully carved wooden doors lead from the street to spacious courtyards, and cool cellars 15 metres (50 feet) deep provide a retreat from the heat of summer. Victorian glass chandeliers are a reminder of the family's vast wealth in the last century. A tour of one of the houses can be arranged through the PTDC at Dean's Hotel.

The **Gor Khatri** is a large Moghul caravanserai crowning the hill at the top end of Sethi Street. A huge Moghul gateway leads into a courtyard over 200 metres (650 feet) square, which was once surrounded on all four sides by rooms for travellers. The site has been considered holy for nearly 2,000 years. In the second century AD, it was a Buddhist shrine and monastery known as the Tower of Buddha's Bowl. With the decline of Buddhism, it became a Hindu shrine, and in Moghul times Shah Jahan's daughter built a mosque here and surrounded it with the caravanserai. The Sikhs knocked down the mosque during their 19th-century rule and replaced it with a temple to Gorakhnath. This still stands in the southeastern corner of the courtyard, with a shrine to Nandi beside it. The Sikhs closed the caravanserai and installed their governor in the compound. Since that time it has housed government offices.

Once again, start at Chowk Yadgar and follow Katchery Road (the main street going north) past a row of shops selling holsters for guns and bandoleers for ammunition to the Grand Trunk Road. There, brooding over the highway to the north and the old city to the south, squats **Bala Hisar Fort**, which was built by the Sikhs in 1834 on the site of Babur's earlier fort. The army still uses it, so it is closed to the public.

The Cantonment

Peshawar's cantonment sprawls along the west side of the railway line and was laid out by the British as graciously and grandly as any other. Between the old city and the cantonment is the **Saddar Bazaar**, an area full of hotels, restaurants and shops stocked with antiques and carpets.

Peshawar Museum, formerly Victoria Memorial Hall, was built near the east end of the Mall in 1905. (Its long hall, flanked by side galleries and with a raised platform at the end opposite the door, was the ballroom.) The museum has one of Pakistan's best collections of Gandharan art, and the pieces are well arranged and labelled, with sculptures illustrating the life of Buddha placed in chronological order. The fasting Buddha here is even more haunting than the one in Lahore Museum. The ethnological section, the Hall of Tribes, has wooden carvings from the Kalash people in Chitral. There is also a Muslim Gallery. Guided tours are scheduled daily at 10 am and 4 pm, but they do not always materialize. Telephone 72252 or 74452 for details and opening times.

St John's Church is the oldest in Peshawar, dating from 1851, the second year of the British presence. The Christian cemetery is not beside the church, however, being located instead at two places beyond the residential area on the road to the Khyber Pass. The oldest graves are cemented into the wall closest to the road and tell evocative tales of death on the frontier. One Lieutenant Colonel Walter Irvine was the chief medical officer of the NWFP 'who lost his life in the Nagoman River when leading the Peshawar Vale Hunt, of which he was Master, 26 Jan 1919'. The Rev Isidor Loewenthal was a 'Missionary of the American Presbyterian Mission who translated the New Testiment into Pushtoo and was shot by his Chokeydar [watchman], April 27 1864'. There are many sad tiny graves similar to the one for 'Our Little Mavis, born September 6th 1903, died May 1st 1904. The dearly loved child of Arthur and Maud Tyler.' Donations for the upkeep of the cemetery are welcomed by the bishop at St John's Church.

The **Peshawar Club**, on Sir Syed Road near the Mall, is reserved for members and their guests, but anyone can go in to look around and browse in the library. The swimming pool is surrounded by large shade trees and is open to the public. In the morning, half of it is curtained off by a *shamiana*, behind which swim women in *purdah*. Bells ring loudly just before noon to warn the ladies that they are about to be exposed.

Edwardes College, one of Pakistan's prestigious boarding schools, was founded in 1855 as the Sir Herbert Edwardes Memorial School. It has splendid Moghul Gothic buildings replete with ornate cupolas, baubles and pillars.

Khalid Bin Walid Bagh is the narrow park on the Mall full of beautiful chinar trees. It is all that remains of an old Moghul Shalimar Garden.

University Town lies about seven kilometres (four miles) from the centre of Peshawar on the road to the Khyber Pass. Its oldest building is Islamia College, which was founded in 1913 to educate the sons of Pathan chiefs. If the elegant Moghul Gothic hall looks familiar, you may have noticed it on the hundred-rupee note. The college formed the nucleus of the University of Peshawar when it was founded in 1950. Various research departments in the area include the Pakistan Academy for Rural Development and the Pakistan Forest Institute. The surrounding residential area is a sprawling garden town of red brick buildings among watered lawns.

Trips from Peshawar

Khyber Pass

The Khyber Pass is closed to foreigners. However, UN officials, diplomats and accredited journalists can apply to the Provincial Home

Secretary and the Minister of Tribal Affairs for permission to drive through the pass. Pakistanis should apply to the Political Agent.

The Afghan border at Torkham is 56 kilometres (35 miles) from Peshawar, about an hour's drive. The road runs west from the cantonment and through University Town, after which the fields on either side of the road are covered with refugee camps. After the camps are the compounds of Pathan tribesmen, their high mud walls furnished with turrets and gunslits, their entrances guarded by huge corrugated-iron gates.

Jamrud Fort, 18 kilometres (11 miles) from Peshawar and at the mouth of the Khyber Pass, is as far as you can go without a permit. The fort, coarsely constructed of stone daubed with mud plaster, was built by the Sikhs in 1823 on the site of an earlier fort. The modern stone arch spanning the road dates from 1964.

The eastern end of the pass is wide and flat, bounded on either side by low, stony hills. Every small hillock in the area is capped with a picket manned by the Frontier Force. The road zig-zags up, passing two viewpoints that look back into the Vale of Peshawar, until it reaches **Shagai Fort**, which was built by the British in the 1920s. It then starts down into a small valley in which stand fortified Pathan houses and the Ali Masjid. Perched high above this mosque on a commanding spur is the **Ali Masjid Fort**, which overlooks the entire length of the pass and guards the gorge that is its narrowest point. The road here hugs a narrow ledge beside the river bed in the shadow of high cliffs on either side. Until the way was widened, two laden camels could not squeeze past each other, and even now the road is one way. (The return road and the railway follow separate ledges higher up on the opposite cliff, affording a less exciting view of the gorge.)

In the cemetery here are the graves of British soldiers killed in the Second Afghan War of 1879. Regimental insignia are carved and painted on to the rock faces at several places along the road, with the Gordon Highlanders, the South Wales Borderers, and the Royal Sussex, Cheshire and Dorset regiments standing in one doughty group.

After the gorge, the pass opens out into a wide fertile valley dotted with Pathan villages. True to form, however, these villages look more like forts, with high, crenellated mud walls running between watch-towers pierced with narrow gunslits.

Sphola Stupa, a Buddhist ruin dating from the second to the fifth centuries AD, stands to the right of the road and above the railway at the village of Zarai, 25 kilometres (16 miles) from Jamrud. The stupa has a high hemispherical dome resting on a three-tiered square base. Some beautiful Gandharan sculptures were found here when the site was excavated at the beginning of this century. Some of the finds are

now in the Peshawar Museum. The side of the stupa facing the road
has been restored.

Landi Kotal, at the end of the railway line and eight kilometres
(five miles) from the border, is a smugglers' town. Electrical goods,
cloth and drugs are the main commodities in the bazaar below the road
to the left. The road forks here: right to the Khyber Rifles'
headquarters, left to the border. A viewpoint beyond the town looks
out across tank traps of closely packed cement pyramids to the border
post at **Torkham**, the last oasis of green before the barren brown of the
Afghan plain.

On a hilltop to the left of Torkham is the ruined **Kafir Fort**, a
Hindu relic of the ninth century AD. On this ridge in 1919, the British
and Afghans fought one of the last engagements of the Third Afghan
War. The top of the hill is now Afghan territory, with a commanding
view down on Pakistani installations and forts.

The Khyber Train

For rail enthusiasts, the Khyber Railway from Peshawar to Landhi
Kotal is a three-star attraction. The British built it in the 1920s at the
then-enormous cost of more than two million pounds. It passes
through 34 tunnels totalling five kilometres (three miles) and over 92
bridges and culverts. The two or three coaches are pulled and pushed
by two SG 060 oil-fired engines. At one point, the track climbs 130
metres in little more than a kilometre (425 feet in 0.7 miles) by means
of the heart-stopping Changai Spur. This is a W-shaped section of
track with two cliff-hanging reversing stations, at which the train
wheezes desperately before shuddering to a stop and backing away
from the brink.

The Khyber train currently carries no foreign passengers, but it is
easily seen at Peshawar Station except on Friday, the day it makes its
run to Landhi Kotal.

Darra Adam Khel

Darra is the gun factory of the Tribal Areas, located 40 kilometres
(25 miles) south of Peshawar on the road to Kohat, a drive of about 40
minutes. Foreigners need a permit from the Home Secretary of the
NWFP to leave Peshawar on this road.

The Darra arms 'factory' fired up in 1897. In return for turning a
blind eye to this illegal Pathan enterprise, the British were guaranteed
safe passage along the main roads. In any case, the British believed it
better that the Pathans have inferior weapons of their own making
than stolen British-made guns.

Afghan Refugees
by John Elliott of the Financial Times

Visit some of the small carpet shops near Greens Hotel in the border city of Peshawar, and you might find rugs decorated with Kaleshnikov rifles, hand grenades, rocket launchers and Russian helicopters. This new twist to ethnic art and the region's traditional carpet business is the work of some of the three to three and a half million Afghan refugees who have fled to Pakistan since Soviet armed forces occupied their country in 1979.

The carpets are made in refugee camps outside Peshawar. These and other handicrafts are produced, marketed and exported to the United States and other countries with the help of the Save the Children Fund and the Salvation Army, two of the many aid organizations operating in the area.

Peshawar, always a colourful border town near the famous Khyber Pass, was transformed in the early 1980s, when it became not only the centre of a massive international aid effort to look after the refugees but also the headquarters for the main Mujahideen guerilla groups. The University Town area is the centre of the activity and is now full of modern jeeps and station wagons filled with refugee representatives, guerilla fighters and journalists.

Outside the city are huge refugee camps, which have populations of over 200,000 each and are divided into distinct villages complete with streets of brick and mud dwellings, bazaars and small businesses. Refugees start off when they arrive with a tent from aid agencies. As devout Muslims, they quickly build outer walls to shield their women — then more walls under canvas roofs. Finally, they add permanent roofs.

In all, about 340 villages have sprung up to house as many as three million of the refugees. About two-thirds of the people are in the North-West Frontier Province, of which Peshawar is the capital. Another 20 percent are further south in Baluchistan, with a smaller number in the Punjab. Some refugees have merged into the Pakistan community, with many engaged in the transport business, an important component of which has always been Pathans from the North-West Frontier, where the border dividing Pakistan and Afghanistan is vague and disputed.

In addition to the refugees in Pakistan, an estimated two million live in Iran, a half million mostly middle-class Afghans are scattered in the West, and as many as three million more are displaced within Afghanistan.

Pakistan has been able to absorb its massive influx of people with relatively little tension partly because of the generous economic and military aid that has poured into the country, mostly from the United States. The Afghan conflict has, however, created in Pakistan rapidly worsening gun-running and drug-addiction problems, making the Pakistanis ever more hopeful that an end to the Soviet occupation of Afghanistan would gradually allow the refugees to return home.

Either way, Peshawar will never be the same.

Darra's main street is lined on either side with small forges at which guns are made by hand. The tools are astonishingly primitive, yet the forges turn out accurate reproductions of every conceivable sort of weapon, from pen pistols and hand grenades to automatic rifles and anti-aircraft guns. The copies are so painstakingly reproduced that even the serial number of the original is carried over. Much of the craftsmanship is very fine, but the materials are sometimes wanting: gun barrels are often made from steel reinforcing rods diverted from the building trade. The main street constantly erupts with the roar of gunfire, as tribesmen step out to test prospective purchases.

Gandharan Remains

The three most interesting archaeological remains from Gandhara are Takht-e-Bahi (a ruined Buddhist monastery), the Ashokan edicts (two inscribed boulders) and Charsadda (an excavated mound that was once the capital city). These three places can be visited in a one-day outing from Peshawar or *en route* between Peshawar and either Islamabad or Swat. An interesting loop takes in Charsadda and Takht-e-Bahi on the way up to Swat via the Malakand Pass, then the Ashokan edicts on the way down from Swat via the Ambela Pass.

The kingdom of Gandhara centred on the Peshawar area from the sixth century BC to the 11th century AD and enjoyed its high period from the first to the fifth centuries AD under the Kushan kings. This was a time of great international contacts, and Buddhist Gandhara was at the hub of Asia, trading with China, the Mediterranean and India. The kingdom is remembered chiefly for its Buddhist art. Museums all over the world display the fine stone and stucco sculptures of Gandhara, works that reflect a society that was mature, prosperous, advanced and (in the best Buddhist tradition) gentle.

The first capital of Gandhara was Pushkalavati — the Lotus City — on the banks of the Swat River just north of its junction with the Kabul, at a place now called Charsadda. Under the Kushans, the capital moved to Peshawar, and under the Hindu Shahi kings from the ninth to the 11th century the capital was at Hund, on the Indus. After Mahmud of Ghazni conquered the area and converted it to Islam in AD 1026, the name Gandhara disappeared. Only a few ruins and the civilization's great art remain.

Though there is little to see, it is still exciting to stand on the mound where the Lotus City once flourished and to imagine Alexander the Great's army attacking in 327 BC, to read Ashoka's edicts of 260 BC at Shahbaz Garhi, and to visualize the life of a Buddhist monk at Takht-e-Bahi in the third century AD.

Charsadda

Charsadda, the site of Pushkalavati, is 28 kilometres (17 miles) northeast of Peshawar. Pushkalavati was the capital of the ancient kingdom of Gandhara from about the sixth century BC to the second century AD. Even after the capital moved to Peshawar, Pushkalavati remained a centre of pilgrimage until the seventh century, thanks to the presence of an important Buddhist shrine.

The **Bala Hisar** is a mound about 800 metres (half a mile) to the left of the road from Peshawar, about a kilometre (half a mile) before Charsadda. It has been excavated twice, by Sir John Marshall in 1902 and by Sir Mortimer Wheeler in 1958. You can climb to the top. The millions of pottery sherds amid the round, beautifully coloured stones at your feet are only the top layer of 2,500 years of debris, for the Bala Hisar was occupied from the sixth century BC to the 18th century AD.

In about 516 BC, Gandhara became part of the seventh province of the Achaemenid Empire and paid tribute to Darius the Great of Persia. According to Herodotus, the Greek historian, Darius sent the explorer Scylax of Caryanda to sail down the Indus and find the sea. Scylax probably set out from Pushkalavati, as the river is navigable from here down.

Gandhara probably remained within the Achaemenid Empire for the next 200 years, until its overthrow by Alexander the Great in the fourth century BC. Alexander first captured Persia and Afghanistan, then in 327 BC he split his army, taking half of it north to subdue Swat. The other half he placed under the command of Hephaestion, with orders to go directly to Gandhara, capture the main towns, proceed to the Indus and build a bridge across it. The able Hephaestion laid siege to Pushkalavati and, after 30 days, took the city and killed its defender, Astes. He built his bridge by lashing together a line of boats from one bank to the other at Hund. He secured the surrender of Taxila through negotiations. By the time Alexander got to Gandhara, he owned it.

In 322 BC, Chandragupta Maurya rose to power, bringing Gandhara under his sway some years later. By this time, Taxila, with its famous university, had grown more important than Pushkalavati. The Mauryan emperor Ashoka built stupas containing relics of Buddha at both cities. The mound believed to enclose the stupa at Pushkalavati has not been excavated.

The Bactrian Greeks were the next rulers of Gandhara. They arrived from Balkh in Afghanistan in about 185 BC and laid out new cities at both Pushkalavati and Taxila. The city at Taxila is now called Sirkap. The one at Pushkalavati, now called Shaikhan Dheri, is a kilometre (half a mile) northeast of the Bala Hisar. From the top of

Gandhara Art

Between the first and fifth century AD, the Buddhist kingdom of Gandhara in northern Pakistan enjoyed a period of unparalled peace and prosperity. It stood at the hub of the trade routes linking China, India and the Mediterranean — a cultural and commercial crossroads. The heart of the kingdom was in the plains of Peshawar along the Kabul and Swat rivers, its capital near their confluence. The prosperity resulted in the growth of cities able to support a large community of Buddhist monks living in about 1,600 monasteries along the two rivers, always within easy reach of the towns where the monks went daily to beg.

Each monastery had its stupa, a solid domed structure (usually on a square base) representing Buddha and sometimes containing some relic of Buddha or of a revered Buddhist holy man. To facilitate their devotions, the monks decorated their stupas and monasteries with stone and plaster statues of Buddha and scenes telling the story of his life. This Gandharan sculpture was so vivid and alive — and the kingdom so powerful — that the artistic tradition continued for five centuries.

The strength of Gandharan sculpture came from the depth of belief and devotion of the artists, whose work was their expression of veneration of Buddha. They created an exciting new mix of eastern and western art, incorporating ideas from India, Persia, Greece and Rome. The various influences are evident in the Corinthian and Persepolitan capitals of pillars carved in relief and in the centaurs, garlands, vine motifs and Atlas figures that ennoble one piece after another. The earliest sculptures refrain from direct representation of Buddha in human form, resorting instead to symbols — a stupa, lotus, tree or wheel. In the second century AD, Kanishka, the greatest Kushan king, convoked a council on Buddhism, which decided to popularize Buddhism by encouraging sculptors to represent Buddha, for the first time, as a man. The first Buddha figures had Greek faces and wore Roman-style robes, carved with deep folds. This western look later gave way to a more mask-like expression, representing the inner serenity, the private ecstacy, achieved through deep meditation.

Buddha is shown either standing, sitting cross-legged or lying on his deathbed. His hands are frozen in certain gestures recognized by the faithful as prayer, preaching, blessing or accepting gifts. His hair is wavy or curly and tied in a bun on top of his head, which was later mistaken for a protuberance from his skull. His earlobes are usually elongated, and the middle of his forehead bears a round mark. He is normally crowned with a halo.

Buddha never visited Gandhara, but the Buddhist belief in reincarnation made it easy for sages to borrow from local oral tradition, turning the hero of any local legend into Buddha living some previous life. Important shrines sprouted on the supposed sites of miracles performed by these earlier incarnations, each shrine decorated with scenes from the Jataka stories, as the legends came to be known.

The Tibetan-styled Baltit Fort (left) was occupied by the mir *of Hunza until 1960. A Hunzakut shepherd (right) guides his flock across almost barren scree.*

Bala Hisar mound it is visible across the river; only dedicated archaeologists gain much by going to take a closer look.

Though the Bala Hisar had fallen into permanent decline by the second century BC, it was never entirely abandoned, and people continued to live here right up to the 18th century. It was used as a fort then, which is the meaning of *hisar*.

Charsadda is surrounded by hundreds of hectares of graves, all decorated with black and white stones in geometric patterns. The graveyard here is considered especially holy, like Makli Hill in Sind (see page 72). The road running south from the crossroads at the centre of Charsadda leads to Prang, the site of several high, completely unexcavated mounds — the debris of thousands of years of occupation.

Takht-e-Bahi

The Buddhist monastery at Takht-e-Bahi, 14 kilometres (nine miles) northwest of Mardan on the road to Swat, is the most impressive and complete ruin of its kind in Pakistan. A visit here yields a good idea of what life as a Buddhist monk was like. The top of the hill behind the monastery affords a view of the Peshawar plains on one side and, on the other, the Malakand Pass and the hills of Swat.

To reach Takht-e-Bahi directly from Charsadda, turn left (north) at the crossroads in Charsadda. After exactly two kilometres (1.2 miles), turn right into a single-lane, surfaced road leading through rich irrigated farmland. Keep to the main road and after 22 kilometres (14 miles) come out on the main Mardan-Swat road. Turn left here and proceed one kilometre (half a mile) to Takht-e-Bahi.

To get to the ruins, cross the level crossing in the centre of Takht-e-Bahi and, after 500 metres (0.3 miles) turn right at the sign, 'Archaeological ruins of Takht-e-Bahi 3 km' (two miles). Cross the railway, turn left at the gate of the sugar mill and, a little further on, turn right down a dirt road. Now you will see on top of the hill to the right the ruins of the large, eighth to tenth-century Hindu Shahi Fort. Continue to the end of the track. The ruins of the monastery are straight ahead. It is a steep 500-metre walk up the hill to the site, and another 500 metres to the top of the hill.

The monastery and stupas at Takht-e-Bahi were founded in the first century AD and abandoned in the sixth or seventh century. On the ridge above the monastery to the south, and on the spurs to the east and west, are the ruins of private houses, some of which are three storeys high.

You approach the monastery from the east. On the right, just before the entrance of the main ruin, is a two-storey block of four monks' cells. In each cell are two niches for the monk's lamp and other belongings.

The **court of stupas** is the first you enter at the top of the path. Alcoves or chapels open to the court on three of its sides. Originally, these contained single plaster Buddhas, either sitting or standing, the statues dedicated to the memory of holy men or donated by rich pilgrims. The largest statues must have been ten metres (33 feet) high, and all would have been gilded or painted. Carved friezes in high relief showing scenes from the life of Buddha once ringed the walls of the chapels. Carved on slabs of stone, they were attached to the walls with iron nails.

The remains of 38 votive stupas and some more chapels are scattered haphazardly round the centre of the court. They also were built as offerings by pilgrims and were full of gilded and painted statues and reliefs depicting Buddha and his life. One stupa is unusual in that it is octagonal.

The **monastery court** is north of the court of stupas up some steps. It has monks' cells ranged round three sides, and a second storey once contributed 15 more cells. According to the Chinese pilgrim Xuan Zang, writing in 630 AD, the walls of the cells were plastered and painted different colours and the wooden doorjambs and lintels were decorated with carvings. In each cell are two niches for the monk's lamp and belongings, and a small window.

The water tank stands in the southwestern corner of the court and was probably filled by rainwater draining from the roofs. The kitchen and dining-room are east of the monastery court, with stairs leading up from the kitchen to the second floor. On the outer wall of the kitchen are two projecting buttresses that may have been the latrine.

The **court of the main stupa** is south of the court of stupas up some steps. The single large stupa standing in the centre of the court was once about ten metres (33 feet) high, with its umbrellas projecting higher. The square base was surmounted by a hemispherical dome, and the entire structure would have been decorated with gilded and painted Buddhas and scenes from his life. Like the court of stupas, this court had on three sides roofed alcoves or chapels that once housed statues of Buddha.

The **assembly court**, where the monks met together, is on the northwestern corner of the complex and surrounded by high walls. The two cement water tanks in the centre of the court are modern.

Opposite the entrance to the assembly court, at the southeast corner of the court over the vaulted chambers, is a small chapel. It contains two tiers of ornamental trefoil panels divided by pilasters. This chapel may have housed a small stupa to commemorate an individual who was either especially holy or especially rich.

The ten vaulted chambers beneath this court, and reached through arched doorways, were used either for meditation or storage. Two more arched doorways lead west from these rooms out to a large open court, but what purpose this court served remains a mystery.

In the covered area south of the open court are two small stupas. Their elaborate decoration of red and gold paint was in perfect condition when they were excavated in 1910, but little decoration remains today, despite the protecting shed.

Private houses are scattered up the hill above the monastery and for more than a kilometre (half a mile) along the ridge. Some houses have rooms set around a central court, but most are two-storey structures consisting of two small rooms set one above the other. Each is entered by a low door and lit by one small sloping window. Staircases run up the outside and consist of flat slabs of stone protruding from the wall.

Options from Takht-e-Bahi are to continue north up to Swat (see page 156) or to turn south to Mardan, 14 kilometres (nine miles) away, from where you can continue east along the ancient trade route.

Mardan

For nearly 200 years a major military base, Mardan is the headquarters of the elite Guides Corps, which was organized in 1846 to guide regular units in the field, collect intelligence and keep the peace on the North-West Frontier. British soldiers at the time wore uniforms of brilliant red and blue, making them easy targets for Pathan snipers. The Guides were the first to wear khaki, which is the local word for 'dust'.

The **Cavagnari Arch** in the centre of Mardan is dedicated to those Guides who died in Kabul in 1879. The plaque reads:

The annals of no army and no regiment can show a brighter record of devoted bravery than has been achieved by this small band of Guides. By their deeds they have conferred undying honour not only to the regiment to which they belong, but on the whole British army.

The Guides' cemetery and church are also worth a visit. For an account of the Guides in action, see Charles Miller's *Khyber* or M M Kaye's romantic novel, *Far Pavilions*.

Ashokan Inscriptions at Shahbaz Garhi

Shahbaz Garhi is 13 kilometres (eight miles) east of Mardan on the road to Swabi. It was once an important city at the junction of three major trade routes: the main road from Europe, through Afghanistan

to India via Pushkalavati; the more northerly route through Afghanistan via Bajour, Dir and Swat; and the route from China via the Indus Valley and Swat. From Shahbaz Garhi, the combined routes continued east to cross the Indus at Hund.

The outline of the ancient city is now difficult to trace. Its centre was at the modern road junction, and the three modern roads pass over the sites of its three gates. Two Chinese pilgrims who visited in AD 520 and 630 wrote of a thriving Buddhist centre surrounded by stupas and monasteries.

The Ashokan inscriptions were written in the third century BC for the information and edification of travellers such as these. They are down a dirt track to the right (south) a few hundred metres (yards) before the left (north) turn to Rustam, the Ambela Pass and Swat. The inscriptions are on two rocks on a hill about 300 metres (yards) to the left (east) of the track and 400 metres (yards) from the main road.

They are the most important and complete of Ashoka's proclamations. Written 2,250 years ago, they are also the oldest historically significant writings extant in the subcontinent.

The Mauryan emperor Ashoka (272–231 BC) was one of the greatest monarchs the world has ever known, ruling over almost the whole of the Indian subcontinent from his capital at Pataliputra (now Patna) on the banks of the Ganges River in India. Tolerant of all religions, he may have been a Buddhist himself. He ordered that a series of edicts, announcing state policy and instructing his subjects, be inscribed on rocks and pillars all over his empire.

Ashoka's inscriptions were written in the script best understood by the people of the locality in which they were placed. Thus, the two in Pakistan (here at Shahbaz Garhi and at Mansehra) were in Kharoshthi, the Gandharan script derived from the Aramaic scripts of Iran. The inscriptions at Kandahar in Afghanistan were in Greek and Aramaic, and those in more southerly parts of the subcontinent were in Brahmi.

At Shahbaz Garhi are 12 edicts on the first rock and two on the second. They describe Ashoka's remorse at the terrible destruction and slaughter accompanying his overthrow of Kalinga in eastern India and announce that, in the future, his conquests will be achieved through 'righteousness and *dharma*' and thus infused with love. They go on to promise that wherever he may be — at table or in his ladies' apartments, on horseback or in his pleasure orchards — he is always available to hear petitions from his people. This is his duty.

The duties of his subjects are to honour their parents, relatives and friends, to give alms to the priests and the poor, and to eschew extravagance. The slaughter of animals is forbidden, with pilgrimage suggested as an alternative to hunting trips. Many religious rites are trivial and useless, the edicts warn, and the best ways of gaining merit are showing self-control, respect and generosity. All are commanded to show tolerance to people of other religious sects.

Finally, the edicts order that hospitals be founded for the treatment of both man and beast, and that medicinal herbs be planted to ensure a ready supply. Fruit trees should be planted and wells dug along the roadside for the refreshment of travellers.

A surfaced road leads from Shahbaz Garhi north to Swat via the Ambela Pass. The road east leads to **Swabi**, where it forks left to Tarbela and right to Attock. From Swabi to Islamabad is 119 kilometres (74 miles) via Attock, a drive of an hour and a half, and 137 kilometres (85 miles) via Tarbela, a drive of two hours. A ford before Tarbela could prove difficult for cars during the monsoon.

Hund

Hund is known to history primarily as the place to cross the Indus. Not the least of those to use this spot, Alexander the Great and his army of 50,000 men (35,000 of whom had come all the way from Europe) crossed with their animals over a bridge of boats. It was also the capital of Gandhara from AD 870 to 1001 under the Hindu Shahi kings, only to be utterly laid waste by their nemesis, Mahmud of Ghazni. The main crossing place moved 20 kilometres (12 miles) downstream to Attock in the 16th century. Now, Hund is a place for history enthusiasts only, as there is little to see.

Here, above Attock Gorge, the Indus sprawls lazily across the mountain-edged plain, flowing wide, slow and shallow. In winter, it can be forded on horseback, and even in summer, when it is swollen by melting snows and monsoon rains, it can still be crossed, albeit somewhat precariously, on inflated cow-skin rafts or upturned pots used as floats.

Among the Buddhist, Hindu and Muslim remains at Hund, the most noticeable are the walls of Akbar's fort, which were built in the 16th century and completely surround the modern village. The fort is square, with a gate at the centre of each wall. The road enters the village through the northern gate and exits by the south gate to the river, its cobblestones descending to the crossing place.

The Hindu remains have been badly damaged by the river, but still visible on the cliff at the riverbank is a section of the city wall with two square bastions of diaper masonry.

The Swat Valley

Swat is the most historically interesting valley in Pakistan. It is also one of the most beautiful — certainly much greener and more fertile than the valleys further north, because it lies within the monsoon belt. In Lower Swat, the valley is wide, the fields on either side of the river are full of wheat and lucerne, and the villages are prosperous and surrounded by fruit trees. In Upper Swat, the river tumbles through pine forests hemmed in by snow-capped mountains. For the historian and amateur archaeologist, Swat offers several hundred archaeological sites spanning 5,000 years of history. For the sportsman and trekker, it offers good fishing and hiking.

Getting to Swat

Mingora is served daily except Friday by a 50-minute flight from Islamabad (Rs210) and a twice-weekly, 40-minute flight from Peshawar (Rs170). Regular bus and minibus services run from Peshawar.

Three roads lead to Swat, all passable by ordinary car. The shortest is via Mardan across the Malakand Pass, about 250 kilometres (150 miles) and four and a half hours from Islamabad, and about 120 kilometres (75 miles) and three hours from Peshawar. The most attractive route is via Shahbaz Garhi and the Ambela Pass to Buner, and thence across the Karakar Pass, about five and a half hours from Islamabad (see page 166). From Swat, the traveller can continue north on a dirt road to Chitral, or east on a paved road to the Karakoram Highway and thence to Gilgit and China.

When to Go

Ranging in altitude from 1,000 to 3,000 metres (3,300−9,800 feet), Swat is good to visit in all seasons. Ordinary cars can get half-way up the valley in winter and, from May to November, to the very head of the valley.

History

Stone Age people lived in Swat at least as early as 3000 BC. In 1700 BC, there arrived from Central Asia a wave of Aryans, forerunners of the Hindus and the composers of the Rigveda, the oldest religious text in the world. In one of the 1,028 hymns extant, a chief sings of a victory won on the banks of the River Suvastu, the Swat River.

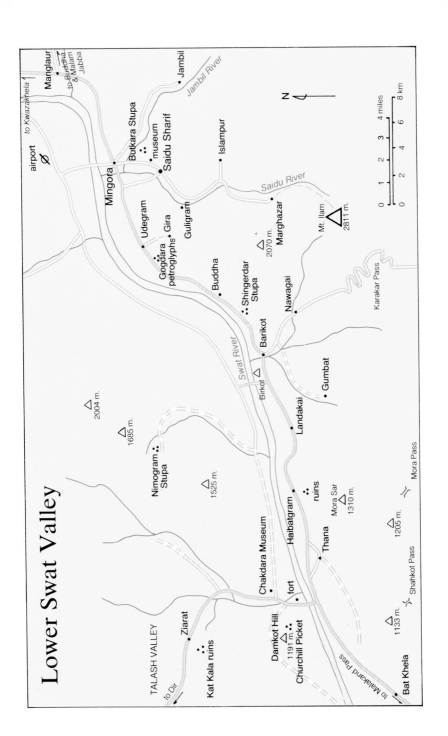

Lower Swat Valley

to Kwazakhela

airport

Manglaur

to Buddha & Malam Jabba

Jambil

Jambil River

Butkara Stupa

museum

Saidu Sharif

Mingora

Islampur

Saidu River

Udegram

Gira

Guligram

Gogdara petroglyphs

Buddha

Shingerdar Stupa

△ 2070 m.

Marghazar

Mt. Ilam △ 2811 m.

Nawagai

Barikot

Karakar Pass

Swat River

Birkot △

Gumbat

Landakai

△ 2004 m.

△ 1685 m.

Nimogram Stupa

△ 1525 m.

Haibatgram

ruins

Mora Sar △ 1310 m.

Mora Pass

Chakdara Museum

Thana

fort

△ 1205 m.

TALASH VALLEY

Ziarat

to Dir

Kat Kala ruins

Damkot Hill △ 1191 m.

Churchill Picket

Shahkot Pass

△ 1133 m.

to Malakand Pass

Bat Khela

N

0 1 2 3 4 miles
0 2 4 6 8 km

In 327 BC, Alexander the Great invaded Swat on his way from Afghanistan to the Indus and fought four battles here. From the second century BC to the ninth century AD, Buddhism flourished in the valley, leaving behind a legacy of beautiful sculpture and more than 500 monasteries. The Hindu Shahi kings built their fortified cities on the tops of many of the hills of Lower Swat from the eighth to the tenth century, and massive stone walls still crown the peaks on every side.

Mahmud of Ghazni took the valley in the 11th century after a fierce battle at Udegram, where his commander Kushal Khan was killed and buried. A mosque dating from the 11th century stands on the hill at Udegram. The Moghuls came to Swat in the 16th century but failed to add it to their dominions. Babur at least gained a wife from Swat, but Akbar only suffered a disastrous defeat in the Karakar Pass.

The Akund of Swat, who rose to power in the 19th century, was a Sufi ascetic with a highly charismatic and warlike personality. He united the Swatis around his capital at Saidu Sharif and has been immortalized in the West by the poem by Edward Lear (1812–88):

Who or why, or which, or what,
Is the Akund of Swat?
Is he tall or short, or dark or fair?
Does he sit on a stool or a sofa or chair, or squat,
The Akund of Swat?
Is he wise or foolish, young or old?
[...And plenty more in that vein]

The Akund's death in 1877 inaugurated 40 years of tribal feuding until the Akund's grandson, Miangul Wadud, aided by the British, was accepted as *badshah*, or king. The British acknowledged Swat as a sovereign state in 1926 and recognized Miangul Wadud as its *wali*, or ruler. Miangul Wadud abdicated in 1949 in favour of his son, Miangul Jehanzeb, who continued to develop the valley by building roads, schools and hospitals and instituting land reform. Not until 1969 was Swat fully absorbed into Pakistan as Swat District.

Suggested Itinerary

Three days and two nights from Islamabad by car, October to April:

Day 1   Drive up via the Malakand Pass, stopping *en route* to visit:
— Takht-e-Bahi, Buddhist ruins and monastery
— Chakdara Museum, collection of first to seventh-century Buddhist sculptures
— Churchill's Picket

— Shingerdar Stupa, third to fourth-century Buddhist ruin
— 11th-century mosque at Udegram and Raja Gira's castle
— Check into hotel at Saidu Sharif or Mingora
— In the evening, drive to Marghazar, 13 kilometres (eight miles) up the Saidu Valley

Day 2   Drive slowly up the valley as far as you can. Visit:
— Swat Museum
— Butkara Buddhist Stupa
— Stop for shopping in Khwazakhela, Madyan and Bahrain

Time allowing, explore more sites in Lower Swat:
— Birkot Hill
— Nimogram Stupa

Day 3   Drive slowly back to Islamabad via the Shangla Pass and Abbottabad. (If the road is blocked by snow, via Ambela Pass.)

May to September:

Day 1   Drive straight to Swat over the Ambela Pass. (It will be too hot to make any stops enroute to Swat.) Spend the night in Miandam.

Day 2   Drive up to Kalam, stopping for shopping in Madyan and Bahrain. Continue beyond Kalam to the end of the road and walk. Spend the night at Kalam.

Day 3   Drive back to Islamabad via the Shangla Pass.

To Saidu Sharif via the Malakand Pass

Go from Islamabad to Mardan via Attock and Swabi, or via Tarbela and Swabi. The quickest but least interesting route is via the Grand Trunk Road to Nowshera.

There is an unmarked bypass round Mardan to the west, but it is interesting to drive through the centre of Mardan to see the Cavagnari Arch (see page 152).

Takht-e-Bahi is 13 kilometres (eight miles) north of Mardan. As the climb to the Buddhist monastery is a steep 500 metres (0.3 miles) up a completely shadeless hill, this site should be visited only in cool weather.

The Malakand Pass begins at Dargai. The road over the pass is good, but is always crowded with a stream of trucks crawling up and careering down.

The viewpoint about a kilometre (half a mile) before the top of the pass overlooks the British-built Swat Canal, by which irrigation water is diverted from the Swat River through a tunnel under the Malakand

Pass to the plains of Mardan. The old Buddhist road winding round the side of the hill about 15 metres (50 feet) below the modern road once led to a monastery below the pass. Unfortunately, the monastery was destroyed during the blasting of the canal tunnel.

Malakand Fort, on the left at the top of the pass, guards the road. Here, 1,000 Sikh infantry under British command held off 10,000 tribal warriors led by the so-called Mad Mullah at the outbreak of the Pathan uprising in 1897, until reinforcements eventually arrived from Mardan.

On the other side of the pass, the road descends through the market town of Bat Khela and continues past the headworks of the Swat Canal to the Swat River. The first bridge across the river is at Chakdara, from which issues the road to Dir and Chitral.

Chakdara was an important centre for thousands of years, because it was here that the trade route from Afghanistan via Bajaur crossed the Swat River. (In 327 BC, Alexander the Great, *en route* to Taxila, crossed here with half of his 50,000-man army.) The area has many archaeological sites, including graveyards in use for 3,500 years and the remains of Buddhist monasteries from the first to the seventh century AD. Eighth to tenth-century Hindu Shahi forts crouch on the hilltops.

Chakdara Bridge, built in 1896 by the British, is guarded by Chakdara Fort, which was built the same year on the foundations of a 16th-century fort built by the Moghul emperor Akbar. The fort is still used by the army. Expect to be asked to show identification papers at the check post at the bridge.

Damkot Hill overlooks the bridge and fort at Chakdara — and the whole valley from Malakand Pass to Barikot. The top of the hill is covered with excavated ruins from different periods, including a Buddhist monastery and Hindu Shahi fort. The newest building is **Churchill's Picket**, a small fort built in 1896. Winston Churchill served here during the Pathan uprising the following year and wrote with youthful exuberance in a dispatch to the *Daily Telegraph* (later included in *My Early Life*) that he had been sent to

> …chastise the truculent assailants. The chastisement was to take the form of marching up the valley…destroying all the crops, breaking the reservoirs of water, blowing up as many castles as time permitted, and shooting anyone who obstructed the process.

If it is not too hot, the 15-minute walk up the path to the top is rewarding, both for the view and the sense of history. Sometimes, though, the army prevents tourists from climbing the hill.

Chakdara Museum is in the village two kilometres (one mile) from Chakdara Bridge along the road to Dir and Chitral, on the right at the junction. Its small but excellent collection of first to seventh-century

AD Buddhist Gandharan sculpture from nearby sites is well arranged and labelled. It is also of considerable importance, as many of the sculptures were found in their original positions in the Buddhist monasteries, allowing them to be chronologically dated. The museum also displays Hindu Shahi and local 19th- and 20th-century artefacts.

Chakdara to Saidu Sharif

Haibatgram is a village on the main Malakand-Saidu road eight kilometres (five miles) from Chakdara Bridge and overshadowed by an enormous Hindu Shahi fort of the eighth to the tenth century. Its walls cascade for more than two kilometres (about a mile and a half) to the village below.

Landakai, 12 kilometres (seven miles) from Chakdara Bridge, is the gateway to Swat. A rocky spur juts down from the hilltop to the river, forming a natural defence for the valley. Hindu Shahi forts crown each of the low ridges that run down from Landakai Spur to the eastern bank of the side stream. All visitors must register here before continuing into Swat District.

Nimogram Buddhist Monastery and Stupa are signposted on the left, seven kilometres (four miles) from Landakai. The Nimogram remains are 21 kilometres (13 miles) away on the other side of the river and up a rough road. Nimogram is unique in that it has three main stupas, one for each of the three principles, or jewels, of Buddhism: Buddha the Teacher, *Dharma* (Truth) and *Sangha* (Order). A number of votive stupas surround the main stupas, and nearby is an unexcavated monastery. None of the Gandharan sculpture found here remains on the site.

Birkot Hill is the site of the ancient town of Bazira, which was sacked by Alexander the Great in 327 BC. It is on the left (north) side of the main road, just past the turning to Nimogram and just before the town of Barikot.

It is an easy walk to the top of Birkot Hill. There are no remains from Alexander's time, but there are the ruins of the eighth to tenth-century Hindu Shahi fort, with one impressive stretch of defensive wall rising to a height of 15 metres (50 feet). This is visible in the distance from the main road beyond Barikot.

The road from the Ambela and Karakar passes joins the main Swat road at Barikot.

Mount Ilam, on the right-hand (south) side of the road, is 2,811 metres (9,222 feet) high, making it the highest hill in Lower Swat. According to legend, it has been sacred since prehistoric times, when it was believed to be the seat of tribal deities and ancestors. At the top

are big, square blocks of natural stone that may have been used as prehistoric altars. The mountain features prominently in the mythology of many religious groups, including the Buddhists, Lamas, Hindus and Muslims. It was probably the Mount Aornos described by the historians of Alexander the Great. (When Alexander defeated the Swatis, they fled to their mountain stronghold, the Rock of Aornos. Alexander pursued them and won a decisive victory on its top.) An annual Hindu pilgrimage up the mountain to the 'throne of Ramachandra' was celebrated until Partition in 1947.

Shingerdar Stupa is on the right (south) side of the road three kilometres (two miles) past Barikot. In the third and fourth centuries AD, the stupa's dome was covered with gold, and its base was plastered and painted and surrounded with Gandharan carvings illustrating the life of Buddha.

A large **Buddha** is carved on the cliff face directly beside the road 1.5 kilometres (one mile) beyond Shingerdar Stupa. This dates from about the sixth century, and its face is very battered.

A flight of cement steps to the left of this image leads up to a natural grotto containing more carvings. These are also very battered, but you can just make out a bearded figure standing on a pedestal supported by lions and flanked by smaller figures. The central figure has a halo round his head and wears a long coat over Cossack trousers tucked into top boots. This Central Asian costume, still worn in China's westernmost city of Kashgar, was the same as that worn by the Kushan rulers, as shown by their coins of the first to the third century AD.

The Gogdara rock engravings are about six kilometres (four miles) past the carved Buddha, about 100 metres (yards) to the right of the road just before the village of Udegram. A sign on the roadside points the way. The rock has recently been seriously defaced by local villagers, who have scratched their names all over it, but you can still see some of the engravings of stick figures driving two-wheeled war chariots (like those driven into Swat by the Aryans around 1700 BC), horses, ibex, leopards and oxen. Dating from about 1000 BC, these carvings are among the earliest petroglyphs found in Pakistan.

Buddhist carvings from the sixth or seventh century AD are higher up on the same rock, with more Buddhist carvings on a rock face on the right about 100 metres (yards) further along the path. These depict Padmapani, the lotus-bearing bodhisattva, seated with his right leg tucked up and flanked by two attendants.

Udegram is one of the most historically interesting villages in Swat. It was the site of the ancient town of Ora, where Alexander the Great fought one of his battles in 327 BC. It was also the capital of the Hindu

Shahi rulers in Swat from the eighth to the tenth century. The massive Hindu ruins of Raja Gira's Castle are scattered up the hillside above the village. The earliest mosque in Swat, built in the 11th century at the time of Mahmud of Ghazni, was excavated in 1985 just below the Hindu Shahi fort.

For those who enjoy walking and exploring, there is plenty to see on the hillside above Udegram. It is worthwhile to go to the top of the hill, which takes about an hour and a half. The best time to go is in winter or, if during the summer, at dawn. It is too hot to climb during the heat of a summer day.

The first excavations, on the left near the modern village, date from the fourth century BC. This was the bazaar area of Ora, and most of the buildings were shops.

The **Shrine of Pir Khushab (or Khushal) Baba** is surrounded by a grove of trees at the foot of the hill. This is the grave of the commander of the army of Mahmud of Ghazni, who subdued Swat in the 11th century and introduced Islam. The commander was killed during the long siege of the fortress of Raja Gira, the last Hindu ruler of Swat. Arrowheads and human bones are scattered all over the hillside below the fortress.

The 11th-century **mosque** is in the centre of the hillside, about half-way between the saint's shrine and the main defensive wall of the fort. It is unlabelled, but ask any small boy for the *purana masjid*, and he will show the way. The south wall of the mosque, protected by the mountain, still stands about seven metres (23 feet) high. The west wall is also in quite good condition, with the arched *mehrab* (prayer niche facing Mecca) in the centre. The bases of the ten pillars that supported the roof over the prayer hall survive, as does the metre-deep (three-foot) ablution pool, which is surrounded by stone seats in the centre of the courtyard.

Massive, eighth to tenth-century AD defensive walls surround **Raja Gira's Castle**, which is entered up a monumental flight of steps eight metres (26 feet) wide. Inside the citadel are the foundations of many rooms separated by corridors. Nothing is labelled.

The walls of the town climb from the citadel for about one kilometre (half a mile) up to the crest of the hill, then follow the top of the sharp ridge separating the Swat and Saidu valleys. The view is magnificent in every direction, taking in Mount Ilam, the lower length of Swat Valley to Chakdara and the snow-covered mountains far to the north at its head. From the top of the hill the wall runs along a precipitous, rocky spur down the eastern side of the ruined town to a spring at the head of the gully. This spring was the town's sole water supply and was heavily defended. The water was brought from the well along a series of channels to holding tanks at the foot of the giant stairway. Italian excavators working the site lined one of these tanks with cement and filled it using the existing system.

To Saidu Sharif via the Ambela and Karakar Passes

This route to Swat is quieter and more scenic than the Malakand Pass. The roads are metalled the entire distance.

From Islamabad, go to Shahbaz Garhi either via Attock and Swabi or via Tarbela and Swabi. From Peshawar, go to Shahbaz Garhi via Charsadda and Mardan, or via Nowshera and Mardan, this last route being the fastest but least interesting. At Shahbaz Garhi, turn north to Rustam, thence east across the Ambela Pass to Buner.

From the **Ambela Pass** you can see down over the Peshawar Valley. This was the scene of the Ambela Campaign in 1863, when British troops spent two foggy winter months trying to subdue 15,000 Mujahideen freedom fighters (or 'Hindustani fanatics', as the British called them) who had been raiding the Peshawar Valley from their hideout at Malka, in Buner. The ruins of several British forts still dot the pass.

The main road climbs up across the 894-metre (2,935-foot) **Buner Pass** and comes down to **China** (pronounced *Cheena*). After four kilometres (2.5 miles) you come to **Daggar**, from where a newly repaired road leads left (west) to Jowar. If you have time, though, an interesting detour is north via Pacha to **Pir Baba**, the Shrine of Syed Ali, reputedly the grandson of the Moghul Emperor Babur.

Pir Baba is one of Pakistan's most popular shrines, to which devotees flock by the thousand, particularly at the death festival of the saint. The path to the shrine is lined on one side with beggars and on the other with pretty boys selling traditional cosmetics — khol for the eyes and perfume. Behind the shrine is a separate mosque for women, and behind this is the *baithak*, a place of meditation for fakirs and Sufi holy men.

The 45-kilometre (28-mile) road from Pir Baba to Barikot passes the sacred Mount Ilam (see page 161) on the right before rising through mature pine forests to the 1,336-metre (4,384-foot) **Karakar Pass**. Here, in 1586, the Moghul Emperor Akbar lost most of his 8,000-man army in a vain attempt to invade Swat. From the top of the pass down to Barikot is a well-engineered road through pine forests.

For a description of the road from Barikot to Saidu Sharif, see page 161.

Saidu Sharif and Mingora

Saidu Sharif and Mingora are twin towns two kilometres (one mile) apart. Saidu Sharif is the administrative capital of Swat Division, while Mingora is the district headquarters and main bazaar area. Both are 990 metres (3,250 feet) above sea level.

Flights operate six times weekly from Islamabad and twice weekly from Peshawar. The Tourist Information Centre is at the Swat Serena Hotel (telephone 2220), where cars and jeeps are for hire.

Mingora has been an important trading centre for at least 2,000 years. Its bazaars are interesting to explore for semi-precious stones, locally woven and embroidered cloth, and tribal jewellery. Saidu Sharif has, in addition to government buildings, the Swat Museum, the Tomb of the Akund of Swat and the archaeological remains of the Butkara Buddhist Stupa.

Places of interest nearby include, in addition to the places described below, Raja Gira's Castle (a distance of six kilometres (four miles); see page 165), Birkot Hill (16 kilometres (ten miles); see page 161), Chakdara (36 kilometres (22 miles); see page 160) and the Karakar Pass, briefly described on page 166. There is a golf course near the airport.

Swat Museum is on the east side of the street half-way between Mingora and Saidu. It has a disappointing collection of Gandharan sculptures taken from some of the Buddhist sites in Swat. Many are, in fact, reproductions. The ethnographic section has some local embroidery, carved wood and tribal jewellery. There are also a few coins and some weapons. Hours are 10 am−4.30 pm October through March; 8 am−noon and 3−6 pm, April through September.

Butkara Stupa, one of the most important Buddhist shrines in Swat, is near the museum. Take the dirt track on the left (north) side of the museum for one kilometre (half a mile). The stupa is 400 metres (a quarter of a mile) from the track across the fields to the left (north).

The stupa, which dates from the second century BC, was possibly built by the Mauryan emperor Ashoka to house some of the ashes of Buddha. In subsequent centuries, it was enlarged five times by encasing the existing structure in a new shell. Italian excavators working in 1955 exposed the successive layers of the stupa, each layer illustrating a stage in the evolution of building techniques.

The stupa was enlarged three times before the birth of Christ. At the beginning of the third century AD, the peaceful rule of the Kushans brought unprecedented prosperity, and Buddhism in Swat approached its zenith. Butkara was a bustling shrine and centre for pilgrimage. The stupa was enlarged again and richly decorated with stone and plaster carvings of the life of Buddha, and the whole was gilded and painted and topped by a stack of stone umbrellas.

Most of the carvings have been removed, but two of green schist (a crystalline rock) dating from the fifth century have been left in place on the great stupa. One is a headless Buddha low down on the east side, and the other is a Buddha standing on a lotus flower between three rows of acolytes on the north side. A few other small fragments of statues still stand around the base of the stupa.

Votive stupas were built around the main stupa by wealthy pilgrims hoping to gain merit. There were 215 of these, all decorated with statues, painted, gilded and topped with stone umbrellas. Only the bases remain. The best-preserved ones are on the north side of the main stupa. You can still see some of the decoration: green schist columns, lions with full curly manes, eagles, stylized lilies, cupids on lotus flowers, and a few traces of red and blue paint. Scattered all around the site and looking like millstones are circular stone umbrellas that have fallen from the various stupas. Some pilgrims preferred to erect columns surmounted by statuary, and the stone lions (some of limestone) crouching on their haunches east of the main stupa probably came from the tops of such columns.

The Jambil and Saidu rivers run on either side of Butkara and have often flooded the site, which is also frequently jolted by earthquakes arising from the nearby fault line between the Indian and Asian geological plates. During times of plenty, the faithful repaired the damage, but in the seventh century devastating floods swept through the area, and the monastery was abandoned for a time. In the following century coarse repairs were made, but by this time the Hindu Shahi kings ruled the area and Buddhism had evolved into its tantric form. Butkara was soon abandoned.

Marghazar is a small village at the top of the Saidu Valley, 1,287 metres (4,220 feet) above sea level and 13 kilometres (eight miles) from Saidu Sharif. Here the Saidu stream cascades down off Mount Ilam. The Marghazar Hotel was once the summer palace of the first Wali of Swat. Beside the stream behind the palace runs the old Hindu pilgrim path up Mount Ilam, a superb all-day hike to the top and back.

Islampur is a village two kilometres (one mile) off the main Saidu-Marghazar road, where visitors can see handloom weaving and buy handwoven shawls and blankets.

Upper Swat Valley

The Swat Valley becomes more beautiful the higher you go. In winter it is blocked by snow above Bahrain, but in summer you can drive up beyond Kalam and from there trek north to either the Chitral Valley or the Gilgit Valley. From Khwazakhela, the road across the Shangla Pass to the Karakoram Highway is open only from May to November.

Minibuses to Kalam leave from the General Bus Station in Mingora. The fare is about Rs10. The buses from the New Road Bus Station are slightly cheaper but are very slow and dirty and are not recommended. Buses to the Karakoram Highway cost about Rs15.

The **Jahanabad Buddha** is three kilometres (two miles) off the main road, along the side road to Malam Jabba. The Buddha is four metres (13 feet) tall and carved on a rock on the other side of the river. It dates from about the seventh century AD and shows a fat-faced Buddha sitting cross-legged, his hands folded on his lap. To reach the carving, cross the river by the next bridge in Jahanabad village and walk back.

The metalled side road continues to the ski resort of **Malam Jabba**, due to open in 1988 with a 50-room hotel, one ski run and, in summer, pony trekking and mini-golf. The scenic drive through steep, terraced hills to Malam Jabba takes about an hour.

Khwazakhela is about 30 kilometres (19 miles) from Mingora on the east bank of the Swat River, where the road across the Shangla Pass to the Karakoram Highway leaves the Swat Valley. It is 69 kilometres (43 miles) from here to Besham on the Indus (a two-hour drive), and 70 kilometres (44 miles) to Kalam at the top of the Swat Valley. Well placed at the junction of two trade routes, Khwazakhela is the largest commercial centre in this part of the valley. The main street is worth exploring for silver tribal jewellery, locally woven and embroidered fabrics, carved wood, semi-precious stones and 'ancient' coins. The manufacture of fake ancient coins is a thriving business in Swat, so very few, if any, of the coins for sale are as old as they appear. Similarly, most of the 'antique' wood-carvings are newly carved and blackened.

Miandam is a small summer resort ten kilometres (six miles) up a steep side valley and 56 kilometres (35 miles) from Saidu Sharif, making it an hour's drive. The metalled road passes small villages stacked up the hillside, the roofs of one row of houses forming the street for the row of houses above. Tiny terraced fields march up the hillside right to the top.

Miandam is a good place for walkers. Paths follow the stream up past houses with bee-hives set into the walls and good-luck charms whitewashed around the doors. In the graveyards are carved wooden grave posts with floral designs, like those used by the Buddhists 1,000 years ago.

Madyan is a tourist resort on the Swat River. At 1,321 metres (4,335 feet) above sea level, it is neither as cool nor as beautiful as Miandam, but it is a larger town and has many hotels in all price ranges and excellent tourist shopping. Antique and modern shawls, traditional embroidery, tribal jewellery, carved wood, and antique or reproduction coins are sold along the main street.

The central mosque at Madyan has carved wooden pillars with elegant scroll capitals, and its mud-plastered west wall is covered with relief designs in floral motifs. Both bespeak the Swatis' love of decoration.

Bahrain is ten kilometres north of Madyan and only slightly higher, at about 1,400 metres (4,500 feet). It is another popular riverside tourist resort, with bazaars worth exploring for their handicrafts. Some of the houses have carved wooden doors, pillars and balconies. These show a remarkable variety of decorative motifs, including floral scrolls and bands of ornamental diaper patterns almost identical to those seen on Buddhist shrines and quite different from the usual Muslim designs.

At **Kalam**, 29 kilometres (18 miles) from Bahrain and about 2,000 metres (6,800 feet) above sea level, the valley opens out, providing room for a small but fertile plateau above the river. On this plateau are

administrative offices, the police station, the PTDC motel and information office, and the Falakseer Hotel. Down by the river are more hotels (some of which are cheaper) and the mosque, which features some excellent wood-carving. Gigantic scrolls form the capitals of the pillars, and some of the beams are ten metres (33 feet) long. Kalam is cool in summer and a good base for hikers.

Beyond Kalam the road divides. Dirt roads follow the Ushu and Utrot rivers, both passable in ordinary cars in summer. The modern Muslim graves in this area are surrounded by intricately carved wooden railings. There are rest houses at **Utrot**, **Gabral**, **Ushu** and **Matiltan**. From Matiltan, the road is jeepable almost to **Mahodand Lake**, the 'Lake of Fishes'. It is safe to camp in the grassy fields by the lake, and the walking and fishing are excellent. A fishing permit is required. Bring your own tackle.

The Chitral Valley

Chitral is an isolated valley about 300 kilometres (190 miles) long in the northwestern corner of Pakistan. It is dominated by Tirich Mir, the highest mountain in the Hindu Kush, which separates Chitral from the narrow Wakhan Corridor in Afghanistan and the Soviet Union beyond.

The tourist season is April to November. At some 1,500 metres (5,000 feet) above sea level, Chitral town is snow-bound in winter, but not too hot in summer.

Getting to Chitral

The easiest way to reach Chitral is by air from Peshawar. There are two flights most days, provided that the weather is clear, which it often is not. Book several days in advance and be prepared for cancellation. The flight takes 50 minutes and costs only Rs195. The view is spectacular.

The drive to Chitral town from Peshawar over the 3,118-metre (10,230-foot) **Lowari Pass** takes between ten and 15 hours. The road is blocked by snow from November to May. Driving from Chitral town to Gilgit over the 3,734-metre (12,250-foot) **Shandur Pass** takes two days — if the jeep road is open. The only motorable route from Upper Swat to Chitral is back via Saidu Sharif, Chakdara, Dir and the Lowari Pass.

All visitors to Chitral must register with the police on arrival. A permit from the Deputy Commissioner is needed to visit the valleys of the Kafir Kalash. If you wish to see the Kalash women dance, you need a second permit from the Deputy Commissioner.

Sights

The main attractions of Chitral town are the bazaar, the fort and the mosque by the river. The summer palace of the ex-ruler of Chitral is on the hilltop above the town.

The **Kafir Kalash people** are the tourist attraction for which Chitral is most famous. This non-Muslim and culturally distinct tribe live in three valleys close to the Afghan border, about an hour's drive from Chitral town. They are the last unconverted survivors of the Kafir ('heathen') tribes that so fascinated the first European visitors to what was then called Kafiristan. Kafir Kalash women are of particular interest, as they are not in *purdah*, but wear instead extraordinary head-dresses decorated with cowrie shells and buttons and, around their necks, countless strings of red beads set off by their black robes. (*Kalash* means black. The other Kafir tribes that used to live in Afghanistan wore red robes and were called Red Kafirs.)

About 3,000 Kafir Kalash live in about 20 villages in the three valleys of **Birir**, **Bumburet** and **Rambur**. They make offerings to several gods, each of which protects a different aspect of life and livelihood: animals, crops, fruits, family and so on. They build their houses of timber and fill the cracks between the logs with mud and pebbles. In summer, the women sit on a wide verandah on the second storey to cook, spin and weave. In winter, they cook inside, the smoke escaping through the central hole in the cantilevered wooden ceiling.

The wooden temples of the Kalash are often elaborately carved, especially around the doors, pillars and ceilings. Some of the holy places are closed to women, both Kalash and foreign. The dead are left in wooden coffins above ground in Kalash graveyards, where the lids often fall off, exposing skeletons to view.

The Kalash love music and dancing and perform different dances for their various festivals, which are celebrated in May, August, November and December.

Garam Chashma (Hot Springs) is a town 45 kilometres (28 miles) from Chitral town along a spectacular drive up the Lutkho River through a deep and narrow gorge. The sulphurous hot springs are believed to cure skin diseases, gout, rheumatism and headaches.

Upper Chitral Valley

The main jeep track up the Chitral Valley follows the Mastuj River for 107 kilometres (66 miles) to **Mastuj** and, from there, jogs south to cross the **Shandur Pass** into the Gilgit Valley. Tourists need a permit from the Deputy Commissioner to make this journey.

The Kaghan Valley

The Kaghan Valley was the old summer route to the Northern Areas before the advent of the all-weather Karakoram Highway. It is over 160 kilometres (100 miles) long and climbs from about 900 metres (3,000 feet) at its mouth to 4,173 metres (13,690 feet) at the **Babusar Pass**. A jeep road over the pass (open July to September) connects with the Karakoram Highway at Chilas. The narrow and beautiful Kaghan Valley is terraced from river to hilltop and clothed in forests of huge Himalayan pines. Just on the edge of the monsoon belt, it is wet enough for cultivation without irrigation.

Balakot, the gateway to the Kaghan Valley, is about a four-hour drive, without stops, from Islamabad. **Naran**, the main tourist centre in the valley, is 82 kilometres (51 miles) from Balakot. At 2,427 metres (7,963 feet) above sea level and furnished with a PTDC motel and several good-value local hotels, this is the best place to stay. Fishing and walking are the main attractions, in addition to scenic side trips to **Shogran** and **Saif-ul-Muluk Lake**.

From Naran to the top of Babusar Pass is 66 kilometres (41 miles), a jeep drive of about five hours. The 37 kilometres (23 miles) from the top of the pass down to Chilas zig-zags across difficult scree.

The Karakoram Highway

The Karakoram Highway, or KKH, is the greatest wonder of modern Pakistan and one of the most spectacular roads in the world. Connecting Pakistan to China, it twists through three great mountain ranges — the Himalayas, Karakorams and Pamirs — following one of the ancient silk routes along the valleys of the Indus, Gilgit and Hunza rivers to the Chinese border at the Khunjerab Pass. It then crosses the high Central Asian plateau before winding down through the Pamirs to Kashgar, at the western edge of the Taklamakan Desert. By this route, Chinese silks, ceramics, lacquer-work, bronze, iron, furs and spices travelled west, while the wool, linen, ivory, gold, silver, precious and semi-precious stones, asbestos and glass of South Asia and the West travelled east.

For much of its 1,284 kilometres (799 miles), the Karakoram Highway is overshadowed by towering, barren mountains, a high-altitude desert enjoying less than 100 millimetres (four inches) of rain a year. In many of the gorges through which it passes, it rides a shelf cut into a sheer cliff face as high as 500 metres (1,600 feet) above the river. The KKH has opened up remote villages where little has changed in hundreds of years, where farmers irrigate tiny terraces to grow small patches of wheat, barley or maize that stand out like emeralds against the grey, stony mountains. The highway is an incredible feat of engineering and an enduring monument to the 810 Pakistanis and 82 Chinese who died forcing it through what is probably the world's most difficult and unstable terrain. (The unofficial death toll is somewhat higher, coming to nearly one life for each kilometre of road.)

The **Karakorams** and the **Himalayas**, the newest mountain ranges in the world, began to form some 55 million years ago when the Indian subcontinent drifted northwards and rammed into the Asian land mass. India is still trundling northwards at the geologically reckless rate of five centimetres (two inches) a year, and the mountains are still growing. The KKH runs through the middle of this collision belt, where there is an earth tremor, on average, every three minutes. *Karakoram* is Turkish for 'crumbling rock', an apt description for the giant, grey, snow-capped slag heaps that tower above the gorges cut between them.

The **Indus River** flows northwest, dividing the Himalayas and the Karakorams, before being knocked south by the Hindu Kush. The KKH hugs the banks of the Indus for 310 kilometres of its climb north, winding around the foot of Nanga Parbat, the ninth highest mountain in the world and the western anchor of the Himalayas. The highway then leaves the Indus for the Gilgit, Hunza and Khunjerab rivers to take on the Karakoram Range, which contains 12 of the 30 highest mountains in the world. By the time the road reaches the 4,733-metre (15,528-foot) Khunjerab Pass, it has earned the name of the highest metalled border crossing in the world.

From Islamabad to Kashgar is a four-day journey (about 30 hours, driving time), provided that there are no rockfalls. A second option is to fly the 603 kilometres (375 miles) to Gilgit, from which the remaining 681 kilometres (423 miles) to Kashgar can be covered in two or three days. The Khunjerab Pass is open to tourists from 1 May to 30 November (weather permitting), though the Chinese authorities usually stop allowing access from their side two or three weeks earlier.

The flight from Islamabad to Gilgit must be one of the most exciting in the world. The PIA pilot of the small Fokker Friendship plane flies by sight up the Kaghan Valley and over the Babusar Pass, then skirts round the shoulder of 8,125-metre (26,660-foot) Nanga Parbat for a peek at the 'sleeping beauty', who is fancied to be lying on her back across the top. The mountain is so massive that the plane takes fully ten minutes to fly past it. The pilot invites passengers into the cockpit to see Pakistan's 82 peaks over 7,000 metres (23,000 feet), which stretch, range after range, as far as the eye can see. The sharp triangle of K-2, the second highest mountain in world, is clearly visible on the horizon. As the flight can operate only in clear weather, it is often cancelled.

Distances

Islamabad — Abbottabad	121 km (75 mi)	2 hours
Abbottabad — Besham	151 km (94 mi)	3.5 hours
Besham — Komila/Dassu	74 km (46 mi)	2 hours
Komila/Dassu — Chilas	129 km (80 mi)	3 hours
Chilas — Gilgit	128 km (79 mi)	3 hours
Gilgit — Aliabad/Karimabad	105 km (65 mi)	2 hours
Aliabad/Karimabad — Passu	56 km (40 mi)	1 hour
Passu — Sost	33 km (21 mi)	40 minutes
Sost — Khunjerab	64 km (40 mi)	2 hours
Khunjerab — Pirali	32 km (20 mi)	40 minutes
Pirali — Tashkurgan	96 km (60 mi)	2 hours
Tashkurgan — Kashgar	295 km (183 mi)	7 hours

Suggested Itineraries

Four days

Day 1   Drive from Islamabad to Chilas, ten hours without stops

Day 2   Chilas to Karimabad, five hours (plus lunch stop in Gilgit)

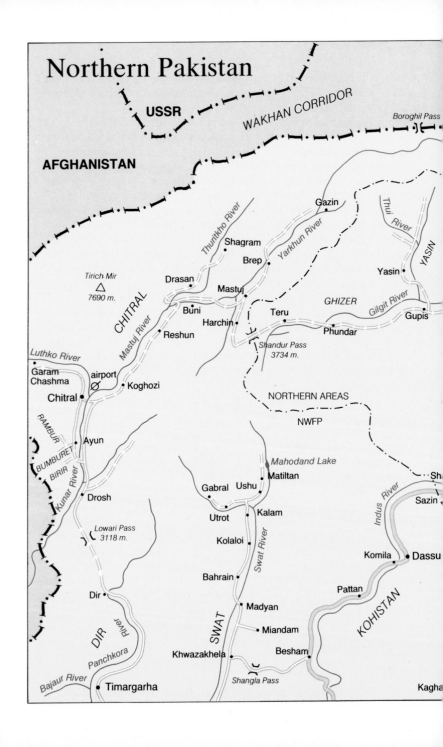

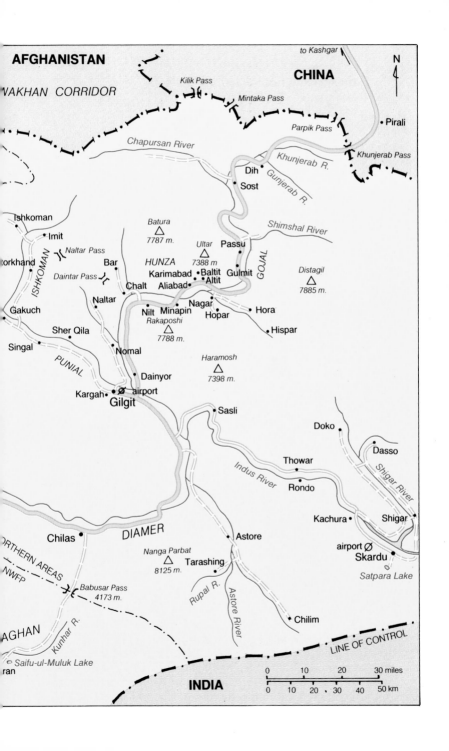

Day 3   Karimabad to Tashkurgan, seven hours
Day 4   Tashkurgan to Kashgar, seven hours

Five Days

Day 1   Drive from Islamabad to Saidu Sharif in Swat via Buner
Day 2   Saidu Sharif to Chilas via the Shangla Pass
Days 3–5   As above

Six Days

Day 1   Drive from Islamabad to Nathia Gali
Day 2   Nathia Gali to Besham
Day 3   Besham to Gilgit
Day 4   Gilgit to Passu or Sost
Days 5 and 6   To Tashkurgan and Kashgar

All of the above itineraries involve long days of driving. The most beautiful area is between Gilgit and Sost. It is a good idea to break your journey at least at Karimabad. Do not be tempted to rush through Northern Pakistan in your haste to reach China. The scenery is more beautiful along the Pakistani portion of the highway, and the tourist facilities are better developed.

When to Go

The pass is closed at least from 1 December to 30 April. Gilgit and Hunza are most beautiful in April, when the fruit trees bloom, and October, when the autumn colours reach their brightest. July is very hot in Gilgit and along the Indus Valley.

Islamabad to Gilgit

The first day's journey up the KKH passes through Hazara, a long, narrow district between the Indus and Jhelum rivers with its capital at Abbottabad.

Abbottabad, at 1,220 metres (4,000 feet) is named after James Abbott, a British administrator who served in Hazara in the 1840s and '50s. It is a military town, full of soldiers exercising, parading, playing polo and practising the bagpipes. The cantonment area, a reminder of the British era, is full of spacious bungalows surrounded by gardens and pine trees, in addition to a church and a club at the top of the hill.

Mansehra, 24 kilometres (15 miles) from Abbottabad, was an important junction of ancient trade routes. The roads from Kashmir (now closed) and Kaghan meet the KKH here, and there is a set of **Ashokan edicts**, like those at Shahbaz Garhi, outlining the Mauryan emperor's state policy and providing his subjects with moral instruction (see page 152).

The Karakoram Highway climbs through pine forest before dropping down to join the Indus River about 100 kilometres (60 miles) from Mansehra. The Chinese-built bridge across the Indus is carved with lions, lanterns, butterflies and flowers.

Besham, a small bazaar on the west bank of the Indus 28 kilometres (17 miles) beyond the bridge, is half-way between Islamabad and Gilgit and a good place for an overnight stop. The road from Swat joins the KKH here, and Besham can be very crowded in summer, so book in advance.

From Besham, the KKH follows the Indus River round the base of Nanga Parbat and through one of the wildest and most inhospitable areas of Pakistan. This is the line at which the Indian geological plate noses under the Asian plate, pushing up the mountains at an annual rate of seven millimetres (a quarter of an inch). The heaving and settling of the mountains makes this the most geologically unstable part of Pakistan. Rockslides frequently block the road, but the army usually has them cleared within a few hours. This area is particularly interesting to geologists, for crushed and tilted northwards between the two large continental plates is a small island plate. The Hunza, Gilgit and Indus rivers cut a section through this plate, from its lower face near Pattan to its upper face at Chalt, near Hunza. The KKH provides convenient access.

Chilas, another recommended overnight stop, is a small bazaar town that was once an important junction on the ancient trade route. The jeep track over the Babusar Pass from the Kaghan Valley joins the KKH here. The town itself is three kilometres (two miles) south of the KKH, out of sight of the road, but the Shangrila Hotel, police post and petrol pump are right on the highway.

Petroglyphs, rock carvings and inscriptions, cover hundreds of rocks along the banks of the Indus at Chilas. They date from the first century BC to modern times and were carved by invaders, traders, pilgrims and locals. The earliest drawings show warriors on horseback and lifelike leopards and antelopes. Later, Buddhist pilgrims and missionaries travelling to and from China carved thousands of Buddhas and stupas as prayers for safe journeys. They wrote inscriptions in various languages, often giving the date, their destinations and the purpose of their journey. The inscriptions and drawings of different periods are all jumbled together, often with inscriptions in four different languages and written centuries apart sharing a single rock.

(previous page) A porter strides at Khaplu in Baltistan.

The two most interesting groups of drawings are down a jeep track before the Shangrila Hotel and down another jeep track leading to the bridge to Thalpan just after the petrol station. The best carvings face the river, and there are some particularly good ones on the north bank, across the Thalpan bridge. From the first century BC, a warrior with a huge knife slaughters a goat that he holds up by the back leg, and a snow leopard attacks an ibex. On some rocks, whole scenes are portrayed: drinking parties, a ruler with captives, a horse festival (or polo game), a ploughman, and a royal couple. Buddhas and stupas are numerous and of various types.

East of Chilas, the Indus and the KKH pass through a desert at about 1,200 metres (4,000 feet). North of the river, barren mountains rise as high as 5,000 metres (16,000 feet) and, south of the river, Nanga Parbat looms a dizzying 3,000 metres (10,000 feet) higher than that, thus towering an awesome 7,000 metres (23,000 feet) above the river. Within the gorge, the scenery looks just like Tibet. High mud cliffs studded with round boulders, glacial remains and flood debris flank the road, while huge sand dunes, untouched by monsoon rains, roll down to the river. Summer is cruelly hot, and biting winds howl through the gorge in winter.

The best views of Nanga Parbat are looking back from about ten kilometres beyond the bridge that crosses the Indus at Raikot. The mountain's massive bulk rises serene and white in the distance. Ahead is a clear view of the triangular points of Rakaposhi and Domani. To the east, on the other side of the river, towers the snow-covered Haramosh Range. Just a bit upriver is the confluence of the Indus and Gilgit rivers. The KKH leaves the Indus and follows the Gilgit — and then the Hunza — towards China.

A metalled road follows the Indus River southeast through narrow gorges to **Skardu**, the capital of Baltistan, sometimes called Little Tibet. Also accessible by air, Skardu is the starting point for some of the world's best mountaineering. Nowhere else is there such a concentration of high mountains, 60 of which are over 7,000 metres (23,000 feet), culminating in the 8,611-metre (28,250-foot) K-2.

Gilgit

Gilgit, the capital of Pakistan's Northern Areas, is a thriving frontier town that has expanded rapidly since the Karakoram Highway opened in 1978. It sits in a wide, irrigated bowl 1,500 metres (5,000 feet) above sea level, surrounded by barren mountains. The Northern Areas enjoy very little rainfall, so all agricultural land must be irrigated by water from the melting snows of higher altitudes. The tiny, terraced fields and fruit groves stack one upon the other up the lower slopes of the mountains around Gilgit, their greenery contrasting vividly with the surrounding desert.

Getting to Gilgit

The flight from Islamabad to Gilgit takes one hour and costs Rs220. The best views are on the right going north and the left going south (see page 177). The plane flies only in clear weather, and cancellations can lead to a backlog. Confirm your return flight on arrival. Buses (NATCO and Masherbrum Tours), minibuses and wagons (Prince Tours) ply the road daily between Rawalpindi and Gilgit, taking 15–20 hours (Rs120).

NATCO (Northern Areas Transport Company) runs public buses and minibuses further up the KKH to Hunza. Other companies run wagons and jeeps all over the region, and Suzuki vans run wherever the road is suitable. Jeep taxis up the Gilgit Valley leave morning and afternoon from the Punial Road bus stop beyond the Aga Khan Polo Ground. They tend to be very crowded. NATCO buses, wagons and jeeps leave from NATCO in the main bazaar. Check for their schedule. The Sargin wagon services up the Hunza Valley leave from near the Nasim Cinema. NATCO, PTDC, Walji/Avis and Mountain Movers have private jeeps for hire.

History

Gilgit has been inhabited for thousands of years. The various waves of invaders that passed through lower Pakistan also reached Gilgit, bringing their customs and religions with them. The animism of the early inhabitants gave way to fire worship brought in from Iran, which was replaced in turn by Hinduism following the Aryan invasion. From the first century BC, Gilgit, like Kashgar, was an important staging post on the Silk Route from China, and the Chinese wielded considerable influence in the area.

From the third to the 11th century AD, Gilgit was Buddhist and, with Upper Chitral, was called Little Bolor. (Baltistan was known as Great Bolor.) Early in the eighth century, three great powers — China, Arabia and Tibet — jostled for control here. A Chinese force of 10,000 troops sent to occupy Gilgit and Baltistan was ousted by Tibetans, as was an Arab force in Upper Chitral that had invaded via the Baroghil Pass. In 725, the kingdoms of Great and Little Bolor merged into one under Tibetan suzerainty. Kashmir was an up-and-coming power about this time, and the Tibetans enlisted the Kashmiris in an alliance to keep the Arabs out.

By the 11th century, the Gilgit area had developed into the powerful and independent kingdom of Dardistan and was equal in strength to Kashmir. Sometime after the 11th century, the whole area was converted to Islam. Today, the people of the Northern Areas are divided fairly equally into three sects of Islam: Sunni, the majority in the whole of Pakistan; Shia, the majority in Iran; and Ismaili, the followers of the Aga Khan. The Sunni sect came via Swat, the Shia via Kashmir and the Ismaili via Afghanistan.

The valleys are so isolated that, when the strong central power declined, each valley became a small kingdom, each with its own language and customs. The better situated of these grew rich by taxing the traffic to and from China, and Marco Polo remarked after passing through the area in the 13th century that it was 'noisy with kingdoms'.

In 1846, the Northern Areas were placed under the nominal control of the maharajah of Kashmir, but repeated military campaigns in the 1850s and '60s failed to bring the kingdoms to heel. The British became interested in the region because of its strategic importance near Russia and China and, in 1877, set up the Gilgit Agency, the most isolated outpost of the British Empire, to guard against a possible Russian thrust through the mountains to the Vale of Kashmir. This was the world of Kipling's *Kim* and the 'Great Game' (see page 188).

At Partition in 1947, the Northern Areas were designated part of Hindu-ruled Kashmir. The overwhelmingly Muslim population objected and staged a successful coup against the Kashmiri governor. Between 1972 and 1974 the kingdoms were dismantled, and the whole area was incorporated into Pakistan. The Northern Areas are now divided into three administrative districts: Diamer (Chilas), Baltistan (Skardu) and Gilgit, the last of which includes Hunza.

Sights

Gilgit is the only market town for hundreds of kilometres in every direction and the meeting place for traders from Central Asia, the Punjab and Sind. Mountain men from the remotest valleys walk for days to bring their goats to market. Except on Fridays, the bazaars are always bustling and photogenic. The single-storey, box-like shops sell an extraordinary range of goods, from paraffin lamps and camp stoves to fragile porcelain and lustrous silks from China, from powdered milk and iodized salt to tough climbing boots and ice axes. Bakeries and bookshops do brisk business, as do the markets selling vegetables, fruit, meat and spices.

The **polo tournaments** in June, August and November are engaging and exciting. Polo originated in the Northern Areas, and the version still played here is much less staid than the international game. The field is unusually long and narrow, and the ponies are small and vigorous. Six players make a team (instead of four), and the same ponies are used throughout the match. If a player manages to catch the ball, he can charge through the goal posts to score. The spectators become wildly involved, shouting and jeering in a solid mass. But drowning out all else are the excruciatingly loud *surnai* (clarinets) and the *damal* and *dadang* (drums) of the band, a carry-over from the days when kings directed their troops in battle by signalling with different tunes. The band now relays musical messages from the coach. In addition, each player has his own signature tune. These, as well as the commands, are readily recognized by the crowd.

Trips from Gilgit

A visit to the **Kargah Buddha** is the most popular outing from Gilgit. The Buddha is carved half-way up a cliff-face at Kargah Nullah, ten kilometres (six miles) west of Gilgit on the road to Punial. You can drive to the Buddha (about a 20-minute ride), then walk back along the irrigation channel cut along the hillside, an easy two-hour stroll through fields, groves and villages featuring magnificent views down

The Great Game

by Peter Fredenburg

The second half of the 19th century saw intense rivalry between Russia and British India for domination of the high ground of Central Asia, an unmapped sprawl of mountains from Afghanistan in the west to Tibet in the east. While the Russians probed for a route through this no man's land to the markets and warm-water ports of the subcontinent, the British sought to remove the threat of a Russian invasion by establishing hegemony over a string of buffer states in the mountains. In this contest, information was everything.

The blanks on the maps that so perplexed and distressed military strategists energized explorers, who risked (and often lost) life and limb gathering the information needed to fill them in. The 'pundits', native graduates of the spy school run at Dehra Dun by Captain Thomas Montgomerie, posed as holy men to penetrate and map Tibet, where no European could go. Afghanistan and Chinese Turkestan — and the tangled knot of mountains in between — were explored by British and Russian military men, either active or 'retired', some travelling with official status, others without, maintaining for their government (to use the modern phrase) 'plausible deniability'. The world they uncovered was as complex ethnologically as it was topographically, to the delight of anthropologists and linguists but the exasperation of the soldiers and civil servants whose job it was to bring the myriad mountain kingdoms — isolated, backward and fractious — under imperial sway.

Kipling fictionalized the Game in *Kim* and *The Man Who Would be King*, but the real world of such players as Nikolai Prejevalsky and Francis Younghusband was hardly less entertaining to the armchair adventurers who immersed themselves in the geography and intrigues of the Karakorams, the Pamirs and the Hindu Kush, convinced that the fate of empires hinged on events in narrow clefts with names like Ladakh, Baltistan, Hunza, Chitral and Dir.

The British had mapped most of India's northern frontier by 1893. They completed their *cordon sanitaire* two years later by affixing the Wakhan Corridor to Afghanistan, thus stretching the reluctant amir's domains to the Chinese frontier. (This arrangement held until 1981, when the Marxist Kabul regime formally ceded Wakhan to the Soviet Union.) By 1913 it was clear that there was no pass over which Russia could invade India, but the Bolshevik Revolution four years later — and Lenin's plan to take India through revolutionary subversion rather than invasion — rendered the question academic.

Though the Great Game proved in the end to be a comedy of hysteria and anticlimax, the journals published by the explorers of Central Asia remain an exciting record of exhilaration and drive, of deprivation and despair, of heroics and death. Interest stimulated by tourism and the popular histories of Peter Hopkirk and John Keay has recently brought back into print many of these books.

over Gilgit and the valley. The channel ends near Serena Lodge, from where you can catch a Suzuki back to Gilgit for Rs2.

The three-metre (ten-foot) Buddha was carved in the seventh century. A monastery and three stupas about 400 metres (a quarter of a mile) upstream from the Buddha were excavated in 1931, yielding the Gilgit Manuscripts. Written in Sanscrit, the manuscripts contain Buddhist texts and the names and dates of some of the rulers of the area and the more illustrious pilgrims. The manuscripts are now divided among the British Museum, Rome, Delhi and Karachi.

Jutial Nullah is a valley starting behind Serena Lodge. Follow the irrigation channel behind the lodge to the cleft in the cliff-face, then take the goat path into the gorge, keeping to the right of the stream. Like most valleys in the Northern Areas, Jutial is very narrow at its mouth and considerably wider further up. A six-kilometre (four-mile) walk along the stream, through a steep-sided gorge, takes you in one and a half hours to pine forests and pastureland.

Naltar is the loveliest full-day outing from Gilgit. About a two-hour drive away, it is an area of alpine meadows and pine forests 3,000 metres (10,000 feet) above sea level and surrounded by snow-capped mountains. The road up from Nomal climbs steeply through a rocky gorge to emerge on the fertile, high-altitude pastures. Those who wish to stay can choose among the Public Works Department rest house, the very basic local hotel, or camping. Naltar is the perfect base for gentle walks through the forest or up to Naltar Lake, where the fishing is excellent. The village is also the starting point for more energetic treks across the 4,000-metre (13,000-foot) **Naltar Pass** to the Ishkoman Valley, or across the 4,800-metre (15,700-foot) **Daintar Pass** to Chalt. The two ski-lifts at Naltar are reserved for army use.

The Road to the Shandur Pass

The jeep road to Chitral across the Shandur Pass follows the Gilgit River east for 240 kilometres (150 miles), a tortuous 12-hour journey not recommended for the faint-hearted. The dirt track — barely wide enough for a jeep — is cut along the cliff-face on the south bank of the river. Passing through the former kingdoms of **Punial** and **Gupis**, with **Ishkoman** and **Yasin** up side valleys to the north, the road connects Gilgit town with all the tiny village oases of the upper Gilgit Valley, which is also known as **Ghizer**.

In August, a polo match between Gilgit and Chitral is played in the Shandur Pass. At that time, there are plenty of public jeeps going up to the pass from both sides. During the rest of the year, however, public transport runs only as far as Teru, 225 kilometres (140 miles) from Gilgit and, from Chitral, as far as Mastuj. Transport across the pass is hard to find.

Phundar, nine hours from Gilgit, is the recommended overnight stop *en route* to Chitral. The good PWD rest house sits on a ridge overlooking on one side the Gilgit River, as it meanders along its flat, stony bed, and on the other a steep slope into the deep blue of Phundar Lake. If not pressed for time, plan to spend two or three nights here. The trout fishing is excellent both in Phundar Lake and a little up a side valley in Handrap Lake.

The **Shandur Pass** is 3,734 metres (12,250 feet) above sea level. The top is flat, open summer pastureland with two small lakes. The pass is blocked by snow from November to May.

From Gilgit to the Khunjerab Pass

The Karakoram Highway from Gilgit over the 258 kilometres (160 miles) to the Khunjerab Pass on the Chinese border follows the Hunza and Khunjerab rivers through barren gorges, past terraced oases and round the bases of the mountains Rakaposhi, Distaghil and Ultar, all three of which are over 7,300 metres (24,000 feet) high. It is an unforgettable six-hour drive, along which magnificent views emerge around every corner and the snouts of two glaciers press right down to the road.

Those planning to cross into China need a valid visa, which is obtainable at the embassy in Islamabad. China-bound travellers must clear the Pakistani border post at Sost by 11 am, while arrivals from China are processed until 4 pm. No private vehicles are allowed into China, but they can be taken as far as the border for sightseeing. The pass is closed in winter (see page 9).

Gilgit to Hunza

Two roads connect Gilgit with the KKH. If you have a small jeep, the shorter and more fun route is across the longest suspension bridge in Asia, which crosses the Hunza River near its confluence with the Gilgit River. This road joins the KKH at Dainyor. The main road from Gilgit joins the KKH ten kilometres east of Gilgit on the south bank of the Gilgit River.

The KKH follows the east bank of the Hunza River, skirting half-way around Mount Rakaposhi and passing through a series of bleak gorges with sheer walls running up to towering mountains and down to the river rushing below. Wherever there is a patch of more or less flat land between the gorges, tiny settlements with terraced fields cling to the bases of the barren mountains.

The old jeep track that was once the only southern access to Hunza runs along the opposite side of the river. The first settlement of any consequence on the west side of the river is **Nomal**, 33 kilometres (21 miles) from Gilgit and from where the jeep track leads up to Naltar. (There is no bridge here; access is from Gilgit only.) A memorial to those who died building the KKH stands on the highway opposite Nomal.

Beyond the first long gorge is the large settlement of **Chalt**, also on the opposite side of the river, but connected to the KKH by a bridge. This is where the island plate ends and the Asian land mass begins (see page 181). A sign on the cliff reads, 'Here two continents collide.'

Chalt — with its near neighbour, **Chaprot**, and **Nilt**, nine kilometres (six miles) further on — was the scene of a rather smaller but better-documented collision in 1891 between British forces and the warriors of Hunza and Nagar. E F Knight, accompanying the British as a correspondent for the *Times*, described the action (for which three Victoria Crosses were awarded) as 'one of the most brilliant little campaigns in military history' and later wrote a stirring account of the battle in his book, *Where Three Empires Meet*.

The British needed three weeks to defeat the locals. They then crossed the Hunza River and occupied the palace of the *mir* (king) of Hunza in Baltit. The *mir* fled to his relations in Kashgar, and all resistance came to an end. The palace was ransacked in the search for 'the treasures of many a pillaged caravan and the results of many a raid', but little was found except some beautiful books and a secret chamber containing gunpowder and garnet bullets.

The KKH turns east at Chalt and hugs the Hunza River round the north side of **Rakaposhi**, at 7,788 metres (25,550 feet), the 27th-highest mountain in the world. As you drive along, you catch intermittent glimpses of glaciers, precipices and gleaming white peaks and ridges surrounded by wide expanses of smooth snow. Two of the best views of Rakaposhi are two kilometres (one mile) past the petrol pump at the turning to Chalt, where you come round a corner to find the great mass of Rakaposhi staring you down, and nine kilometres (six miles) further on, where a sign in English says, 'Visitors please Rakaposhi on your right.'

Beyond Chalt, the ex-kingdoms of Hunza and Nagar begin — Hunza on the north side of the Hunza River, and Nagar on the south. Once one ancient kingdom, Nagar and Hunza were divided between warring brothers in the 15th century and have remained traditional enemies ever since. The conflict is exacerbated by religion, as the Hunzakuts are Ismailis, followers of the Aga Khan, and the people of Nagar are Shias, admirers of the Ayatollah Khomeini of Iran. The slopes of Hunza face south to the warming sun, while Nagar slopes north, often shivering in the shadow of Rakaposhi. Consequently (it is said), the Hunzakuts have a warm, open nature, while their neighbours across the river are known for their dour temperament.

The KKH runs through Nagar territory for about 20 kilometres (12 miles) before crossing over to Hunza at Nazirabad on another of the elegant Chinese bridges guarded by two rows of ornamental lions. About ten kilometres (six miles) from the bridge, the road turns a corner and the Hunza landscape opens up before you, a dramatic contrast to the grim desolation of the earlier gorges.

Hunza

Called by Eric Shipton, 'the ultimate manifestation of mountain grandeur', Hunza, at 2,400 metres (8,000 feet), is indeed a fairytale land, 'rich, fecund and of an ethereal beauty'. The fields ripple in tiny terraces down the mountainside, as neatly arranged as fish scales, each supported by a high, mortarless stone wall. Everywhere, slender poplar trees cut strong vertical lines perpendicular to the horizontal terraces or stand out sharply against the glacier-scarred rock. The colours change with the seasons, the emerald green of spring deepening in summer and giving way to the golden yellow and orange of autumn. Above all, guarding the valley on all sides, stand Rakaposhi, Ultar and Distaghil.

The scene vanishes again as the road heads up the Hasanabad gorge to find a place to cross. Visible to the left (north) from the Hasanabad Bridge is the terminal moraine of Hasanabad Glacier, which ends a little way above the road and from which issues a stream. **Aliabad** straddles the KKH two kilometres (one mile) further on, while **Karimabad**, the capital, sits on the mountainside about one kilometre (half a mile) above Aliabad, accessible by two jeep roads. With its panoramic views and many hotels, Karimabad is the better place to stay. Walkers are happy here for days on end; non-walkers feel they have seen it all in 24 hours.

History

The 30,000 inhabitants of Hunza have been ruled by the same family since the 11th century. Legend has it that the Hunzakuts are descended from five wandering soldiers from the army of Alexander the Great. The fair skins and blue or green eyes of many of the people may lend credence to the legend, but little else does. The people of central Hunza speak Burushaski, an aboriginal language apparently unrelated to any other. In Gojal (Upper Hunza) they speak Wakhi, which is similar to the speech of Khotan in the Xinjiang region of China.

Like Gilgit, Hunza was an important staging post on the Silk Route, as caravans traversing the Kilik, Mintaka, Parpik and Khunjerab passes all came through here. Hunza lived off the fruits of raiding these caravans and its neighbours — and the resulting slave trade. Its isolation ensured its independence until the British conquest in 1891, and it did not become part of Pakistan until 1974.

Hunza functions co-operatively rather than competitively, and there is remarkably little disparity of wealth. Each family grows enough wheat, maize, apricots and walnuts for its own use. However, Hunza's traditional self-sufficiency in virtually all items of daily life, including clothing and utensils, is now a thing of the past, as the KKH has made it easy to bring in goods from China and the south.

Almost everyone in Hunza is Ismaili, members of Islam's most progressive sect. The women wear bright clothes: a long shirt over baggy trousers and an embroidered pill-box hat, over which they drape a light shawl. They do not cover their faces, but are embarrassed when foreigners attempt to photograph them.

The modern, green-roofed *jamat khanas* (community centres) that dominate every village are the Ismaili places of worship. (They are not open to the public.) They fly the green and red flag of the Aga Khan, and notices in every village announce the development work he has undertaken, reflecting his deep interest in the area. The Hunzakuts converted to the Ismaili sect early in the 19th century when their *mir* visited Aga Khan I in Afghanistan and became his follower.

Hunza was probably John Hilton's model for Shangri-La in his novel, *Lost Horizon* — a place where people do not age. The myth of the longevity of the Hunzakuts was 'confirmed' by an article in *National Geographic*, which said the people were the world's longest living, thanks to a supposed absence of social stress and to a diet high in apricots and low in animal fat. Though old people in good health are evident in Hunza, few, if any, live to the fabled age of 120, and many are not as old as they look. Life is hard in Hunza, as it is elsewhere in the Northern Areas. It is particularly hard in spring, when food stocks run low. Infant mortality is high, and only the strong survive.

This much is true. Fruits, especially apricots, have long been the staple diet. Nothing is wasted: the apricot stone is used for fuel; the kernel is ground into flour, eaten as a nut (similar to an almond) or pounded for its oil, the pulp being used for fodder.

Sights

Baltit Fort, once the palace of the *mir* of Hunza, is perched on a hilltop at the entrance to Ultar Gorge, from where it overlooks the entire valley. It is about 400 years old and reflects Tibetan influence. The local people say that a princess of Baltistan ('Little Tibet') married a reigning *mir* and brought as part of her dowry some Balti masons, carpenters and craftsmen to build Baltit. It was inhabited until 1960, when the *mir* built a new granite house in Karimabad, below the fort.

Baltit is a curious, rambling old place with 53 rooms scattered on three levels. The whole is sturdily built of stones reinforced with timber beams and plastered over with sun-dried mud. You approach the main door up a zig-zag ramp and enter the ground floor into a dark 'hall' with guard rooms off it. On the same floor are guest rooms, prisons, store rooms, kitchens and the queen mother's apartments. A rough wooden staircase with banisters of poplar poles leads up through a square hole to the floor above.

You emerge into a central courtyard, off which are the main reception rooms, where the *mir* held court. There is a throne room, summer and winter living quarters, bedrooms, baths, store-rooms, guards' quarters and an arms depot. There is even a royal balcony, with a view over the kingdom. Behind the balcony is a room containing photographs of the *mirs* and important visitors. In the 'museum room' are coats of mail, weapons and the drums that sounded the alarm when the enemy attacked, warning the villagers to run into the fort for shelter. This was a feudalistic society: in return for his taxes, the *mir* provided protection in time of danger and distributed grain from his store-rooms in times of need.

Another wooden ladder leads to the roof for a view straight across the valley to Rakaposhi. Nestled below are the adjoining villages of Baltit and Karimabad. The polo ground in Karimabad is now used as the school playground. The *mir*'s new palace is visible one kilometre (half a mile) away to the south, and his family graveyard lies beyond. To the east, beyond the fields, village and fort of Altit, the Hunza Valley leads down from China. To the north is a sheer drop into Ultar Ravine, which leads up to Ultar Glacier.

For a spectacular view of the back of Baltit Fort, you can walk out along the irrigation channel that comes from **Ultar Glacier**. It is a steep, three-hour climb up the side of the glacier to the summer pastures and shepherds' hut on the slopes of Ultar Mountain. Follow the irrigation channel into the gorge, then keep to the left as you climb. (The 7,388-metre (24,240-foot) Ultar Mountain remains temptingly unconquered.)

Altit Fort, a two-kilometre (one-mile) jeep ride from Karimabad, is perched on a rocky cliff with a sheer 300-metre (1,000-foot) plunge to the Hunza River. It is even more impressive than Baltit and is probably 100 years older. Like Baltit, it comprises a maze of small rooms on

three levels. A curved passage from the door to the stairs leads past a store-room with a sinister past. Ostensibly where wine was made, it also served as one of the entrances to the rabbit warren of store-rooms and dungeons beneath the fort. The trapdoor in the floor (now blocked) leads to the cells below. The prisoners were kept in total darkness, and food was thrown down to them from time to time. It was also in this room that, three generations ago, the *mir* murdered his two brothers in a struggle for the throne. The wooden pillar beside the trapdoor has some evil-looking notches carved into it, but they represent only the tally of grain collected as revenue.

On the next floor are the royal apartments: the bedroom is to the west, the throne room to the east. Each has cantilevered ceilings, the beams of which are decorated with good-luck symbols. Beside the fireplace in the throne room is a post about one metre (three feet) high on which the lamp stood. Cupboards stand in two corners, and a door leads out to the lavatory and bath. The kitchen is between the bedroom and the throne room.

Stairs lead up to an open courtyard on the roof, with its dizzying view over the battlements to the river. The roof holds both 16th and 20th-century buildings. Dominating all is the watch tower, with carved windows and doors and dated Anno Hijrae 909 (AD 1503). To the right of the tower is a store for arms and ammunition, also with an old, carved door. To the left is a tiny, carved mosque. The passage beside the mosque leads to the 20th-century apartments of the rajah, all strung along a carved verandah with a view up to Baltit Fort and Ultar Glacier. Close under the walls of the fort is the village of Altit, where women work on the roofs of the houses drying fruit and vegetables for the winter.

The **Pakistan Mineral Development Corporation** project in Aliabad is devoted to developing Hunza's mineral wealth. Precious and semi-precious stones are sold here. Some two kilometres (one mile) further on, a path leads off to the left toward some ruby mines.

Ganesh is the village enclosed in the S-bend of the KKH as it snakes down to cross the Hunza River on Ganesh Bridge, six kilometres (four miles) beyond Aliabad. Ganesh is guarded by an old watch tower and fort, with a carved mosque standing at its side. The pool in front of the tower is where all the local boys once learned to swim. The test of swimming ability — and bravery — was to swim the Hunza River. Hunza's defence depended on initiations into manhood such as this.

The **Sacred Rock of Ganesh** is immediately beside the KKH, between the road and the river a few hundred metres (yards) east of Ganesh Bridge. The rock is covered with drawings and inscriptions in five different scripts: Kharoshthi, Brahmi, Gupta, Sogdian and Tibetan. There is a portrait of Gondophares, the Kushan king of Gandhara in the first century AD, labelled with his name and the date. Another inscription reads, 'Chandra sri Vikramaditya conquers', with a date corresponding to AD 419. Chandra sri Vikramaditya was Chandra Gupta II, the greatest of the Gupta emperors, who ruled over most of India in the early fifth century AD. Other names and dates appear in the many inscriptions.

Most of the drawings are of hunting scenes, with ibex figuring in almost every one: ibex being surrounded and shot at by horsemen, and men dancing round ibex. In remoter parts of Hunza, the people still perform ritual ibex dances at festival times. The local *bitan* (shaman) dons an ibex head-dress and falls into a trance, from the depths of which he extracts knowledge of the future.

Nagar is entered by the jeep road that leaves the KKH just beyond the Sacred Rock of Ganesh. The first six kilometres (four miles) of this road are dry and barren, then you cross the Hispar River and climb up into the fertile villages of Nagar. Many kilometres of irrigation channels provide pleasant walks through fields and villages. Beyond Nagar village, the jeep road divides — right for Hopar, and left for Hora. At **Hopar** is a small tent hotel on a ridge, from which is a magnificent view back down the valley on one side and down on to **Hopar Glacier** (also known as Bualtar Glacier) on the other. This is the fastest-moving glacier in the Northern Areas, racing forward at a rate of ten centimetres (four inches) a day. You can cross Hopar Glacier to Barpu Glacier for a spectacular but easy trek up to summer pastures.

The KKH beyond Karimabad

The KKH is at its most spectacular between Ganesh and Gulmit. The road rides high on the eastern side of the river, twisting and turning round the barren foot of the Hispar Range, which boasts six peaks over 7,000 metres (23,000 feet). On the opposite bank, villages cling impossibly to the side of the 7,388-metre (24,240-foot) Ultar Mountain. Between the villages, grey scree slithers down to the river, looking in the distance like piles of fine cigarette ash. Above, the jagged teeth along the ridge hide the highest snow-covered peaks from view.

The KKH crosses back to the west bank at **Shishkot Bridge**, from which the view upstream of the serrated ridge of mountains above the river is one of the most photogenic prospects of the whole drive. From here to Tashkurgan in China, the people speak Wakhi.

Gulmit, eight kilometres (five miles) past the bridge, is a fertile plateau 2,500 metres (8,200 feet) high, with irrigated fields on either side of the road. This is a good place to spend a night or two, marking the half-way point between Gilgit and the Khunjerab Pass. The small museum here belongs to the ex-ruler, Rajah Bahadur Khan, and is full of interesting ethnic artefacts.

The rock and gravel-covered **Ghulkin Glacier** comes right down to the road about one kilometre (half a mile) past Gulmit. The road crosses the snout of the glacier at the very edge of the river, then climbs up on to the lateral moraine — a great, grey slag heap. About five kilometres (three miles) further on, you round a corner to find **Passu Glacier** straight ahead. It is shining white and deeply crevassed — exactly as you would expect a glacier to look. Above the glacier to the left is the jagged line of the Passu and Batura peaks, seven of which are over 7,500 metres (25,000 feet). On the opposite side of the river, the valley is hemmed in by a half-circle of saw-toothed summits, down the flanks of which slide grey alluvial fans.

Passu is a village of farmers and mountain guides 15 kilometres (nine miles) beyond Gulmit. This is the setting-off point for climbing expeditions up the Batura, Passu, Kuk and Lupgar groups of peaks and for trekking trips up the Shimshal Valley and Batura Glacier. The Passu Inn, right beside the road, is the meeting place for mountaineers and guides.

The KKH passes through four more villages before reaching the immigration and customs post at **Sost**, 33 kilometres (21 miles) from Passu. Outgoing traffic must pass through Sost before 11 am. It is a four- or five-hour drive from here to Tashkurgan, and you must allow time for clearing Chinese customs and immigration at Pirali. The time difference between China and Pakistan is three hours, so it will be around 7 or 8 pm, Chinese time, before you arrive in Tashkurgan. Incoming traffic is processed until 4 pm, Pakistani time.

NATCO runs daily buses from Sost to Pirali, but a lack of passengers sometimes results in cancellation. The 96-kilometre (60-mile) journey costs Rs150.

For the first 30 kilometres (19 miles) from Sost, the valley is narrow and barren, the cliff-face shattered into huge cubes and slabs that peel off and tumble down to the road, where they lie like forgotten building blocks belonging to giant children. The road leaves the Hunza for the Khunjerab River, and there is more of the same, with alluvial fans flowing down every gully, frequently blocking the way.

Khunjerab National Park begins 30 kilometres (19 miles) from Sost. The hills move back from the road, the valley opens out and the Khunjerab River dwindles to a tiny mountain stream with the odd tuft of grass, willow or birch along its banks.

The check post at **Dih** consists of six lonely stone houses. The last 30 kilometres (19 miles) to the top of the pass are easier driving, as there is less mountain above and the slopes are gentler. The road follows the banks of the stream before winding up round 12 wide, well-engineered hairpin bends to the top.

The **Khunjerab Pass**, at 4,733 metres (15,528 feet), is the highest metalled border crossing in the world. A red sign announces 'China drive right', and a rival green sign says 'Pakistan drive left'. A monument declares that the highway was opened in 1982 and indulges in a bit of hyperbole by saying that the pass is 16,000 feet. The Khunjerab is on a continental watershed. All water on the Pakistani side flows down to the Indian Ocean, while that on the Chinese side is swallowed by the Taklamakan Desert, whose name means, 'if you go in, you don't come out'.

It is 32 kilometres (20 miles) from the top of the pass to the Chinese border post at **Pirali**. The scenery is remarkably different on the two sides of the pass. The Pakistani side is a vertical world of desert gorges devoid of any sign of human life for the last 30 kilometres (19 miles), except for the road itself. The Chinese side is wide open and grassy, a high-altitude plateau with grazing herds of yaks, sheep and goats tended by Tajik herders. Children and dogs romp among round felt tents called *yurts*. The Tajiks are a smiling and friendly lot, and the women are as happy to be photographed as the men. Even the camels are altogether different animals. Pakistani camels are tall, short-haired, one-humped beasts, while their Chinese cousins are squat, two-humped Bactrians that seem to wear hairy, knee-length shorts.

Hotels, Restaurants, Shopping

Karachi

Hotels

International standard and Expensive: Rs900−6,000

International-standard hotels are often fully booked, so it is wise to make advance reservations.

Sheraton, Club Road. Tel 521021. The best. (Rs1,100−6,000)

Holiday Inn, Abdullah Haroon Road. Tel 522011, 520111. Its popular all-night coffee shop is a fashionable meeting place. (Rs1,100−5,000)

Pearl Continental, Dr Zia-ud-din Ahmed Road. Tel 515021. (Rs900−3,000)

Avari Towers, Fatima Jinnah Road. Tel 525261. Tallest building in Pakistan. (Rs1,000−4,000)

Taj Mahal, Shahrah-e-Faisal. Tel 520211.

Moderate: Rs100−800

Midway House, Star Gate Road, near airport. The usual in-transit hotel. (Rs300−1,000)

Beach Luxury, Maulvi Tamiz-ud-din Khan Road. Tel 551031. Excellent seafood restaurant in garden. (Rs250−1,500)

Metropole, Club Road. Tel 512051. Oldest hotel in town. (Rs350−700)

Mehran, Shahrah-e-Faisal. Tel 515061. (Rs350−850)

Jabees, Abdullah Haroon Road. Tel 512011. (Rs300−600)

Imperial, Maulvi Tamiz-ud-din Khan Road. Tel 551051. (Rs250−500)

Gulf, Dr Daud Pota Road, Saddar. Tel 515834. (Rs200−400)

Columbus, Clifton Road. Tel 511311−4 (Rs160−325)

Airport (The Inn), Star Gate Road, near airport. Tel 480141−5. (Rs250−300)

Hostellerie de France, opp Star Gate, airport. Tel 481101−2. Popular with tourists. (Rs200−250)

National City, Sarmad Road, Saddar. Tel 513850. (Rs150−250)

Royal City, Sarmad Road, Saddar. Tel 512378. (Rs150−250)

Inexpensive: Rs25−100

Most cheapies are in and around Saddar Bazaar and Empress Market, with some more around Cantonment Station, Boulton Market and along Shedi Village Road in Lee Market.

Al-Farooq, Summerset St, Saddar. Tel 511031−2. (Rs55−100)

North Western, 26 Beaumont Road, near PIDC House. Tel 510843. (Rs50−100)

Al-Salatin, Dr Daud Pota Road, Saddar. Tel 516362. (Rs50−100)

Khyber, Preedy St, Saddar. Tel 710359. (Rs45−60)

Ambassador, Dr Daud Pota Road, Saddar. Tel 514820, 514200. (Rs50−65)

Shalimar, Dr Daud Pota Road, Saddar. Tel 529491, 527671. (Rs40−50)

International, Sh Chand St, Saddar. Tel 511471. (Rs40−50)

Estate, Rajah Ghazanfar Ali Road, near Empress Market. Tel 511411. Good value, popular with backpackers. (Rs35−50)

Royal, I I Chundrigar Road, near Habib Plaza. Tel 211089. (Rs 30−50)

Sunshine, Cantonment Station. Tel 512316. (Rs25−50)

Hostels

Amin House Youth Hostel, 2 Maulvi Tamiz-ud-din Khan Road. (Rs15−25)

YMCA, Strachen Road, opposite Governor's House. Tel 516927, 513022. (Rs25−50)

YWCA, M A Jinnah Road. Tel 71662. Recommended for women travelling alone.

Salvation Army, Frere Road, behind Empress Market. Tel 74262. Dorm only. (Rs30)

Restaurants

Karachi now has hundreds of good restaurants, especially in Clifton shopping centre and along Airport Road.

Beach Luxury Hotel, Casbah Restaurant. Tel 551031. Excellent grilled seafood; good ambience (outdoors).

Pearl Continental Hotel, Chandi Lounge on 9th floor. Tel 515021. International food and seafood.

Avari Towers, Teppanyaki Restaurant on rooftop. Tel 525261. Japanese cuisine, magnificent view.

Pioneer, Abdullah Haroon Road. Good vegetarian food on Tuesdays and Wednesdays.

Red Carpet, Seabreeze Centre, Boat Basin, Clifton. Barbecue and curries.

Seagull, Seabreeze Centre, Boat Basin, Clifton. Tel 531244.

Dolphin, Boat View Arcade, Khayaban-e-Saadi, Clifton. Tel 537429, 533874.

Shezan Kohsar, Hill Park. Tel 428628. Good Pakistani food.

The Village, Merewether Road. Tel 512880. Barbecue.

Bundu Khan, M A Jinnah (Bundar) Road. Chicken tikka and parathas.

Star of Pakistan, Boulton Market. Tel 225219.

The best cheapies are in Lee Market near the bus station. Also good value (Rs8−20) are the stalls in Burns Road, Napier Road and Hill Park — and the Chinese stalls near Merewether Tower.

Shopping

Good buys in Karachi are new Pakistani carpets and old tribal rugs (from Baluchistan, Afghanistan and Iran), leather, furs, jewellery (antique and modern), cotton bedspreads, antique and modern brass and copper, embroidered table linen and handicrafts. Most carpet shops are on Abdullah Haroon Road. Keep to the hotel lobbies and shopping plazas for leather, furs and modern jewellery. The best antique jewellery is in Sarafa Bazaar, north of Boulton Road. For the

(previous page) Bathers in the tank at a Hindu temple at Ketas, in the Salt Range

rest, try the Saddar Bazaar area, especially Zainab Market. Two recommended handicraft shops in Zainab are Marvi Handicrafts and Village Handicrafts. Zainab Market also sells very good and extremely cheap cotton shirts, ready-made *shalwar-kameez*, and general export rejects. Bargain hard everywhere.

Boutiques

Iridescence, 10 A-7 Amir Khusro Road, off Karsaz Road and opposite the American school. Tel 436987. Latest Pakistani fashions and modern Western dress. Block-printing on the premises.

Haveli, 10 C-1 Gizri Lane, DHS IV, Tel 537514, 542237. Saris, traditional *shalwar-kameez* and Western clothes.

Chaman, 43 B-4 Block IV, PECHS. Tel 430430. Also F-31 Block 1V, Kehkashan, Clifton. Tel 532515, 533334. Hand-printed fabrios and traditional Pakistani ready-to-wear.

Cleos, Hilltop Shopping Centre, 4 D-2 Gizri Boulevard, DHS IV. Modern *shalwar-kameez* and some Western clothing.

Fusun, 9 A-1 Khayaban-e-Shujaat, DHS V. Tel 536085. Western export clothing. By appointment only.

Koel, 36-1 Khayaban-e-Hafiz, DHS V. Hand-block-printed and embroidered traditional Pakistani clothing, cushion covers, table linen, wall hangings, silver jewellery. Block-printing and hand embroidery on the premises.

Sehr, opposite back entrance to Metropole Hotel. Tel 514404. Export clothing and *shalwar-kameez*.

Nicky Malik, C178-2 PECHS Main Tariq Road, above International Furnishers. Tel 442233. Smart Western clothes.

Aliya Iqbal, 16-1-2 3rd Zamzama St. Clifton. Western couture.

Other

Tourist Information Centre, PTDC, at Metropole Hotel, Club Road. Tel 510234.

International Arrivals Lounge, Karachi Airport. Tel 482441.

Pakistan Tourism Development Corporation, Karachi. For booking PTDC motels in Sind, tel 510234, 516397.

Sind Wildlife Management Board, Strachen Road. Tel 523176.

Archaeological Office, Karachi. Tel 431821.

Passport Office, Saddar Bazaar. Tel 510360.

Lahore

Hotels

Expensive: Rs900−3,000

Lahore's better hotels are often fully booked, so it is wise to make advance reservations.

Pearl Continental, Shahrah-e-Quaid-e-Azam (the Mall). Tel 67931, 69931. International class, with all facilities.

Hilton International, Shahrah-e-Quaid-e-Azam (the Mall). Tel 310281−10. International class, with all facilities.

Moderate: Rs200−800

Faletti's, Egerton Road. Tel 303660−10. A once-gracious old building with arcades and a garden. More atmosphere than at the big hotels. (Rs450−800)

International, Upper Mall. Tel 870281−7, 880196−8. (Rs450−650)

Ambassador, 7 Davis Road. Tel 301861−8, 302890. All facilities; good value. (Rs250−400)

Amer, 46 Lower Mall. Tel 320101−3, 65072−3. (Rs200−400)

Indus, 56 the Mall. Tel 302850, 302856−8. (Rs200−400)

Shalimar, Liberty Market, Gulberg. Tel 870331−3. (Rs225−350)

Cheaper: Rs50−300

Country Club Motel, 105-A the Mall. Tel 311361−2. (Rs200)

Orient, 74 McLeod Road. Tel 306794−6, 320261. (Rs100−300)

Lahore, Kashmir Building, McLeod Road. Tel 320257−69, 320250. (Rs60−350)

Menora, 41 McLeod Road. Tel 224028−9, 224031. (Rs60−300)

Uganda, 45 McLeod Road. Tel 56077, 310553. (Rs60−200)

Moghul, 3-K Main Building, Gulberg. Tel 882211. (Rs100−150)

Asia, near railway station. Tel 57429, 57997, 68685. (Rs80−100)

Parkway, near railway station. Tel 54507, 57259, 58553, 69838. (Rs50−100)

Shabistan, McLeod Road, near railway station. Tel 56744. (Rs50−100)

Liberty, 44 Commercial Zone, Liberty Market. Tel 870561. (Rs20−50)

Inexpensive

The cheap hotels in Lahore, particularly those near the railway station and along McLeod Road, are not safe. Problems range from stolen travellers' cheques to planted drugs and blackmail. Recommended are:

Railway Retiring Rooms (s/d Rs20/30)

Youth Hostel, 110-B/3 Firdous Market, Gulberg 111. Tel 83145. Good, but a bit far from the centre. Camping allowed. (dorm Rs10)

YMCA Hostel, the Mall, near GPO. Tel 54433. Easy to miss, as it is in part of a large building. Usually full. (dorm Rs20)

YWCA Hostel, Fatima Jinnah Road. Tel 304707. Camping allowed in garden. (s Rs45, dorm Rs30)

Salvation Army Hostel, 35 Fatima Jinnah Road. Camping allowed in garden. (dorm Rs10−30)

Restaurants

Restaurant food in Lahore is probably the best in Pakistan. Some of the best-known restaurants are:

Gulberg Kabana, Main Boulevard, Gulberg. Tel 871062, 872255. Pakistani food; quail especially good.

Kababeesh, Main Boulevard, Gulberg. Tel 873218. Pakistani food.

Menage, Main Boulevard, Gulberg.

Rendezvous, Main Boulevard, Gulberg.

Tung Fung, Main Boulevard, Gulberg. Tel 87561. Chinese.

Tai Wah, Main Boulevard, Gulberg. Chinese.

Saloos, WAPDA House, the Mall. Tel 325257.

Lords, the Mall. Tel 312235.

Shezan Oriental, the Mall. Tel 54450.

Kabana, Davis Road. Tel 305489.

Kabana, Fortress Stadium, Cantt. Tel 370550.

Tolenton Kabana, the Mall.

Cathay Restaurant, opp. American Express on the Mall. Chinese.

Salt and Pepper, Liberty Market. Most popular of the fast food places — beefburgers and chips!

Polka Parlour and Carvel, both popular ice-cream parlours on Main Boulevard, Gulberg.

Yummy 36, Liberty Market. Ice-cream parlour.

Cheaper Eating

Mozang Bazaar, for chicken tikka.

Gamal Mandi area, near old city, for fried fish.

Anarkali Bazaar, for local dishes of every kind.

Abbott Road wayside stalls, cheap meals.

Shopping

Good buys in Lahore are new Pakistani carpets, antique brass, silk and cotton cloth, and embroidered table linen.

Lahore is famous for its carpet-weaving. New hand-made carpets are for sale in the shops around Charing Cross, along the Mall and in the hotel lobbies. Some antique Persian and Afghan carpets are also for sale. Carpet-weaving started on a large scale here after 1947, when Muslim carpet weavers from old, established centres in Amritsar and Shahjahanpur moved over the border from India. There are now many large carpet factories using the finest wool and making carpets in any design.

Old brass and copper ware is available in the shops around Charing Cross and from Faletti's Hotel arcade. Some good buys can be found in the brass bazaar in the old city, where prices are usually cheaper (see page 102). Here, though, the brass is often unpolished or still coated in tin, so it is difficult to see what you are getting. (Brass must be coated or it will poison food.)

In Mozang Bazaar, south of Charing Cross, you will find the best cotton and silks. The calico printing shop, selling hand-block-printed cloth, bedspreads and table cloths, is near the Mozang *tonga* stand.

Other handicrafts can be found in the shops along the Mall near Charing Cross. Especially recommended is the Technical Services Association, 65 the Mall, which has beautiful shadow-work embroidery at reasonable prices. Ichara Bazaar has the best buys for cloth of all sorts.

Anarkali Bazaar is a treasure-trove, with virtually everything from handicrafts to transistor radios, tin saucepans to refrigerators. This is a good place to look for costume jewellery. It is a maze of lanes and alleys stretching northwards from the Central Museum end of the Mall. Shopping is more fun here than in the shops along the Mall, and prices are lower. Bargain hard.

Other

Tourist Information Centre, PTDC, at Faletti's Hotel, Egerton Road. Tel 303660, 303623−4.

Director of Archaeology, Northern Circle, Lahore Fort, Lahore 8. Tel 56747.

Passport Office, Muslim Town, near Canal Bank. Tel 854202.

Islamabad

Hotels

Expensive: Rs800−2,000

Holiday Inn, Aga Khan Road, F-5/1. Tel 826121−35. International class; all facilities.

Islamabad Hotel, Municipal Road, G-6/2. Tel 827311−31. Air-conditioned; all facilities.

Moderate: Rs170−500

All air-conditioned.

Ambassador, Khayaban-e-Suhrawardy. Tel 824011−6.

Shah Bagh Motel, near Rawal Dam. Tel 828492.

East West Motel, near Rawal Dam. Tel 826143.

Pak Tours Motel, near Rawal Dam. Tel 824503.

Motel Inn Garden, near Aabpara Market. Tel 825273, 824162, 823361.

Cheaper: Rs60–160

New Garden Motel, near Rawal Dam. Tel 821025. Fan.

Blue Star, T & T Colony, G-8/4. Tel 852810, 852717. Fan.

Camping ground (Rs10), opposite Aabpara Market, near Rose and Jasmine Garden.

Restaurants

Tabbak, 13 West Blue Area. Tel 812535. Pakistani, Chinese and English.

Kim Mun, Jinnah Market. Chinese.

White House, Super Market. Tel 828213. Pakistani and continental.

Orient Express, Round Market, F-7/3. Pakistani and continental.

Kashmirwalah's, Daman-e-Koh Viewpoint.

Kao Wah, Aabpara Market. Khayaban-e-Suhrawardy. Tel 829898. Best Chinese in town.

Golden Dragon, Round Market F-7/3. Tel 827333. Chinese.

Mariah's, Blue Area.

Bunny's, Blue Area. Fast food beefburgers, chips and chicken-corn soup.

Moods, near Jinnah Market. Good steaks and Pakistani food.

Mr Chips, near Jinnah Market. European and Pakistani.

Shopping

Shopping in Islamabad is agreeable and easy, with most shops concentrated in designated shopping areas. The oldest shopping area is Aabpara Market on Khayaban-e-Suhrawardy, G-6/1, where you can buy household goods, fabrics, hardware, spices and food. Melody Market, in the centre of G-6, has souvenir, brass and carpet shops, while Super Market, in the centre of F-6, and Jinnah Market, in the centre of F-7, concentrate on clothing, jewellery, leather goods, shoes, books, furniture and souvenirs. Covered Market, in G-6/3, sells meat, vegetables and groceries and has the best photography and haberdashery shops.

The Juma Bazaar (Friday Market), G-6/4, near Aabpara, is Islamabad's most interesting market for tourists — at least, for those in Islamabad on Friday. Behind the main market, Afghan refugees lay out rows of carpets for sale, as well as jewellery, antiques and souvenirs. This is the best place to search for gifts.

Handicraft Shops

Threadlines Gallery, Super Market. A government-sponsored handicraft shop with some excellent pieces at reasonable prices.

Behbud Boutique, Super Market, G-6. Good selection of ready-made dresses, *shalwar-kameez*, table linen and some traditional embroidery and tribal jewellery. Very reasonable prices. Profits go to charity.

Afghan Handicrafts and Maharajah Handicrafts, in Super Market.

Fancy Handicrafts and Kraftman, in Jinnah Market.

Chiltan Handicrafts, Pakistan Handicrafts, and Asian Arts and Crafts, in Blue Area.

Boutiques

Erums and Behbud, Super Market. Good selection of ready-made shirts, trousers and *shalwar-kameez*.

Creation, Adam and Eve, Crystal II, Sundip, and Guys and Dolls, in Jinnah Market. Ready-made clothes, as above.

English Tailor. Good tailor in Jinnah Market.

Bookshops

Vanguard and Book Fair, in Jinnah Market.

Mr Books and Lok Virsa, in Super Market.

London Book Shops, in Kosar Market.

Old Bookshop, in Melody Market. Second-hand books.

Carpets

Pak Persian and Qureshi's Carpets, in Melody Market.

Baluch Carpets, Lahore Carpet House, Shiraz Carpets, Nabeel Carpets and others, in Blue Area.

Other

Tourism Division, Ministry of Culture and Tourism, College Road, Jinnah Market, F-7/2. Tel 820856.

PTDC Head Office, 2, 61st Street F-7/4. Tel 826327.

Telegraph and Telephone Office, behind Holiday Inn, F-5.

GPO, Post Office Road, G-6/2.

PIA, Nazim-ud-din Road, Blue Area, F-6/4.

Passport Office, Aabpara Market, near National Bank. Tel 826837.

Rawalpindi

Hotels

Expensive: Rs850−3,000

Pearl Continental, the Mall. Tel 66011−21, 62700−10. International class; all facilities.

Shalimar, off the Mall. Tel 62901−21. All facilities.

Moderate: Rs120−700

Flashman's, PTDC, the Mall. Tel 64811−17. All facilities. (from Rs375)

Kashmir Wala's Tourist Inn, the Mall. Tel 68081−85. (from Rs425)

Pine Hotel, Iftikhar Janjua Road, behind Pearl Continental. Tel 63660, 68017−8. Good value and quiet. (Rs120−215, 3-bed dorm Rs75/bed)

Silver Grill, the Mall. Tel 64719, 64729. Very small. (from Rs220)

Marhaba, Kashmir Road. Tel 66021−2, 65178. (Rs150−300)

Parkland, Bank Road. Tel 66080. (Rs150−200)

Sandhills, Murree Road, near railway bridge. Tel 70651. (Rs150−220)

Potohar, Murree Road. Tel 74398, 74366. (Rs150−200)

United, Gulnoor, National City and Park, all on Murree Road.

Cheaper: Rs20−75

The best at the upper end of the cheap range are in the Massey Gate area of Saddar Bazaar.

Maharajah, Murree Road at Committee Chowk. Tel 71011. (s/d Rs50/75)

Al-Azam, Melad Chowk. Tel 65901, 65904, 66404. (s/d Rs40/70)

Al-Hambra, Shah Taj, Al-Khalil, all on Adam Jee Road. Popular with backpackers. (s/d Rs25/40)

Lalazar, Kashmir, Rex, all on Adam Jee Road. (s/d Rs20/40)

Corner (Tel 61671), Nadir (Tel 60687), Al-Aziz, all in Pir Wadhai area near the bus station. (s/d Rs25/40)

Palace (Tel 70672), Al-Hayat (Tel 70979), New Savoy Grill (Tel 71619), Adil (Tel 70730), Pakeeza (Tel 74071, 74100), all in Liaquat Road area.

Inexpensive hotels by the railway station are often full of Afghan refugees, and many will not accept foreigners. There are, however:

Railway Retiring Rooms. Bring your own bedding.

Youth Hostel, 25 Gulistan Colony, near Ayub Park. Too remote.

YWCA, 65-A Satellite Town. Women only. A bit rundown, but cheap and safe.

Restaurants

Aside from the restaurants in the chief hotels, most of the best-known restaurants are along the Mall or just off it.

Shezan, in Kashmir Road. Tel 65743.

Kamran (Tel 67995), Super (Tel 63063) and Shalimar (Tel 68486), in Bank Road.

Chung Wah, in Murree Road. Tel 43803.

The best inexpensive restaurants (about Rs10) are in the Saddar Bazaar area and around Raja Bazaar, the railway station and Pir Wadhai bus station.

Shopping

Sarafa Bazaar, in the old city, is the place to go for old tribal jewellery. Saddar Bazaar, in the Cantonment, is best for leather, carpets, cashmere shawls, furniture and tailors. The heart of the bazaar is along Kashmir Road and Massey Gate.

Shamas Din, in Massey Gate, sells boots, shoes, suitcases, saddles and pouffes. Carpets, brass and antiques are on Canning Road, behind Flashman's, and on the Mall in front. They are also in the lobby of the Pearl Continental Hotel. Men's tailors and cashmere shawls are on Haider Road, but ladies' tailors are in Kamran Market, off Kashmir

Road. English Book House and Pak American Bookshop (Tel 66648) are on Kashmir Road.

The best brass shop is Shaukat Ali's, in Satellite Town, 170 D-Block (Tel 842813), which has a large selection of quality, ready-polished brass and copper. The shop is in an unmarked private house. Entering Rawalpindi from Islamabad on Murree Road, turn right at the first traffic light to Satellite Town, then take the second left. The house is the fifth on the right, about 100 metres (yards) along.

Other

Tourist Information Centre, PTDC, Flashman's Hotel, the Mall. Tel 64811−2.

PIA, the Mall. Tel 67011, 66231.

American Express, Murree Road. Tel 65617.

GPO, Kashmir Road. Tel 65691.

Telegraph and Telephone Office, the Mall. Tel 65854, 65809.

Foreigners' Registration Office, Rashid Minhas Road, Civil Lines. Tel 63866.

Passport Office, 6th Road, Satellite Town. Tel 840851.

Peshawar

Hotels

Expensive: Rs1,000−1,800

Pearl Continental, Khyber Road. Tel 76361−9. International class; all facilities.

Moderate: Rs100−800

Dean's, Islamia Road, Tel 76483−4, 79781−3. PTDC-run. Old-style building with verandahs, a pretty garden and some charm. (s/d Rs460/600)

Jan's, Islamia Road. Tel 76939, 72056, 73009. (s/d Rs100−200/170−300)

Green's, Saddar Road. Tel 76035−7. Comfortable and popular. (s/d Rs100−150/Rs150−200, dorm Rs40)

Galaxie, Khyber Bazaar. Tel 72738−9. (from Rs150)

Inexpensive: to Rs115

Habib, Khyber Bazaar. Tel 73016−7. (s/d Rs65/115)

Neelab, Khyber Bazaar. Tel 74255, 62314. (s/d Rs35/55)

International (Gul's), Saddar Road, Tel 72100, 72250. (s/d Rs40/60)

Sindbad, Saddar Road. Tel 75020. (s/d Rs40/60)

Sabir, Chowk Fawara. Tel 75922. (s/d Rs25/40)

Salatin, Cinema Road. Tel 73779, 73770. Very good food. (s/d Rs20/40)

Kamran, Khyber Bazaar. Tel 72345. (s/d Rs20/40, dorm Rs15)

Khyber Tourist Inn, Saddar Bazaar. (s/d Rs15/30)

There are other cheapies in Saddar Road, Chowk Fawara, Namak Mandi, Cinema Road and along Grand Trunk Road. In summer, some hotels let you sleep outside for Rs8/bed.

Youth Hostel, Peshawar University. Remote.

YMCA Hostel, near Peshawar University. Equally remote.

Railway Retiring Rooms, Peshawar Cantonment Station.

Camping is allowed about 100 metres (yards) from Jan's Hotel for Rs10.

Restaurants

Salatin, Cinema Road. Tel 73779, 73770. Best Pakistani food in Peshawar and famous for its Pathan atmosphere.

Nanking and Hong Kong, both on the Mall. Good Chinese.

Pearl Continental, Dean's, Jan's and Green's, at the respective hotels. All serve European and Pakistani food.

The street food in Peshawar is famous as some of the best in Pakistan. Try the stalls along Khyber Bazaar and Qissa Khawani, where you can eat well cheaply. In and around Saddar Bazaar are more cheap eating places.

Shopping

Best buys in Peshawar's bazaars are tribal silver jewellery, copper, Gardner china, Astrakhan hats, shawls and hand-printed cloth. See the bazaar tour description for where to look. Also excellent value are silk and lace in Saddar Bazaar.

Peshawar is also famous for its wooden furniture with brass inlay work. If ordering furniture for export, try to find out if the wood is properly seasoned, otherwise it will crack, and the brass inlay will pop out. The best-known factories are: M Hyatt & Bros, who have a showroom opposite Jan's Hotel and a factory in the Jamrud Industrial Estate; Royal Furniture; Peshawar Woodworks; Khyber Wood Factory; Pak/Danish Industries and Pak/German Industries. You can arrange factory tours.

Wax worked on cloth is another handicraft for which Peshawar is well known, though it is not suited to every taste. You can find it in Saddar Bazaar and in the arcade of the Pearl Continental Hotel. The designs show a Chinese influence, especially the birds in brilliant colours and the dragons.

The Afghan Metal Works, behind the Pearl Continental Hotel on Pajjagi (Ashab Baba) Road, is open 8 am−4 pm and welcomes visitors. You can watch the moulding, beating, engraving, tinning and polishing of the various copper and brass utensils for sale.

Smoked meat and sausages are available at Brzybrowski's, in the Jamrud Industrial Estate, the only place in Pakistan offering these European delicacies. Tel 50647.

Other

Tourist Information Centre, PTDC, at Dean's Hotel. Tel 724238, 76481, 76431.

Peshawar Museum, Tel 72252, 74452.

Banks and **GPO** are in Saddar Bazaar.

Telephone and Telegraph Office is on the Mall.

Passport Office, Gunner Road. Tel 78931.

Swat Hotels

In the off season, from October to April, hotel prices are cheaper, and hard bargaining in the smaller hotels will make them cheaper still.

Saidu Sharif and Mingora

Moderate: Rs200−400

Swat Serena, Saidu Sharif. Tel 4215, 4604. Or book through Serena,

Karachi, tel 537506−9, telex SERENA PK. International standard, with good food and service in old, colonial style.

Pameer, GT Road, Mingora. Tel 4926, 4306. In the centre of town.

Cheaper: Rs25−80

Udyana, GT Road. Mingora. Tel 4876. (s/d Rs40/80)

Holiday, Makan Bagh, Saidu Sharif Road. Tel 4443. (Rs40)

Abaseen, New Madyan Road, Mingora. Tel 2122. (s/d Rs25/40)

There are about 30 other middle-range and cheap hotels in Mingora along the Grand Trunk Road, Madyan Road and around Green Chowk. The real cheapies do not accept foreigners.

The **Tourist Information Centre** is in the Swat Serena Hotel. Tel 2220. You can change travellers' cheques in this hotel.

Marghazar

Marghazar Hotel, the converted summer palace of the first Wali of Swat. Well-positioned at the end of the valley, ten kilometres (six miles) from Saidu Sharif. (s/d Rs160/250)

Malam Jabba

Due to have a 50-room hotel in 1988. There will be one ski run and, in summer, pony trekking and mini-golf.

Miandam

At 1,800 metres (6,000 feet), this is the best place to spend your first night in Swat in summer. There are four hotels, all moderate in price.

PTDC Motel. Tel 10. Or book through PTDC Rawalpindi, tel 64811, 66231. Well positioned, with a lovely garden and helpful staff. If all the rooms are full, you can take a spare bed outside and sleep under the trees in the garden. (s/d Rs225/300)

Miandam Hotel. Tel Miandam 10. (s/d Rs130/220)

Pameer Guest House. Book through Pameer Hotel, Mingora. Tel 4926.

Karashma Hotel. (s/d Rs50/100)

Camping is allowed.

Madyan

Madyan Hotel. Tel 2, 34. Right on the river. (Rs200–300)

Mountain View. Tel 7. (s/d Rs100/200)

Nisar. Tel 441. (s/d Rs70/140)

Shalimar. Tel 14 (s/d Rs40/60 in season; Rs20/40 off)

Parkway (s/d Rs25/40 in season; Rs15/30 off)

Summer Hill, Hunza Inn and Mauambakhan are all cheaper and adequate. (s/d Rs15/25)

Kalam

Moderate

PTDC Motel. Tel 14. Or book through PTDC, Rawalpindi. Tel 64811, 66231. Nice position, with a large garden. (s/d Rs225/300)

Falakseer. Tel 10. Good position. (d Rs225 in season; Rs150 off)

Khalid. Tel 6. Down by the river. (d Rs200 in season; Rs50 off)

Inexpensive

Heaven Breeze and Falak Naz (Rs100–150)

Mehran and Kalam (d Rs45 in season; Rs25 off)

Camping is free in the PTDC Motel garden. It is not recommended elsewhere, as the people in the area (Kohistanis) are sometimes hostile.

Chitral Hotels

Moderate

Mountain Inn, Ataliq Bazaar. Lovely, peaceful central garden; nice atmosphere. Best in town. (s/d Rs155/225)

PTDC Tourist Complex. Tel 683 or book through PTDC Rawlapindi, tel 64811. Poor value. (s/d Rs225/300)

Inexpensive

Fairland (s/d Rs80/105)

Dreamland (s/d Rs60/100)

Tirich Mir View, down by mosque. Splendid view. (d Rs65)

Garden (s/d Rs15/25)

Shabnam. Basic. (dorm Rs10)

Afghan-run hotel in Shahi Bazaar. Good food. (s/d Rs15/25)

Saif (dorm Rs6)

There are several other cheap hotels in Shahi Bazaar.

Kaghan Hotels

Balakot

PTDC Motel, Tel 8 or book through PTDC Rawalpindi, tel 64811, or PTDC Abbottabad, tel 2728. (s/d Rs215/270)

Park. Tel Balakot 23. Pleasant position. (s/d Rs70/105) The Park Hotel runs two rest houses at Shogran. Book through the Park Hotel at Balakot.

Pakistan (d Rs100−150)

Bangash, Lalazar, Mashriq and Seerab are all reasonably cheap and adequate. (s/d Rs15/25)

Youth Hostel, near PTDC Motel. (Rs10/bed)

Naran

PTDC Motel. Book as for Balakot. (s/d Rs260/320)

PTDC tents. Book as above. (Rs70/tent)

Vershigoom and Shaheen. Both good value. (s/d Rs15/25)

Youth Hostel, three kilometres (two miles) before Naran on the right. (Rs15)

There are several other cheap local hotels and restaurants. Camping is safe.

Karakoram Highway

Besham Hotels

PTDC, one kilometre (half a mile) south of Besham on the banks of the Indus. Book through PTDC Rawalpindi, tel 66231, 64811, 64830. (s/d Rs220/300)

The five local hotels are basic but cheap. There are plenty of local restaurants in the bazaar.

Prince. Tel Besham 56. Nine rooms. (s/d Rs30/50)

International. Tel Besham 65. 14 rooms. (s/d Rs30/50)

Azam. Tel Besham 27. Five rooms. (d Rs20)

Hazara. Tel Besham 12. Eight rooms. (d Rs20)

Besham. Eight rooms. (d/t Rs25)

Chilas Hotels

Shangrila, on KKH. Tel Chilas 69, or book Rawalpindi 73006, 72948, or Karachi 520703, 520801, 520261−5. Good and modern, with 29 rooms. (d Rs345)

Marhaba, main bazaar. 12 rooms. (d Rs25)

The various local hotels are very cheap, and new hotels are being built as we go to press.

Gilgit

Moderate Hotels

Serena Lodge, Jutial, Gilgit. Tel 2330−1. Or book through Serena, Karachi. Tel 537506−9, telex SERENA PK. Outside town, with a magnificent view of Rakaposhi. Best food in Gilgit. (Rs300−500)

Chinar Inn, PTDC, Chinar Bagh. Tel 2562. Central and popular with tour groups. (s/d Rs225/300)

Hunza Inn, Chinar Bagh. Tel 2814. The best value in town, and popular with independent travellers. Nice atmosphere; good meeting place; good food. (d Rs60−200, dorm Rs25)

Park, Airport Road. Tel 2679. Central and modern, but slow service. (d Rs125−200)

Inexpensive Hotels

Golden Peak Inn, Bank Road, Rajah Bazaar. Central, popular with backpackers, camping allowed. (d Rs70, tent Rs10)

Vershigoom Inn, Airport Road. Tel 2991. Central, popular with backpackers. (s/d Rs40/60)

Mountain Movers Inn. Tel 2967. Other side of river; helpful management.

Tourist Cottage, Jutial. Tel 2376. (d Rs40)

Riverside Tourist Lodge, Chinar Bagh.

Masherbroom Inn, Airport Road. Tel 2711. (d Rs50−80)

Mount Balore, Airport Road. Tel 2709. (Rs50−80)

Jubilee, Airport Road. Tel 2843. (d Rs40)

Firdous, Jamat Khana Road. Tel 2778. (d Rs20)

Haidry, near polo ground.

Sargin Inn, Shahrah-e-Quaid-e-Azam. (s/d Rs45/90)

Shopping

Chinese silks, embroidered table linen, porcelain, irregular seed pearls, garnets and rubies are the best buys in Gilgit. The Chinese emporia near the Airport Chowk (roundabout) are the best sources of anything Chinese. Precious and semi-precious stones are available in the bazaar in Xama, opposite the Park Hotel. Know your stones and bargain hard. Pearls, cardigans and sweaters are in the bazaar near the mosque.

Other

Banks in Gilgit cash travellers' cheques denominated only in US dollars or sterling. The rate is slightly less than in Islamabad.

Tourist Information Centre, PTDC, at Chinar Inn.

Hunza Hotels

Moderate

Serena Lodge, Karimabad. (Opening 1989). Book through Serena, Karachi, tel 537506−9, tlx SERENA PK.

Hilltop, Karimabad. Tel 10. Convenient; good food. (s/d Rs125/200)

Mountain View, Karimabad. Tel 17. New, large, with good view. (d from Rs150)

Tourist Park, Karimabad. Tel 45. (d Rs100−150)

Rakaposhi View, Karimabad. Tel 12. (d Rs100−175)

Inexpensive

Rainbow, Karimabad. New, good view. (d Rs65)

Hunza Inn, Karimabad. Tel 17. (d Rs60−80)

New Hunza Tourist, Karimabad. Popular with tourists. (d Rs60)

Happy Day Inn, Karimabad. (d Rs80−150)

Karim, Karimabad. (d Rs50−150)

PTDC camping ground with facilities, Aliabad. Tel 60. (tent Rs60)

Prince, Aliabad. Local meeting place.

There are several other cheap hotels in Aliabad.

Gojal (Upper Hunza) Hotels

Gulmit

Silk Route Lodge, on KKH. Opening 1988. Camping allowed. Moderate rates.

Village Inn, up in village. Tel 12. Traditional room upstairs. (d Rs125−175)

Marco Polo Inn, up in village. Tel 7. (d Rs125−175)

New Hotels opening.

Passu

Passu Inn, on KKH. Tel 1. Popular with hikers; good meeting place. (d Rs70, traditional family room sleeping six Rs200)

Shishper (d Rs70)

Batura Inn (d Rs60)

Boreet, up by lake and cheaper.

Sost

Shangrila. Opening 1988. Book Rawalpindi 73006, 72948, or Karachi 520703, 520810, 520261−5. Moderate rates (under Rs800).

Kunjerab View. Basic; camping allowed. Inexpensive rates.

New hotels opening.

Urdu Glossary

Urdu is a mixture of Persian, Arabic and various local languages. It is similar to Hindi, but is written in Arabic script.

1	ek
1.5	dehr
2	doh
2.5	dhai
3	teen
4	char
5	paanch
6	che
7	saat
8	aath
9	naw
10	dus
11	gyara
12	bara
13	tera
14	chawdra
15	pundra
20	beess
25	pacheess
30	teess
40	chaleess
50	pachaass
100	ek saw
2,000	doh hazaar

(Beware of similar-sounding 25 and 50.)

greeting (Peace be with you)	Salaam alay kum.
reply (With you also be peace)	Waalay kum as salaam.
How are you?	Aapka (*or* Tumhara) kya hal heyh?
I am well.	Teekh heyh *or* Teekh takh.
What is your name?	Aapka (*or* Tumhara) naam kya heyh?
Do you speak English?	Kya aap ungrezi boltay heyn?
I am English/American/French.	Meyn ungrez/amrikan/fransisi hun.
thank you	shukria
good bye	khoodha haafis
yes	jihaan, haanji *or* haan
no	naheen (na'en)
okay/good	achaa

When?	Kub?
three o'clock	teen bujay
morning	subah
evening	shaam
Which way to Lahore?	Lahore kiss turaf heyh?
go	jaana
near	nazdeek
far	dur
food	khana
eat food	khana khana
drink	peena
meat	ghosht
beef	gai ka ghosht
goat meat	bukri ka ghosht
chicken	murghi
fish	muchli
egg	unda
vegetable	subzi
potato	aalu
spinach	palak
lentils	daal
rice	chavel
bread	roti, naan, chapati
yoghurt	dahi
water	pani
tea	chai
salt	namak
sugar	cheeni
home/house	gher/mekaan
bed	pulang, charpai
blanket	kambal
pillow	takya
sheet	charder
fan	punkha
candle	moom butti
hot	guram
cold	thanda (m) thandi (f)
small	chota/choti
big	burha/burhi
clean	saaf
expensive	mengha
How much is this/that?	Yeyh/Voh kitnay ka heyh?
What is this/that?	Yeyh/Voh kya heyh?

Recommended Reading

History

Basham, A.L. *The Wonder That was India* (New York: Grove, 1954; London: Sidgwick & Jackson, 1967; New York: Taplinger, 1968) Excellent introduction to the prehistory, history, art, religion, language and politics of the subcontinent.

Collins and Lapierre. *Freedom at Midnight* (London: Pan, 1977) Flashy, journalistic account of the independence movement and Partition.

Morris, J. *Pax Britannica*, *Heaven's Command*, and *Farewell the Trumpets* (trilogy) (London: Faber and Faber, 1968, 1978) Beautifully written history of the British Empire.

Spear, P. *A History of India II* (London: Penguin, 1965) Concise, readable history covering Moghul period to present day.

Wheeler, Sir M. *Civilizations of the Indus Valley and Beyond* (London: Thames and Hudson, 1966) Well-illustrated prehistory and early history of the subcontinent.

Woodruff, P. *The Men Who Ruled India* (London: Cape, 1954) The British involvement in India and the men who worked there.

Travel and Adventure

Fairley, J. *The Lion River* (London: Allen Lane, 1975) The Indus River from its source to the sea.

Keay, J. *When Men and Mountains Meet* (London: Murray, 1977) Readable narrative of the exploration of the Karakorams and Himalayas from 1820 to 1875.

Keay, J. *The Gilgit Game* (London: Murray, 1979) Continuation of the above, 1865–95, at the height of the Great Game.

Moorhouse, G. *To the Frontier* (New York: Holt, Rinehart and Winston, 1985) A journey around Pakistan with descriptions of people and places.

Murphy, D. *Where the Indus is Young* (London: Murray, 1977) Eccentric Irishwoman's diary of a winter of walking in Baltistan with her six-year-old daughter.

Murphy, D. *Full Tilt* (London: Murray, 1965) Bicycling from Ireland to India via Pakistan's Northern Areas.

Naipaul, V.S. *Among the Believers* (London: Deutsch, 1981) Travels in Iran, Pakistan and Indonesia, comparing Islamic peoples.

Fiction in English

Fraser, G.M. *Flashman in the Great Game* (London: Pan, 1976) Flashman carouses through the First Afghan War — and survives. Terrific read.

Kipling, R. *Kim* (London: Macmillan, 1899) Classic novel of the Great Game.

Lambrick, H.T. *The Terrorist* (London: Benn, 1972) Sindhi rebellion, illustrates the power of the *pirs* (religious leaders). Excellent read.

Rushdie, S. *Midnight's Children* (London: Cape, 1981; Pan, 1982) Extraordinary fictionalized account of Partition. Winner of Booker Prize.

Rushdie, S. *Shame* (London: Cape, 1983; Pan, 1984) Hilarious — sometimes spiteful — novel of modern Pakistan. Excellent read to be approached lightly.

Sinclair, G. *Khyber Caravans* Light and amusing. Describes Quetta earthquake.

Singh, Kushwant. *Last Train to Pakistan* (New York: Grove, 1961) Describes the horrors of Hindu-Muslim slaughter at Partition.

Other

Miller, K. *Continents in Collision* (London: Philip, 1982) Royal Geographical Society scientific expedition to the Karakorams.

Mumtaz, K.K. *Architecture in Pakistan* (Singapore: Concept Media, 1985) Excellent, well-illustrated and readable history of architecture from the Indus Civilization to the present.

Index of Places